Ethics, Knowledge and Truth in Sports Research

The study of sport is characterised by its inter-disciplinarity, with researchers drawing on apparently incompatible research traditions and ethical benchmarks in the natural sciences and the social sciences, depending on their area of specialization. In this groundbreaking study, Graham McFee argues that sound high-level research into sport requires a sound rationale for one's methodological choices, and that such a rationale requires an understanding of the connection between the practicalities of researching sport and the philosophical assumptions which underpin them.

By examining touchstone principles in research methodology, such as the contested 'gold standard' of voluntary informed consent in the natural sciences and the postmodern denial of 'truth' in the social sciences, McFee demonstrates that epistemology and ethics are inextricably linked. Drawing on a wide range of examples, from the laboratory to the sports field, McFee explores the concepts of 'knowledge' and 'truth' in sports research and makes a powerful case for a philosophical deepening of our approach to method and methodology in sport. This book is important reading for all advanced students and researchers working in sport, exercise and related disciplines.

Graham McFee is Professor of Philosophy at the University of Brighton and at California State University Fullerton. He was Vice President of the British Society of Aesthetics. He has written and presented extensively, both nationally and internationally, on the philosophy of Wittgenstein and on aesthetics, especially the aesthetics of dance.

Ethics and Sport
Series editors
Mike McNamee
University of Wales Swansea
Jim Parry
University of Leeds
Heather Reid
Morningside College

The Ethics and Sport series aims to encourage critical reflection on the practice of sport, and to stimulate professional evaluation and development. Each volume explores new work relating to philosophical ethics and the social and cultural study of ethical issues. Each is different in scope, appeal, focus and treatment, but a balance is sought between local and international focus, perennial and contemporary issues, level of audience, teaching and research application, and variety of practical concerns.

Also available in this series:

Ethics and Sport
Edited by Mike McNamee and Jim Parry

Values in Sport
Elitism, nationalism, gender equality and
the scientific manufacture of winners
*Edited by Torbjörn Tännsjö and Claudio
Tamburrini*

Spoilsports
Understanding and preventing sexual
exploitation in sport
Celia Brackenridge

Fair Play in Sport
A moral norm system
Sigmund Loland

Sport, Rules and Values
Philosophical investigations into the
nature of sport
Graham McFee

Sport, Professionalism and Pain
Ethnographies of injury and risk
David Howe

Genetically Modified Athletes
Biomedical ethics, gene doping
and sport
Andy Miah

Human Rights in Youth Sport
A critical review of children's rights in
competitive sports
Paulo David

Genetic Technology and Sport
Ethical questions
*Edited by Claudio Tamburrini and
Torbjörn Tännsjö*

Pain and Injury in Sport
Social and ethical analysis
*Edited by Sigmund Loland, Berit Skirstad
and Ivan Waddington*

Ethics, Money and Sport
This sporting Mammon
Adrian Walsh and Richard Giulianotti

Ethics, Dis/Ability and Sports
Edited by Ejgil Jespersen and Michael McNamee

The Ethics of Doping and Anti-Doping
Redeeming the soul of sport?
Verner Møller

The Ethics of Sport Medicine
Edited by Claudio Tamburrini and Torbjörn Tännsjö

Bodily Democracy
Towards a philosophy of sport for all
Henning Eichberg

Ethics, Knowledge and Truth in Sports Research
An epistemology of sport
Graham McFee

Ethics, Knowledge and Truth in Sports Research

An epistemology of sport

Graham McFee

Routledge
Taylor & Francis Group

LONDON AND NEW YORK

First published 2010 by Routledge
2 Park Square, Milton Park, Abingdon, Oxon OX14 4RN
Simultaneously published in the USA and Canada
by Routledge
711 Third Avenue, New York, NY 10017

Routledge is an imprint of the Taylor & Francis Group, an informa business

First issued in paperback 2011

© 2010 Graham McFee

Typeset in Goudy by Swales & Willis Ltd, Exeter, Devon

British Library Cataloguing in Publication Data
A catalogue record for this book is available from the British Library

Library of Congress Cataloging in Publication Data
McFee, Graham.
   Ethics, Knowledge and truth in sports research : an epistemology
of sport / Graham McFee.
   p. cm.
   includes bibliographical references.
   1. Sports—Research—Methodology. 1. Title.
   GV706.8.M39 2010
   796.07—dc22
   2009022980

ISBN 13: 978-0-415-68861-1 (pbk)
ISBN 13: 978–0–415–49314–7 (hbk)
ISBN 13: 978–0–203–87268–0 (ebk)

Contents

Preface

You are under the impression that the problem is *difficult*, when it's *impossible*. I want you to realise that you are under a spell.
(Wittgenstein, Ms. 158 p. 37: see Wittgenstein, 1993 p. 488; emphasis added)

A great many books introducing research methods for the social sciences are useful for undergraduates in sports studies, or something similar: for instance, Chris Gratton and Ian Jones (2004) *Research Methods for Sports Studies*. But, as MRes programmes in sports studies (and similar) come on stream, the demands of postgraduate study, and perhaps even some advanced undergraduate study, require more sophisticated treatments of the kinds advanced here. Crucial for sound high-level research into sport is the rationale for one's methodological choices. Such a rationale requires understanding the connection between the practicalities of researching sport and the philosophical assumptions which underpin them. While journal articles might partly satisfy that requirement, teaching this material myself convinced me of the value of a text focusing on the theoretical underpinnings of key ideas here. Moreover, it grows from a connection between *ethical* issues for sport research and *epistemological* ones. In sketching an account of such connections, and their consequences, this work offers something to those teaching and learning research methods for sports studies at a higher level. It therefore naturally supplements the primers for such methods.

Further, these problems may be less urgent in natural-scientific enquiries into sport, where the researchers are typically doing what Thomas Kuhn (1970: 10) rightly calls "normal science". For there, researchers are utilizing small numbers of tried-and-trusted methods and assumptions: and need not step outside them (although *some* do!). So this text focuses specifically on the epistemology and ethical demands of broadly *social-scientific* research into sport for researchers, primarily postgraduate researchers: that is, research based in, for instance, sports sociology, sports history, philosophy of sport. For these are my personal interests; and my claim is that there, unless one gets the philosophy clear, much research – otherwise good – becomes hopelessly flawed.

At the centre of the philosophical concern, as in the quotation from Wittgenstein (in the epigraph), is the thought that many issues here set aside as mere *difficulties* for understanding research, and the place within of both researcher and rersearched, are actually impossibilities, reflecting conceptual confusions.

I am conscious, too, that some critics might think that no-one holds the views criticized here. Well, first, while I hope that is true, my experience of teaching fledging researchers, as well as discussions with established researchers and reading what they write, make me doubt it. And some of the examples sketched here suggest that I may be right: indeed, my world seems to teem with the scientistic and the postmodernist, in some variety or other. But, second, were the contemporary situation that happy one where the book was presently unnecessary, I would justify it as an intervention to keep things that way!

Acknowledgements

I would like to thank all those whose comments on texts or presentations were part of the development process of this text, including all the editors of the published work (see Related papers/presentations) – who I also thank for permission to reprint material. Those to be thanked include generations of students (especially research students) at the University of Brighton. A large number of friends and colleagues contributed here, directly and indirectly. Let this alphabetical list stand for them all:

Tom Carter, Scott Fleming, David Gilbourne, Paul Gilchrist, Roger Homan, Mike McNamee, Paul McNaught-Davis, Caroline Marlow, Richard Royce, Andy Sparkes, John Sugden, Alan Tomlinson.

Mike McNamee, who appears as both a friend/colleague and read through the whole first draft, deserves special thanks. And so does Paul McNaught-Davis, and the village of Joncelets, France.

I would especially single out for thanks my wife, Myrene, for all her help, from discussing the topics with me, through making the illustrations, to reading the whole text as proofreader and commentator; but also my grandchildren, Samantha and Ryan, for their input (while Myrene was babysitting all of us); and Al Flores, of California State University Fullerton, for his generous discussion of many of these points, especially those concerning "deceptive" research.

Related papers/presentations

Ideas from this text are prefigured in things I have written, some of which are published: in no case is earlier work simply reprinted here, not least because the items include a fair amount of repetition. (In some instances I identify more closely where in this work to find that contribution.)

1. "Triangulation in Research: Two Confusions" *Educational Research* Vol. 34, 1992 pp. 215–19 – in Chapter Two.
2. (with Paul McNaught-Davis) "Informed Consent? A Case Study from Environmental Physiology" in A. Tomlinson & S. Fleming (eds) *Ethics, Sport and Leisure: Crises and Critiques*, Aachen: Meyer & Meyer, 1997 pp. 111–25.
3. "It's Not a Game: The Place of Philosophy in the Study of Sport" in John Sugden & Alan Tomlinson (eds) *Power Games: A Critical Sociology of Sport*, London: Routledge, 2002 pp. 117–37.
4. "Why Do Sports Psychologists Neglect Freud?" in Mike McNamee (ed.) *Philosophy and the Sciences of Exercise, Health and Sport*, London: Routledge, 2004 pp. 85–116.
5. "The Quest for Understanding Sport: Generating Knowledge through Researching Art and Action", keynote address to the 1st International Conference for Qualitative Research in Sport and Exercise, Liverpool: John Moores University, 18 May, 2004 – in Chapter 6 and Chapter 10.
6. "Research Quality and Qualitative Research in Sport", read at University of Loughborough, February, 2005.
7. "Right Reason: Searching for Truth in the Sports and Exercise Sciences", *European Journal of Sports Science,* 2006 pp. 65–70 – in Chapters 1 and 6.
8. "Ethical Considerations and Voluntary Informed Consent in Sport", read at a conference on "Ethical Issues in Leisure Research", University of Gloucestershire, March, 2005, and published in S. Fleming & F. Jordan (eds) *Ethical Issues in Leisure Research* (LSA Publication No. 90), Eastbourne: Leisure Studies Association, pp. 13–30 – Chapter 7 and 8.
9. "Paradigms and Possibilities", versions read at British Philosophy of Sport Association national conference, May 2005; to Sport & Leisure Cultures seminar, Chelsea School, University of Brighton, May 2006; to European College

of Sports Science, July 2006; and published in *Sport, Ethics and Philosophy*, 2007 pp. 58–77 – in Chapters 5 and 6.

10. "The Researcher's Hat: An Ethical Issue for Conducting and Reporting Research", *LSA Newsletter*, 2008 – in Chapter 9.

11. "The Epistemology of Qualitative Research into Sport: Ethical and Erotetic?", *Qualitative Research into Sport and Exercise* Vol. 1, No. 3 in McFee, 2009 pp. 297–311) – especially Chapter 6.

Part I

Overview

1 A vision of the ethics and epistemology of qualitative research into sport

Introduction

It is becoming a commonplace that researchers must concern themselves, not merely with *collecting* data, but with the nature of that data *as data* (the kind of knowledge it represents) and with the conceptualizations these researchers assume of their methods and practices (see, for instance, Punch, 1998: 46–63). Accounts of the nature of empirical research tend to classify that research, first, as natural-scientific or something else (usually, social-scientific) – where the first is sometimes just called "scientific"!; and, second, as quantitative or qualitative. Indeed, some texts use these contrasts to characterize methodological questions for research. Then the questions become:

1   Is the research design natural-scientific or not?
2   Is the research design quantitative or not?

Faced with this framework, much empirical research involving sport claims to be social-scientific and to be qualitative. At least, the research that is my concern in this text would self-define in these ways (perhaps for want of anything better), although I say something about the alternatives. Similarly, its typical disciplinary self-definition is as sports sociology or sports psychology, although others (such as sports history) are not excluded. But my target in this text begins from the first pair of contrasts (and the associated categories) themselves, rightly lumped together as a concern with the *epistemology of research*: that is, with the view of knowledge that the research presupposes. Thus, to repeat, the specific focus of this text is as a contribution on the epistemology of (broadly) *social-scientific* research into sport, primarily for postgraduate researchers and their supervisors.[1] In such research into sport, human subjects are treated (roughly) as though they were indeed human beings, able to answer (and ask) questions.

As a terminological point, I prefer the term "subjects" for those who are researched. This is presently unfashionable:[2] *participant* is probably the preferred locution. Thus, the code of conduct of the American Psychological Association (APA) no longer makes ". . . reference to the term 'research subject' . . ." (McNamee *et al.*, 2007: 74–75). But my preference here reflects my desire to emphasize the researcher's mastery over his/her research data: he/she is the one who analyses and presents it. Hence I would not dispute the substance of the claim that "[t]he protection of the research *participant* is a key element of research ethics" (McNamee *et al.*, 2007: 189; emphasis mine). But this is not incompatible with calling the involved person a *subject*. For, first, as emphasized throughout, what I call a "subject" is recognized as a *person*, suitable for moral treatment. Were this stress only achievable through adherence to the term 'participant', or something similar, I would use that term, re-writing this text in that way. But, second, my preferred term, "subject", provides a safeguard against conceptualizing these "participants" as co-contributors, or something similar. In not wishing to down-play the powers and capacities of subjects, talk of *participants* can effectively over-rate them – an 'other side of the coin' mistake. The over-rating tendency should be rejected. Yet something crucial is also missed if the agential-subjects in such research are regarded as though they were the comparatively uncomplicated subjects of other research.

Situating our investigation

As noted, this text contributes to discussion of the ethical demands and epistemology of research for researchers, primarily postgraduate researchers, into sport. It specifically focuses on the epistemology of broadly *social-scientific* research into sport: research based in, for instance, sports sociology, sports history, philosophy of sport.

The academic study of sport generates a number of issues which, while not unique to sport, are posed with special intensity in that case. In part, this reflects strong traditions within the academic study of sport invoking the procedures of the natural sciences – such as physiology, biomechanics, psychology (on some conceptions) – but also those deploying social scientific and humanistic investigations, such as those mentioned earlier. So any satisfactory discussion of researching sport should treat each tradition judiciously, while giving appropriate weight to both. Thus the first tradition, which I call "sports science", utilizes the epistemological assumptions and the conception of ethical researching *it* associates with the natural sciences; the second makes similar moves – and a wide variety of them – drawing on assumptions and conceptions from (broadly) the many versions of social scientific investigation.[3]

At first blush, these two research traditions seem incompatible: each conceptualizes knowledge, truth, and research (especially the soundness of research) in its own terms. In doing so, each rejects the conceptions of the other tradition. Further, each foregrounds a style of research which is problematic from the other's point of view. If one's cases for research ethics begin from overt, laboratory-based experimentation with control groups, then covert, broadly ethnographic modes of enquiry can seem methodologically unsound. And vice versa. Rather than give, say, equal treatment to these traditions, this text urges, first, the fairly uncontentious claim that each fundamentally misconceives what the *contrasting* tradition is doing and, second, that each misrepresents the central concepts that are taken for granted in its own tradition. So that, for example, the sports scientists are unreliable guides in their advocacy of the scientific method. Since both traditions are wrong even in their own preferred area, little weight need be given to them here, beyond searching for the insight (if any) that grounds each. Then one moves forward by considering the implications of the realization that each tradition is a mixture of distinct insight (to be preserved) and shared confusion (to be set aside), locating the points of impact. But, throughout, considerations for social theory, such as sociology, provide the primary focus *here*. So the natural scientific enquiries are discussed only insofar as they shed light on such social investigations.

Researching cultural forms and practices

Once we recognize sport as "a constitutive element of . . . popular culture" (Tomlinson, 2005: xiv) or as a set of culturally-valued *practices* (Alderson and Crutchly, 1991), researching it centrally involves researching cultural forms or practices. Yet how are these to be researched? Clearly, lots of methods suggest themselves, especially if we hope to capture that culture as it stands. For instance, participant observation, oral history, and interviews (especially semi-structured interviews) offer the opportunities to investigate cultural contexts with the minimum of disturbance to what would have occurred had there been no research. Other methods, such as formal interviews, focus groups, and questionnaires, may be more intrusive, or they may take the subject out of the sporting activity itself. But what unites such methods for our purposes is their concern with the context-laden activity: hence, with at least some of the culture within which sporting activities take place, as well as with the sporting activities themselves (to draw a tendentious contrast). Moreover this conception of researching sport invites us to take a generous view of what is part of that activity. So that we could consider, not just, say, the team and its results, but also the coaching and training, the fan-base, the location of the stadium, and so on. Further, a concern with the institutional forms and settings of sport may lead us to include the governing bodies, perhaps in relation to competitions and events as well as rule changes. Then international bodies, such as the International Olympic Committee (IOC), may have a place. For these are not mere *adjuncts* to the sporting activity, but can provide the context within which such activities are made possible. We can imagine similar lists drawn up for the variety of sports and the variety of our concerns with them. But, in all cases, the research-question will be inflected by its need to include, or rule out, such material. For that determines the degree to which the research aims at *naturalism*, as well as the scope of that research.

A distinctive aspect of the view here is the close relation of the epistemological questions or issues to the ethical ones, demonstrated later. For example, the conception of the role of the researcher is shown to be essentially ethical: obligations on the researcher to the research community and to the discipline are ethical obligations. But those obligations have implications for the practice of sport research; and hence for its epistemology. Further, conceptions of one topic, and especially misconceptions of it, might be expected to apply more generally. For each element is held in place by that collection of shared assumptions which, in the research context, is called a *methodology* (contrasting it sharply with the kinds of methods it supports). If the issue raised, the question (then) asked, the knowledge (thus) generated, and the treatment of subjects are all part of a unified package – as our use of the term "methodology" here suggests – one would expect to find commonalities for consideration.

So, what conception of knowledge – that is, what epistemology – is presupposed by one's research into sport? In effect, my answer begins with two more (related) questions, and an assertion. The questions:

a   What kind of interest does one have in sport? And
b   What kinds of subjects is one deploying in one's research? And, in particular, are they human subjects (viewed as agents)?

Suppose the first question is answered broadly in terms of the social-science disciplines,[4] which often suggests a broadly naturalistic approach, and the second by granting human agential-subjects. Then our research will be of the kinds centrally discussed here. For the upshot of these responses identifies what might be called a *qualitative* research base (although that would be a new, or technical, use of the term) since it encompasses both concern with human subjects and treating those subjects as *persons*. Then (the assertion) the research epistemology of those engaged in what is thereby classified as *qualitative research* has an ethical dimension.

This text has, in effect, two over-arching ideas. The first, behind the book as a whole, is that high quality research into the social aspects of sport (as into other areas of social research) requires sophisticated consideration of the ethical and epistemological commitments specific to social research, of a kind typically not provided even in quite reliable guides to the detail, or the techniques, of such research.[5] In their justified concern with methods, such books can ignore methodology. Then the second idea, determining the structure of this book, is that the ethical questions interpenetrate the epistemological ones, and vice versa. The obligation to behave well in research is an ethical obligation. But, as an obligation to one's disciplinary background or field of study, it extends beyond simply one's treatment of research subjects. Further, the dependability of one's research designs places obligations on the research. So any satisfactory discussion of research design must address both ethical *and* epistemological questions. Were this right, one could not simply include a small sketch of one issue while elaborating the other. Yet that is what many texts offer. This *pair* of commitments determines the uniqueness of this work.

For a book aimed at sport researchers, sport (or even sport research) is rarely addressed *directly*. Even some examples come from outside sport research. But many traditional distinctions deployed in researching sport (especially that using human beings as 'subject') are misconceived. Thus examples must also be found elsewhere, since much research into sport is flawed in precisely the ways that this text aims to draw out. In particular, the distinction between qualitative and quantitative research is less revealing than is often supposed. And the contrast between research in the natural and the social sciences – sound as far as it goes – fails to capture many crucial features of research into sport: for instance, in neglecting how the research subjects are conceptualized. Further, similar confusions are perpetrated in attempts to characterize researchers' relations to research subjects as independent of how they engage with those subjects. However, actual pieces of flawed research are not typically discussed in detail (say, with quotation) since, in being too specific to this particular piece of research, such discussion readily turns into a critique of that actual piece of research only. Similarly, an example that is too hypothetical seems just a straw man, set up simply for target practice. Thus many of my examples, although based on genuine research projects, are presented abstractly, either to avoid the focus on the detail of the project or to steer clear of modifications the piece's author later introduced. Hence, while research into sport, especially social-scientific research, provides the vast majority of the contexts for the discussions, other broadly social scientific investigations suggest similar topics, giving my points here application in these cases also.[6]

Qualitative versus quantitative

As already mentioned, much research is self-defined as quantitative or qualitative – while granting some reservations about the usefulness of these classifications. Of course, research designs where the outcome is presented as numbers or quantities differ from those where it is not. Moreover, that such-and-such is a good way to present the data tells us something about the nature of those data; hence, about the conception of truth and knowledge supporting these being the data. Sport-researchers call their data or investigations *quantitative* to make points they take to be important. These typically include the data's suitability to statistical analysis, or the ease with which one data-set can be compared with another. So, too, in calling their data or investigation *qualitative*, sport-researchers are usually making an oppositional point to the effect that their research deals with persons; and, as far as possible, recognizes the importance of the contexts which are the sites of the subject's characteristic behaviours – such as playing sport and training for it, or being a sports fan, or some such.

But these 'qualitative' virtues could also be *claimed* by research (for instance using large-scale questionnaires) which is amenable to statistical analysis, and where the interaction with the subjects is at one remove. (This is often achieved by pre-coding of responses, so that subjects are, in effect, merely selecting from a set of responses – including other! – offered by the researcher.) This is very far from the full interaction of two persons, which usually involves their talking with each other. Similarly, much research calling itself qualitative may actually become quantitative in execution: that is, the data generated may be viewed and analyzed in mathematical, and hence quantitative, ways. For instance, ways of coding the data (for instance, using the NUD*IST or Ethnograph computer programmes)[7] can effectively turn data originally based on human discussion – say, as transcripts of discussions or interviews – into data suitable to be treated statistically, where we automatically worry first about reliability and validity, modelling these on reliability and validity from a conception of natural-scientific investigations. Such an outcome can lose, or minimize, the distinctiveness of these data.

So research using persons as subjects should be distinguished from research where, even when the subjects are in fact persons, those subjects are not treated as persons. The simplest example of the second kind is an investigation of the hand in a swimming stroke: we simply recognize that, for instance, our swimmer failed to do as required, but the focus is on her hand, not elsewhere. Here, the subject is, in effect, the hand (or, perhaps, hand and arm) in the swim-tank only. In particular, the person is not typically asked about the stroke: how it seemed to her is beside the point.

Yet our usual mode of interaction with other people is different. Such interaction is characterized by *talk*: by social niceties about the weather; by questions and answers on topics both trivial and profound; by monologues (and attentive listening to them); by jokes; and all the rest. So one key feature of treating one's research subjects *as* persons will be that a place must be found for all this talk. Moreover, worries about its soundness as research-data should not lead us to dismiss it initially. Instead, this should first be taken as data, then consideration should be given as to its soundness. After all, we are pretty good in our daily lives at distinguishing truth from half truths, and these from outright lies, especially with those we know (as we can know our research subjects).

Granting that the researcher here engages in a kind of conversation recognizes the subject's interaction in the research process; and hence the need to treat such subjects morally. Hence research epistemology is connected to its ethics. For recognizing one's research subjects as persons helps clarify the nature of the ethical researcher's obligations to them. In our usual inter-person interaction, moral obligations permit ethical justification of omissions, and occasionally even 'white lies'. Such points carry over to research ethics, making some logical space for ethically-conducted covert research – constraints on such research can then be explored in sport-related contexts.

A human conception of research

A central thread of my conception of research concerns both the nature of human action in human contexts and the moral character of such action. The terms "moral" and "ethical" are used here more or less interchangeably: both indicate the constraints on what one ought, or ought not, to do in a particular situation. Both would be contrasted with kinds of prudential obligation on which one acts in such-and-such a way to secure praise or avoid punishment, or some such. In following the dictates of morality, we neither, on the one hand, follow pragmatic or practical considerations – we do not follow rules merely to avoid penalties, say – nor, on the other, track external goals, with money or fame as the obvious examples. That is to say, I reject the contrast between morality as obligation and 'ethics as ethos',[8] which accompanies a sociological version of ethics, stressing what people usually or normally do. While morality is normative (it proscribes and prescribes behaviour), it does not necessarily reflect what most people in fact do – nor even what is done by most people in a society or at a time. Certainly it need not match this. For its foundation does not reside in whether or not behaviour is typical, or what most people do, since 'most people' could behave badly in some context. Indeed, as with children learning long division, perhaps most of the examples given of long division are wrong! But this does not preclude there being normatively correct 'answers' in context. And similarly for moral obligations.

It is worth addressing briefly a question concerning the force behind ethical obligations. Behind legal conclusions is the force of law: do what the law says, or be fined or sent to jail! Equally, (other) prudential conclusions have such a force: do this, and things will be good for you (or, more likely, don't do it, and things will go badly). But moral judgements are regularly and rightly contrasted with prudential ones; so what is the force of moral obligation? My answer is that, seen one way, there is not, and cannot be, such an external force behind moral judgements since, if there were, our actions would not be flowing from moral reasons but for these others (perhaps prudentially).

Plato's discussion (sometimes called the Euthyphro Problem: see McGinn, 1992: 13–14) brings out this point. Let us assume that some such authority lies behind moral judgements; and then show such a supposition to be self-refuting. So imagine that appeal is made to some authority behind morality. (For ease of exposition, I shall call this authority "God", but nothing much turns on that decision.) Now identify some act uncontentiously morally wrong: again, for short, I shall talk about murder. But other examples make exactly the same point. Then "Thou shalt not murder" has two readings: either (a) murder is wrong because God wills it (that is, it is wrong on God's say-so), or (b) God recognizes the wrongness of murder, and passes that information on. These seem to exhaust the options.

Of course, in option (b) God is not after all an authority. Rather, God simply recognizes the wrongness – it is wrong for . . . well, whatever makes it wrong. But, importantly, on this option God's authority does *not* make murder wrong. So if, as initially assumed, some authority behind moral judgement is needed, this option fails to deliver. So turn to option (a): here, murder is wrong on God's say-so – here God's authority determines that murder is wrong; and nothing but God's decision makes this so. But now it seems entirely arbitrary that murder is wrong, or that friendship is good. It does not depend on specific features or properties of murder or of friendship. Since it *is* arbitrary, God could have made friendship wrong and murder good – she did not; but there is no reason why she did not. Indeed, there could not be such a reason: if there were, God would merely be recognizing that reason, which returns us to option (b)! And one cannot argue independently for the moral rightness of God's conclusion here without detaching that conclusion from God's decision.

Thus, if we imagine an authority behind morality – say, the authority of an author – we must recognize that such a supposition is incoherent; there could not be an authority behind morality, since assuming that means that the conclusions are not moral after all. Of course, nothing here turns on my selecting God as a candidate authority behind morality. For any candidate authority would be in the same position. Hence, granting that there is moral authority here also grants that such authority cannot come from behind (or outside) morality. There is no justifiable demand for an author here.

Let us therefore return to our discussion of the ethical as it applies in sport research. For the ethical realm, and hence morality, is centrally other-regarding. So, with Morgan (2006: 25), I take a moral consideration to be: ". . . one that gives pride of place to the good of others with whom we interact and the good of the projects we share and take up together".

Further, Morgan (2006: 25) rightly quotes with approval Bernard Williams (2002: 20) urging that: "simply to pursue what you want . . . is not the stuff of morality; if [that] is your only motive . . . then you are not within morality and you do not have . . . any ethical life".

It is no accident that the moral is regularly contrasted with the selfish! Thus the central province of morality will be people's actions in the world: in particular, their interactions with others. To some degree, one might (with justice) think that all human actions lie within the realm of moral concern. Certainly it includes our treatment of those others who are our research subjects. This draws straightforwardly on the sense (as discussed earlier) in which researching other people can be seen as locating ourselves in a conversation with them. That follows from our treating them as persons, since conversation, with its moral constraints,[9] is our typical interaction with other persons. It has implications both for the epistemological stance of research with persons and for the sorts of ethical regard offered to those persons as subjects of one's research.

But many researchers into sport would worry, although without justice, that selecting *talk*-based research methods leads automatically to poorly supported research conclusions. If one selected such methods to address "the thoughts and feelings of people . . . [then these] are difficult to quantify" (Gratton and Jones (2004: 25). Moreover, "much of the data will lack focus . . . [and face] . . . problems of recall, misperception, and incorrect knowledge" (Gratton and Jones, 2004: 143). Further, "[r]eliable and valid analysis of qualitative interviews may be *more* difficult" (Gratton and Jones, 2004: 143; emphasis mine) than, say, using a questionnaire. In particular, the fact that this person discussed with another, or listened to him/her, may raise questions about repeatability. Further, considering the need to be theoretically informed, Gratton and Jones (2004: 72, quoting Yiannakis) note that research lacking this theoretical dimension is "likely to generate findings of a narrow and ungeneralizable value". But these issues can be overcome, as they typically are in conversations; and parallel problems can be discerned with other, more formal techniques.

The failure of some sports researchers to recognize the reliability of ideas generated in these ways may be explained partly through a mistaken account of knowledge – and especially of natural scientific knowledge – given by those *not* engaged in researching human action in human contexts. For, as we will see, that view of science is shared, in two different ways, by those whose errors I diagnose; and it supports their misunderstandings. Moreover, failing to grasp both the nature of knowledge and the place of human subjects here tends to leave researchers at a loss when it comes to ethical safeguards for such subjects. Or so I shall argue.

In effect, then, the argument first stresses the connection of the conception of knowledge appropriate to research with human subjects to the fact that such subjects are viewed as persons. But, of course, typical persons are moral agents, able to talk with one another; and thereby to explain their actions. So this concession – seeing one's research subjects as persons – clarifies how those subjects should be treated. Hence, it makes explicit the connection between one's investigation and concerns with research ethics.

The *treatment* of research subjects is our focus here, concerned both with respecting the research subject's *autonomy* and with the demands of avoiding *maleficence* (that is, the causing of harm) as ways of behaving ethically. In addition, moral concerns can also impact on research ethics through the discussion of *beneficence* (or the positive good the research will do).[10] And certainly these are explicit topics for discussion when, say, health-related research (for example, in exercise provision for cardiac rehabilitation) is discussed, under the auspices of the NHS (National Health Service) in the UK, by Local Research Ethics Committees (LRECs). But, as McNamee *et al.* (2007: 53) note, "although ethics committees are charged with the appraisal of the benefit, value or worth of research, . . . there is remarkably little in the literature by way of any frameworks to help with this appraisal". So that some of the deliberations of such committees have more to do with the prudential matter of avoiding harm than with genuinely moral concerns.

Others have, or could have, defended many aspects of the picture of research expounded here. The main differences turn both on the precise *combination* of such aspects and on the particular emphasis provided. Thus, many texts (Punch, 1998: 20–21; Bryman, 2001: 266–67) stress the importance of *the research question* – the need to be clear exactly what one is researching, including connecting such research questions to the methods one can then deploy. But they miss the more general *erotetic* (or question-and-answer) structure of research; and, within it, the contextual nature of the research question. So their perspective here is comparatively limited. For only the erotetic character of research fully explains what may otherwise seem mysterious: how that research question is embedded in the theoretical structures of particular *matrices of disciplinary aims* (Toulmin, 1972: 124). Then the context makes plain how to understand the particular concepts. Hence, the very same words can motivate quite different research investigations, thereby amounting to different research questions – despite being expressed in that same form of words! As chapter 2 grants, the combining of disciplinary matrices implicit in many deployments of multi-methods research designs brings out clearly the connections between the research question, however expressed, and the appropriate methods of answering. These highlight some rarely recognized problems for such designs, issues more usually presented as independent. Similarly, that one's subjects are persons, and hence moral agents, is rarely connected directly to discussions of the researcher's ethical relation to those subjects. Then seeing those issues as integrated here explains features of them that might otherwise seem puzzling.

Some readers may find the examples offered simplified, or abstract, or otherwise unconvincing. Throughout, my examples aim at affording attentive readers a clear view of my contentions. As a work in philosophy, these contentions rest firmly on my *arguments*. Then the examples, if effective, make plain the central cases concerning the analysis here. Giving more (and fuller) examples could improve this text, as some critics will doubtless urge. But doing so would make the present work a great deal longer. And, even with that additional length, the examples offered could still be contested *as examples*: that is, without addressing the points they were supposed to exemplify. Were other examples supplied, those examples too would be susceptible to the same lines of criticism. And readers are invited to supply their own examples and the corresponding analysis of those examples thereby subtended by the principles sketched here.

Some points might still be hard to recognize in the familiar practices of researchers into sport. For instance, on my view, a huge conceptual mistake is made in conceiving voluntary informed consent (VIC) as a 'gold standard' for the ethical treatment of research subjects (see chapter 8). One commentator objected that no actual researcher into sport that he/she knew treated VIC as I have described: instead, very few people treated VIC as I have suggested they should. Yet this response misses precisely my point: that the theoretical account of VIC such people deploy – and hence the criticism they make of the ethical stances of *others* – draws on exactly the conception of VIC that I have outlined. Were that account removed, they would be left with no justification of their practice! Further, just such a commitment to VIC is implicit in the claim that: ". . . volunteers were given a *complete* explanation of procedures and possible risks and discomforts involved in the study and informed consent was obtained" (Engels *et al.*, 1996: 323; emphasis mine).

For what exactly is a "complete" explanation of these things? In using the term "complete", the researchers here claim exactly what I shall be at pains to deny is possible, since its supposed *completeness* assumes a finite totality of topics for explanation and consent.

Thus some difficulties in understanding this work reflect difficulties with philosophy. Sometimes this is simply due to the unfamiliarity with philosophical techniques and practices; but sometimes connecting abstract theoretical concerns to the practical issues (here concerning research) generate more profound problems of understanding. For this reason, within the body of this text such abstract presentations are flagged up clearly but kept to a minimum; and one major discussion is consigned to the Appendix.

Locating Ramsey's Maxim; and our contextualism

But if a failure to recognize its concerns as centrally philosophical gives one reason why this text's project might be misunderstood, another reason is its deployment of a technique not widely familiar even within philosophy – its use of *Ramsey's Maxim* (Ramsey, 1931: 116–17; Bambrough 1969: 10): "wherever there is a violent and persistent philosophical dispute there is likely to be a false assumption shared by both parties".

This strategy, therefore, undermines *both* of a pair of standard oppositions by rejecting an assumption both share. So Ramsey's Maxim does not offer a kind of 'middle way' between two alternatives: here, between two competing views of the place of truth. Rather Ramsey's Maxim involves rejecting a key element of each of the two views (and hence rejecting *both* views) – while recognizing, and retaining, key insights of each of them. Since this argumentative strategy is not especially familiar, it can be missed. But recognizing it is crucial since, from each view Ramsey's Maxim is used to put aside, we will look like adherents of the other view!

For example, truth-deniers (such as postmodernists) recognize problems with the assumption, prevalent in much writing on natural science, of an implied exceptionlessness of any conclusion: that saying such-and-such is true seems to imply that it is true in all situations. Then their thesis becomes roughly that, since there fails to be just one exceptionless account of such-and-such, applicable in all contexts, there is no 'truth of the matter' here. Their thought is reinforced when they see that their opponents are typically urging that truth consists of 'one right answer'. Hence, when the place of truth is defended, truth-deniers take that to endorse 'one right answer'; when exceptionlessness is denied, we are 'convicted' of endorsing their kind of relativism.

In reality, researchers into sport rarely present the matter so starkly. Hence, with a continuum of cases, there are rarely truth-deniers as explicit as Arnd Krüger (2004) who infers from the fact that some of the footage for Leni Riefenstahl's *Olympia* was left on the cutting-room floor – hence the final result is a *selection* from the material – that none of it could possibly be *true*. Or, as Krüger (2004: 34–35) puts it: "... you have a kaleidoscope of distinct ideas about the very same events ... This makes it difficult to come visually to the core of the Games (if there is one) ...".

Take an apparently simple question like, "How many participants were there at the 1936 Olympic Games in Berlin?" Well, some texts report how many athletes competed. But that cannot settle the matter. First, it is not clear that only athletes count as participants: what about, say, officials or coaches? Yet, even when that decision is made (say, in favour of including the officials), and the place – or lack of it – of the audience members is also resolved, since they participate in the experience, there might still be no single, uncontentious answer. For instance, if the US relay team included a reserve who in fact ran neither in any of the heats nor in the final, is such a person a participant or not? Clearly, there is no given criterion for deciding. On that basis, someone might conclude that there was no fact of the matter here about even so straightforward a question. Hence, that many answers are of equal plausibility – each reflecting the preoccupations of this or that interested party. And surely what follows for a relatively simple question such as "How many participants ...?" will be equally problematic for more (apparently) complex questions.

Explicitly aligning his discussion with "the postmodernist", Krüger (2004: 35) asks, rhetorically, "[w]hat then were the original Games? ... were there any original Games?" – taking the "no" answer as obvious! With no "original Games" (of 1936) here, there is no fact of the matter to ground disputes about what did happen at those Games: hence, no truth about what happened. Read this way, his position clearly involves truth-denial.

At the other end of this continuum are those, like Belinda Wheaton (2002: 243), who focus on "the ground between these extreme positions of positivism and postmodernism": they are not *yet* obviously truth-deniers. But can the position be sustained as it stands? Or will it, on consistent interpretation, collapse into truth-denial? If Krüger is *explicit* in grounding his relativism in the denial of a single, exceptionless account of the sporting event (here the 1936 Olympic Games), Wheaton's view too might be read in that way. Our purpose here is less to resolve such questions than to show what follows from recognizing truth-denial.

But the insights driving such positions can be granted – that, when dealing with people, claims are typically not exceptionless, and do not apply in all contexts – without concluding (as our truth-deniers do) that therefore there is no truth. On the contrary, the impact of our contextualism will be very important for any reader who wants to grasp the position here without going to its elaboration later in the work. The idea is *both* that there is not just one truth-value (applied across all contexts) for a particular claim and that this does not preclude truth (or 'facts of the matter') in context. Consider, as a simple example, the claim, "There is an oil tanker in the harbour": this claim will be neither simply true nor simply false even once we identify the time referred to and the harbour in question (Travis, 2008: 235–36). For, in different contexts, the same situation might justify asserting or denying this claim, and rightly. Suppose (with Travis) that the vessel in question is a hovercraft with oil-drums lashed to its deck: for instance, is it really an oil tanker? The oil-hungry might be happy to grant that. And the oil company's decision to use this new kind of tanker in this (shallow) harbour might be enough to decide the matter then. But that need not apply in all cases. So, here, there is no single, unitary truth across all contexts. Some pedants might debate whether the hovercraft is genuinely *in* the harbour. It does not seem that, in all cases, such discussion *must* always be resolved in one way (in that case, which?); nor even that any resolution must hold forever.

As such a case illustrates, different contexts (rightly) justify a certain diversity in answers, with no plausible assumption of exceptionlessness to any of these answers. But that does not imply that there is no truth here. Once we determine in which of these contexts, these 'worlds', we are, there is little difficulty in deciding what the 'truth of the matter' then is. So, in context (but only in context), there may be a correct answer concerning the truth of what is claimed. At least, there is a precise claim to debate.

This contextualism, drawing on work by Charles Travis,[11] is a major philosophical commitment of this text, but appropriately not one presented in full detail. Instead, the body of the text contains two overlapping presentations, using different examples, in the hope of striking a chord with readers: as has been discussed here; and in chapter 2. And the Appendix contains another account.

An erotetic conception of research

Even though it is the topic of chapter 2, it is worth stressing here that a major importance of the contextualism just sketched lies in its explanation of the fundamentally erotetic picture of research. That is, a 'question-and-answer' model explains the relationship between the research project (best understood via the research questions) and the methods deployed in that research, since the selection of those research methods is constrained by the need to address the research question. So a succinct account of the erotetic seems valuable.[12]

To illustrate it, consider two simple cases where this idea misfires. In the first, the selection of methods amounts to a kind of fishing trip for data – there is no precise question driving the research design. Thus, a researcher with the vague aspiration to find out what was going on in her local sports centre has no obvious methods to hand. That is because, so far, there is no precise question. Were such a researcher then to send out questionnaires, organize focus groups, interview the sports centre managers and local government officials, she might certainly seem to be finding out about the sports centre. Yet, with no question, this material is not (yet) data, for it is not evidence in support of this claim or that. So this does not (yet) describe a research project – lacking a question, there is no basis to select methods.

Parallel cases are sometimes encountered in natural scientific investigation of sport, especially for beginning researchers. Asked for their research topic, they say, "I want to use such-and-such piece of equipment" (the latest force-platform, for example). But without a question that the force-platform is recruited to answer, and therefore any discussion of its appropriateness to answer that question, we have not begun research.

So one can start from methods but, in the absence of a question, the research process cannot begin. The second case begins from a question (at least the appearance of one) but no methods. For example, a researcher interested in what occurred in local sports policy but whose methods drew only on what some official thought had occurred, with no possibility of critique (for instance, on the basis of the published documents), would be separating the methods from the question. For those methods were directed at perceptions of the outcome, not the outcome itself, while the question concerns that outcome. And if, for theoretical reasons, one disputed that contrast of perceptions with outcomes, the revised question should reflect that too. In missing the connection urged here, the researcher in this situation has ignored the erotetic character of research.

Or, again, suppose our researcher aims to understand the impact of some theoretical concept (for instance *hegemonic masculinity*) as it applies in the world of some sporting context (for example the local rugby club). What is needed, of course, is to make the question or issue sufficiently sharp so that it both asks what one wants to have explained and allows that data might be collected in some way or other. Suppose one key fact was that "[d]rinking and the pub culture remain a strong part of the . . . [local] rugby league scene" (Spracklen, 1995: 110):[13] how does one go further, first, to validate what (so far) might seem merely anecdotal evidence, and second to explore its bearing on the general topic? Various methods suggest themselves (indeed, just the ones the published research employed): we need to collect data in both the pub context and the club context. One might be investigated ethnographically, using participant observation; the other might form the basis for semi-structured interviews. A key consideration here involves either avoiding *saying* "hegemonic masculinity" to anyone who might not understand it, having opportunities to see who did understand, and explaining it to those who did not. So dividing up the question and organizing the appropriate methods for each part come together. They do so, of course, just because research is erotetic. Recognizing the centrality of these points for the whole text should make it easier to understand.

Structure of the text

Structurally, then, this text is unusual. As noted previously, its motivation is two-fold. The first lies in the increasing practical need for postgraduate researchers to think in more sophisticated ways about the demands of research methodology, especially in the social sciences – in particular for the social scientific investigation of sport. That is, to understand the conception of knowledge (and hence the kind of data) required to resolve their research questions; and the methods needed to arrive at that data. Second, there is a more widespread appreciation of the theoretical requirement that all researchers import (or assume) a plausible epistemology for research designs using the methods they intend to deploy. That, for me, also incorporates a number of ethical matters. To clarify these matters in ways useful to *both* the constituencies sketched earlier, this text combines sketches of the central arguments from this context with vignettes of research designs exemplifying relevant points.

But part of the project here involves disputing or denying the fragmentation implicit in many ways of drawing up the project of sports research, even with human subjects: not, of course, something readily argued for explicitly. One symptom of the attitude disputed here is reflected in questions of research ethics being regularly treated – and taught to students – as though they could be prized-off from the epistemological issues of a particular research design. Yet, first, the conception of the ethical standards deployed is a confused mixture of idealization and nonsense, reflected in the 'dispute' around the status and importance of voluntary informed consent (VIC). Second, epistemological concerns are thought to be really the province of the disciplines – an attitude especially prevalent when disciplines grow from the natural sciences: that they (rather than philosophy of science) will tell us about *the scientific method*, and its implications. Of course, because both thoughts could be defended (if implicitly), it becomes important to determine how each is misguided.

As their titles suggest, my aims in the chapters other than this one are largely negative: to show ways of conceptualizing research protocols and data that are not adequate if we want to conduct good research, in both ethical and epistemological senses. Those chapters, in effect, highlight particular ways for sporting research to be flawed. Thus, the (erotetic) relation between research methods and the questions they aim to answer must be given due weight (chapter 2); and researchers investigating sportsplayers, or sports organizations, or governing bodies (and therefore interacting with *persons*) must recognize that they stand in a moral relationship with their research subjects, just by virtue of their subjects being persons.

One consequence of this relationship is the key role here of *talk*, the conversation between people (chapter 3). Moreover, a more generous view of truth is required to avoid either a misplaced, and scientistic, picture of knowledge, which is inappropriately constraining (chapter 5), or some variety of truth-denial (chapters 6–7). As we will see, giving up the search for truth undermines one's capacity to conduct *genuine* research. For research here presupposes the concept of truth (chapter 4).

Avoiding this set of misconceptions captures an epistemology suitable for, at least, the kinds of social research into sport which stress the culture, or context, in which that sport occurs. But, since the relationship between the researcher and his/her subjects is a *moral* relationship, respecting the subject's autonomy also poses questions reflecting the research protocol, contrasting overt designs (chapter 8) with covert ones (chapter 9). Then recognizing the flaws in the traditionally endorsed 'gold standard' of VIC permits clarification of a morally-responsible *covert* research. Such research typically has a place when confronting sporting culture. Indeed, if the account of fully-overt research offered here is correct, most (perhaps all) research into sport has a covert dimension. If the typical researcher must leave the sporting context as undisturbed as possible, explicitly covert designs will become common. For researchers will recognize that elaborating the research topic or research protocol, or even disclosing that one is a researcher, can compromise the responses of research subjects, when their untrammeled responses are what one requires. For that reason, explicitly covert research may become the usual mode for researching sporting culture. The obligations of the researcher to his/her research must also be recognized (chapter 10): for that permits the researcher's appeal to the constraints from whatever disciplinary matrix he/she recruits.

Thus, despite my commitment to the integrated nature of the picture of research developed here, some central theses can be considered in (relative) isolation from one another – which aids the text's usefulness for others. So it first identifies, in part I, the specific *heresies* I endorse in the epistemology of research for social scientific research into sport, given that one's subjects are human beings, viewed or treated as such. Then it elaborates each *heresy* in turn, grouping them together, and argues for the accuracy of my conclusions.

Parts II through IV reinforce the picture as a whole, but also permit readers to look at the elements one by one, offering cases (sometimes in the form of vignettes) to exemplify those investigative directions or conclusions. Hence, to offer arguments for each without commitment to the picture as a whole. Still, doing so involves acting in a direction contrary to the holistic spirit of this book's contentions. And, since the conclusions are summarized in this chapter, there will be some repetition when they appear again.

Further, my account of both the nature and importance of these features is defended by specific arguments. Then those wishing to differ from me cannot simply deny what I assert, or assert what I deny. A candidate proof in mathematics provides the right comparison. There, an objector cannot simply deny the conclusion, but must show in which of the steps the error occurs. If what is put forward as a proof fails to be one, the objector must show where the proof is defective, by highlighting the error made in line 42, and so on. A similar argumentative structure operates here: the person disputing my conclusions must highlight the flaw in my arguments (if he/she can); only then can my conclusions be set aside.

Moreover, some time has been allocated to demonstrating the validity of an argument form to which I appeal on more than one occasion: that against assuming finite totalities (discussed later in this chapter).

With this in mind, clarity in the exposition of key points becomes especially important, perhaps to the point of bluntness. So readers must grant that "pinch of salt" that Frege (1984: 193) recognizes as necessary when one's target is not the fully articulated, fully theoretical, account of the matter.

Sketch of the picture of research

My strategy involves, first, introducing each of the features clearly in this chapter; second, elaborating each, and exemplifying it, in parts II through IV. Elements of that view, together with some of its argument, include:

a   The problems of stating my picture clearly and briefly: it does not lend itself to summary; and one way it progresses deploys Ramsey's Maxim, denying an assumption shared by advocates of each alternative view.
b   The erotetic character of research – the contemporary picture of the importance of 'the research question' is correct, but does not take us far enough, because it is not rooted in a more general contextualism.
c   The rejection of the centrality of the traditional qualitative/quantitative contrast – the more important idea identifies those research designs that recognize their subjects as human beings.
d   The focus on *persons* typically prioritizes the 'naturalistic' end of the research continuum: that is, the contexts in which those persons *act*, which is especially appropriate for social scientific investigation of sport.
e   The requirement that research designs aim at truth; then standard concerns with the soundness of research data (such as reliability and validity) are seen as aimed at securing truth.
f   The concern with objectivity (and such like) for human-based sport research points once again to a concern with truth.
g   Many large questions about the nature of science reflect this concern with the place of truth: rejecting certain positivistic conceptions allows us to offer the insights from a broadly Kuhnian picture of natural science, with its differentiation from the social sciences.
h   Mention of Kuhn seems to raise the spectre of *paradigms* (hence of paradigm-relativity): but does not do so once it is granted that, for Kuhn, social investigations were not paradigm-relative (having no 'normal science' phase).
i   However, truth-ascription is contextual; hence, although there are reasons, sometimes, to be incredulous about metanarratives, context-relative truths should be recognized as providing all that is needed.

j   Causality in the human world: an intentional account reinforces both the impossibility of finite totalities of properties here, and highlights distinctive features of causality for humans (of the kind relevant in sporting contexts).

k   The recognition that regarding one's research subjects as persons connects ethical matters to research concerns.

l   The integrity of the research means circumscribing the role of research subject.

m   There are issues of exceptionlessness – objecting to the unjustified assumption of *all*, *every* (of finite totalities), regularly occurring in descriptions or evaluations of research designs (discussed later).

A reader content with the earlier exposition on a certain point can focus on the elaboration of those points he/she takes to be contentious. This will speed his/her reading of the text, aiding focus on the issues that *are* contentious, or problematic, or just less clearly elaborated here. But, for convenience in locating similar topics, the features of my position are grouped under three broad headings, reflected in the topics of parts II through IV.

A. *The nature of research*

Concern with the nature and goal of research begins by granting that identifying 'the research question' is fundamental, a demand more powerful than is often assumed. For the research question is erotetic: that is, as part of a 'question-and-answer' structure. Of course, the research under discussion here is not like that conducted in project-development 'R&D' departments. Instead, research is, by its nature, is essentially knowledge-generating, at least in intention. Yet, since knowledge in this context is knowledge *of* what is true, research is inexorably connected to truth. No doubt the connection between research and truth might be exploited in many ways (for example, not *only* through hypothesis-generation). But it would be odd to grant both that such-and-such was research and that it lacked any knowledge-generating capacity.

Two important points follow from this recognition. First, other terms (for instance, *insight*) do not free one from the need for truth – it will only be a genuine insight if what is claimed as a result of it is *so* (that is, it is true). Second, the connection between knowledge and truth means that the target of research can therefore be characterized in terms of truth. This will be important when turning to evaluation of research data: consider in this light what Sparkes (1998: 365) speaks of as a "holy trinity" of:

* *validity*, understood as whether a measure (say) actually relates to the concept it is claimed to examine;
* *reliability*, understood as the consistency of a measure across contexts and researchers;
* *generalizability*, understood as the degree to which conclusions can be extended beyond the population investigated.

These are important (see chapter 4) because they aim to ensure that the data from research are truth-generating. Moreover, methodologies (and then methods) are directed at generating such knowledge, or insight, or whatever; and may be appraised accordingly. But the nature of knowledge appropriately sought in social-scientific investigations provides no special problems for our research designs. Indeed, many of the constraints here are standard constraints on knowledge-claims (such as the *principle of total evidence*: Carnap, 1950: 211) that have application in whatever kind of enquiry one engages. For instance, we are concerned to have *sound* data rather than hear-say or anecdote; we would expect the independence of that data from the whim of the researcher; we take the data we have to be all that is relevant, except in those cases where we have a specific reason to doubt that fact. Since these are quite general requirements on knowledge claims, this is not a place where research on persons is second-best.

Still, the focus of sport means that many of the questions asked concern our understanding of (human) actions occurring in precise contexts; our contextualism reinforces the need to pay attention (as far as possible) to such contexts. This explains why, wanting to investigate an aspect of sporting culture such as windsurfing, one gives close attention to entering that culture without disrupting it – perhaps by negotiating for oneself a role within that culture (say, as a 'core woman' in the windsurfer community, one who actually windsurfs: Wheaton, 2002: 255). Then the research presence will be minimally disruptive of the original context. This in turn suggests that typical research will aim at 'naturalism' or 'real-world' designs, retaining as much of the actual context as possible – a thought pervasive throughout this text.

B. *Truth and knowledge*

Much work concerning the nature of truth and of knowledge is ultimately done by Ramsey's Maxim: that is, by identifying and denying an assumption about truth shared by both the embattled accounts underpinning scientistic and postmodernist pictures of sport-research. And, since our concern is primarily with social research into sport, the natural scientific case need not be addressed in its full generality. Here, that use of Ramsey's Maxim identifies and rejects an ahistorical and universal, 'one right answer', conception of truth which drives many scientistic misconceptions concerning research into human situations, including setting inappropriate goals for social science. But this conception of truth also grounds that deposition of science as a model of knowledge urged by (especially) postmodernist theorists. Rejecting this shared assumption of the two positions allows us to reject them both.

In practice, close attention is needed to each of the pictures thereby *rejected*. First, rejecting naive inductivism as well as other broadly positivistic accounts of science (such as Popper's) involves both dismissing as incoherent what they assume about truth (or science) and articulating something towards an alternative, here exemplified by Kuhn's view of science (chapter 5). The chief error here is a scientism on which knowledge is modelled on scientific knowledge, but with a flawed picture of natural science. Our discussion of Kuhn offers a more accurate account of scientific knowledge, and scientific truth, and lays the groundwork for a more positive account of truth for social-scientific research, such as the research into sport which is our primary focus.

Second, rejecting some versions of postmodernist thinking, and its associated relativism, highlights positive features of truth and knowledge (already argued to be central to this research, see chapter 4). To anticipate a discussion there, there are simple truths in our human contexts. The complex and historically inflected fact that, say, I have an overdraft is partly made true, when true, by other humanly-inspired facts about the banking system. So my having an overdraft might make no sense at some later time. Had the economic system developed differently, the very idea of an overdraft might make no sense; as indeed it might make no sense to conclude that such-and-such a person scored a try. For try-scoring requires at least the human practices of rugby: so it has a certain contingency. But here and now it is a real possibility: and may even be true – that would be for an enquiry to determine. Yet it could only fail to be true now by being false. Could there be some more overarching truths? Nothing argued here precludes it. Indeed, the position here involves a contextual defence of the possibility of such 'metanarratives', in their context. Contrary to what is widely assumed, the rejection of 'one right answer', or Truth with a capital "t", does not require giving up the justified search for truth. Indeed, giving up that search would give up the project of research as understood in this context.

Further, a key distinction is reflected here. The intentional explanation of an event depends on how the event is appropriately characterized (and such like) by its agents. Thus, although it is true that John dated the second tallest girl in London, he did not regard his actions that way: this was not a description under which he behaved as he did. For causality, we characterize both the action and its context independently of how the action might be seen by those involved. Running together these two modes of explanation (the intentional and the causal) will typically be confusing. And the intentional mode of explanation is, of course, the province of persons viewed as persons.

C. *Ethical matters*

In effect, three arguments concerning ethical questions (and their connection to our central epistemological position) are presented. The first (chapter 3) recognizes the centrality of an ethical dimension to research where humans, viewed as humans, are the researched. It follows simply from the need to treat (other) humans ethically. The second (chapter 8) involves identifying the conceptual (as well as practical) limitations of VIC. Were VIC a 'gold standard' for research with human subjects, we would know what ethical treatment of research subjects required. Of course, VIC is rarely if ever achieved in its *full* form (the only form where the 'gold standard' claim might be made). And insistence on VIC precludes many research designs, especially for sport, which seem intuitively ethical (in not being harmful), but where the research protocol requires a degree of covertness.

That is, covertness can be justified, both as the only way of conducting 'necessary' research and as ethically constrained. But VIC in its full form *fails* as a guarantee of ethical treatment: its standard is unattainable in principle as well as in practice. Because the impossibility of meeting the demands set by (full) VIC is *conceptual*, not merely practical, the 'gold standard' of VIC cannot be resurrected by tinkering with its formulation. Further, against it one deploys a form of argument of great power in these contexts: that of disputing the assumption of finite totalities.

Third (chapter 9), we ask what constraints on ethical research with human subjects – at least, for sport – follow from our thinking through the sorts of ethical obligations to others that follow here; and especially those following for covert research designs. For, once granting the previous argument, almost no research on humans can be fully overt. Hence the implications for covert research of central ethical principles, such as *respect for persons*, must be explored.

A further topic *broadly* involving treatment of the research subject combines the ethical concerns with more strictly epistemological ones by considering the researchers' roles, as a way to correctly locate the roles appropriate to a research subject (as subject) in typical research designs, treated in chapter 10. This discussion explains my preference throughout for the old-fashioned-sounding "subjects" (rather than, say, "participants") for referring to the researched. Seen one way, researchers too *participate* in the research; and my use of the term "subjects" does not preclude granting many powers, as well as many rights, to the researched.

Science, exceptionlessness, and finite totalities

In this text, a form of argument occasionally used denies the possibility of a finite totality of properties in a particular context; and thereby denies what those assuming such a finite totality thought followed.

A simple case can introduce this form of argument. We all accept, I think:

- first, that if the *exact* situation occurs on two occasions, there will be the same outcome;
- second, that if the situation is not the same, there is (at most) *no reason* to assume that the same outcome will be the result – the differences might preclude it; further, if we know only that the situation is not the same, we cannot be sure of the outcome here, one way or the other;
- third, that when, in what had *seemed* like exactly the same situation, there was a *different* outcome, this must reflect a difference in the initial situation (broadly conceived), even if we had not noticed one.

These are three plausible intuitions about causality.

As a simplified example showing these three ideas clearly, suppose that, on Monday, one snooker or pool ball (the cue ball) on the table strikes another, and the second ball (the object ball) falls into the pocket. Now (first thought) if, on Tuesday, the balls are in precisely the same configuration, with the cue ball moving as it did on Monday, and the object ball positioned as it was, then the object ball will again fall into the pocket.

But (second thought) we would lack the same confidence in our prediction about the behaviour of the object ball when the situation changed, so that it is not obviously the same as on Monday – say, the snooker table were re-built overnight. Perhaps, in re-building, the engineers gave the table a slope. Or perhaps they corrected a slope from the previous day. Without knowing that these things have *not* happened, we would rightly withhold our assent to the claim that the same thing will happen on Tuesday as happened on Monday – we suspect that the situation is different (although, to anticipate, not whether it is relevantly different). Moreover, regaining our confidence here would involve checking that all the important features of the situation are unchanged. Thus, the baize is now blue instead of green – but, if its other characteristics are the same, this would not alter our prediction. (Yet which are the important features?) We could be confident if we had checked on every feature of the initial situation (Monday) and found it unchanged, or not relevantly changed. (But what exactly are the features of that situation; and how do we check on them *all*?) Then (third thought) when the object ball does not fall into the pocket, we know that something is different – or some number of things are.

This is our simplified model of exceptionless causality. To see my concerns with its application to human action, we need only recognize the problematic character of the idea of exactly the same situation applied to human beings in social settings. The second thought shows that our warrant in predicting the future on the basis of the past (and present) – as I shall put it – runs only to the degree that the future resembles the past (and present). But we have already been alerted to the difficulty in claiming (much less, in knowing) that: what are the features or respects in which we require the past (and present) to resemble the future? Our first two answers might be: "in relevant respects" (for then we have relevantly the same situation); or, "in all respects" (for then we have exactly the same situation). But both answers are unhelpful. For which respects are relevant? Relevant in what way? And how is such relevance to be determined? (As we will see, an answer can be given to these questions for a typical case in natural science. Yet not here.) Or, if we refer to *all* respects, how can we be sure we have got them *all*? These comments are expanded in what follows.

We already have the case for natural science – that if a snooker cue ball is travelling at exactly the same speed and in the same direction on Tuesday as it was on Monday, and if the other balls are in the same position, and nothing else has changed, then the same thing will happen on Tuesday as happened on Monday – say, the object ball will be pocketed. Should this not happen, that shows that there *was* some difference after all (contrary to my assertion). To see the complexity in social-scientific terms, we can include into our picture that the snooker shot is played on Monday by World Snooker Champion John Higgins. The shot on Tuesday will be too, since we aim to replicate the situations. Further, Higgins has neither been injured nor damaged his snooker cue in the meantime. But, while it made sense to think of exactly the same things being in place on the table, and so on, it makes no sense with a person, John Higgins, in the story. First, he cannot be in exactly the situation on Tuesday that he was on Monday – if for no other reason than that, on Monday, he had not potted that ball! So we cannot take him back to his previous state. In fact, we cannot even know where to start looking. Has he had exactly the same meals? Well, even if he has sampled the same menu-items from his favourite Chinese restaurant on both occasions (which is unlikely), he has not eaten the *very same* food. And so on for every feature of his life. Perhaps he had a vital conversation with someone on the Monday evening: that might change his motivation, say. And so on. But, if clear replication is not possible even with one person involved, and a set of relatively closed skills (moreover, skills of which he is a master), how much less likely when there are more persons, more situations and the like? So we will need to think differently about causality with persons.

As far as natural science is concerned – either its formal version, or the everyday science of my snooker-ball example – we specify (on the basis of theory) that certain factors can be ignored; we control for the factors that we can; and we 'handle' the rest by the assumption that 'other things are equal': or, as I shall put it, make a *ceteris paribus* assumption. This device does not involve checking which 'things' are taken to be 'equal'. Instead, we specify that *any* differences can be put aside as irrelevant.

The implicit assumption (though) is that there is, as it were, a complete list of such features if only we knew them, at least in principle: that they comprise a finite totality, so that, if checking, we might first check all-but-two; then all-but-one; and finally *all*. But there is no such finite totality. And that is fundamentally important when we turn to social research.

Of course, there is no such finite totality in natural science, either: there, the 'gap' is *legislated away* with the (real or implied) *ceteris paribus* clause. Yet that seems plausible because – while we do not know *all* of the things relevant in science (there being no *all*: no finite totality) – the *kinds* of scientific investigation in which we are engaged at least show the kinds of factors to be considered. So, the position of the moon is relevant in investigating tides, but not if analyzing some runner's gait. The moon's gravitational effect is granted even in that case – as not exactly irrelevant perhaps, but not significant either. Similarly, some experiments require a Faraday cage to isolate the experimenters from the earth's electro-magnetic field; but others can simply ignore such effects, without compromising their results. These inclusions or exclusions are guided by *theory*; and all are weighed for relevance as factors within that branch of science.

The human world lacks precisely this kind of specificity. Suppose we consider interviews with elite, female cricket players: what exactly are the features or properties of this sporting case? What of the things true of it is (or might be) relevant – in *this* case, if not more generally? And what of the features of our subjects? Having identified them as *elite female cricketers* suggests those as relevant features. But each of them is a certain age: is that relevant? Is hair-colour? Or sexual preference? Perhaps our interviews aim to predict what these people will do in the future. Yet we know, from the second thought from the beginning of this section, that a situation different *in some respects* removes any automatic warrant for assuming that the future resembles the past *unless* we know that the changes are irrelevant (to our discussion). Here, there seems no algorithm to determine what changes have taken place since yesterday, nor which are *all* the relevant ones. Thus, credence as relevant is not usually given to the activity of ants. But if the ants have undermined some part of our house, that *will* often bear on what we do and say: and especially when asking why the snooker table has acquired its slope!

Following Carnap, Hilary Putnam (1990: 98–99) asks us to imagine a world with only three objects. Now, even here, the number of potential relationships between the objects is surprisingly large. But, of course, it is finite and, moreover, countable. So here there *is* a finite totality. Yet that is precisely *not* the situation in the *human* world. Without such a totality, talk of "all", or imagining that one much replace the *ceteris paribus* specification with an enumeration, remains simply an unrealizable aspiration. And with no possibility of listing *all* the factors to consider, we can never consider them *all*.

So the difficulty does not just highlight the huge number of changes in the world since yesterday: rather, having no scale to identify *one* change (as it were, a single change as opposed to a collection or constellation of them), it makes no sense to think of there being some *specific* number of changes; hence, no sense to imagining them as comprising a finite totality ("*all* the changes").

When thinking scientifically about the world around us, natural sciences regularly assume such a finite totality of properties. This picture of the world is *true* for natural science: it is implicitly *made* true (or specified as true) through the use of 'controlling for variables' (say, in an experiment) and, ultimately, by deploying *ceteris paribus* clauses, such that any area of variation not covered through the process of controlling for variables is thereby specified as irrelevant. This explains why general contextual matters need not be considered in natural science: in effect, it constrains the scope or sense of *pertinent* questions in the context of natural-scientific investigations. In contexts where causal necessity *is* (or *can be*) rightly assumed, there will be no room for choice. And only such contexts warrant a blanket assumption of *ceteris paribus*. For an account of causality as causal necessity requires that what is caused is thereby necessitated. That would only follow were all the counter-cases put aside (in these ways; and especially by *ceteris paribus* clauses). That is a simplifying assumption of natural science.

Since there *is* in reality no such finite totality and since the simplifying assumptions of natural science cannot be assumed, these are not the contexts of social-scientific investigation. So we cannot elaborate the argument in that way in social science. Thus the structure which works for natural science makes no sense for social scientific investigations, or for our more general understanding of human agency (at least in its *humanistic* understanding).

This recognition is precisely what is needed to defend the claim of the possibility of agency against the imperialism of natural science: say, through the pretensions of its genetic explanations. Doing so also defends the claims of social science. For humanistic contexts of the kind in which, say, sport is discussed cannot offer us exceptionless generalizations (or 'laws') just because they involve humans, and human choice. Only this misplaced appeal to exceptionlessness gives the force to, say, genetic explanations of human traits. This force is an illusion for, to repeat, those explanations are only compelling where exceptionlessness is assumed in the form either of a *ceteris paribus* clause or of the *controlling* for variables imported by the method of controlled experiment. Yet such assumptions cannot be sustained without detailed elaboration when dealing with humans in the context of social choice and decision; and rarely then – as recognized in treating data about patterns of human decision as *trend-* or *tendency-data*, rather than as exceptionless. In fact even the causality attributable through much natural scientific research here is typically stochastic (or statistical) causation: yes, smoking causes lung cancer – but not in every smoker. This is true to a yet greater degree for social phenomena. That is one reason for the craziness of the idea of a gene for, say, the belief that all bags are carry-on bags:[14] apart from assuming the inevitability of a certain direction to our technological development, this suggestion imports a conception with no room for human choice. There may well be ways we humans often, or typically, or usually behave. But no ways we *always* behave, even *ceteris paribus*. So no exceptionless general claims can be sustained: no 'laws' apply here.

Such a 'law' would be highly implausible applied to the future of humans, even if it held today; for someone who knew this 'law' might decide to act against it. And the only basis for claiming that such a 'law' obtained would involve consideration of *all* the factors that might influence or affect both choice and action. Only then could we consider *all* that might lead to an exception to any claim we make – say, about what would happen next. Only by taking *all* such factors into consideration could we ensure that the world would indeed develop as predicted.

But, recall, taking that view of the *number* of factors to be considered[15] in turn treats this *all* ("*all* the factors") as a finite totality, so that, in principle, we might approach it in stages – *all*-minus-two, *all*-minus-one . . . ah, *all*. Only where there is such a *finite totality* of factors could laws (or similar) be constructed for the relevant behaviour. Also such (assumed) laws explain *this* behaviour, now, in this context only on the assumption that the features of the context too form a finite totality, so that *all* might be taken account of. Yet there is no complete list of the factors that might, in principle, bear on my decision – hence no complete list of the ways my situation differs relevantly from yours when you come to what seems to be the same decision. So this picture misconceives human behaviour (McFee, 2000: 132–34). Then it would be just an empty truism at best to claim that, in the same situation (*ceteris paribus*), we must come to the same decision: all the relevant, or potentially relevant, factors cannot be identified, even in principle. Hence, we cannot *control* for them.

The central difficulty lies in identifying the *relevant* aspects of the situation. Thus, would we act like the title character in the film *Sophie's Choice* (1982)? Which of our children (if any) would we give up to the Nazis, with the likelihood of survival; which would we keep with us in the concentration camp? Well, what factors are *relevant* (McFee, 2000: 124–26)? Might that case be different if one were not Jewish? Or not the mother, but (say) an aunt, or the father – two different cases? The danger for the study of sport lies in thinking that, say, *this* competition or occasion is like *that* one, give or take some irrelevant details; hence, in taking as the same what are crucially different, or taking as different what are centrally the same. Yet that explanation makes the difficulty seem merely practical: that we could resolve it *if only* we could (*per impossibile*) replicate the situation. In fact the objection here is that such a replication makes no sense: *all* the features of that (other) situation cannot be replicated since there is no complete list of these features. There is no *all* here. Although such questions concerning the predicament from *Sophie's Choice* might be approached in the concrete, there is no abstract and general answer here, precisely because there is no abstract articulation of *all* that might possibly be relevant to any consideration of the matter.

Conclusion

This chapter has presented a sketch of the position of this work taken as a whole, together with some of its arguments. In this way, it can structure our later reflections. It has identified some of the work's distinctiveness in disputing the assumptions shared by two major research 'traditions' operative for research into sport. Much of the remainder of the work will be taken up with expansion of this sketch, and defence (by argument) of its central claims.

Some concerns here could be conceptualized as rejecting the use of unthinking or uncritical jargon. Technical expressions, or 'terms of art', have a place, when they are useful; but, sometimes, a jargon-term (and especially a *fashionable* jargon-term, such as "paradigm") is flourished as an alternative to the giving of an explanation. In this sense, I am especially critical here of the unthinking use of "paradigm" and of "triangulation"; but my objections generalize to very many of those terms which are deployed to circumvent the call for explanation.

In the light of the identification of these misconceived assumptions, contrasting conceptions both of truth and reasoning and of ethical obligation in sport research have been sketched. The body of the work develops these sketches. In so doing, it recognizes the *humanistic* dimension of much sport research; and, even when that is not the appropriate conception for a particular investigation, grants to such a humanistic view its own criteria for success. Hence, the view does not over-value the non-humanistic tendencies within natural science: detachment is a virtue, but not the only one. Further, much sport research is ideally located in the precise situations of the sporting competitions or training sessions. So, again, a naturalistic trend reinforces the humanistic one. And these considerations apply both to the epistemological assumptions of sport research and to what one brings to the ethical conduct of sport researchers.

Part II

The nature of qualitative research

2 Research must answer its question

Research as erotetic

Focusing on the research question – erotetic epistemology

As texts on the nature of research widely acknowledge, with justice, research requires close attention to the *questions* being asked (see Punch, 1998: 38). For example, students are regularly taught to focus on the clarity of their research questions. Thus, for the research questions, we can ask: Are the topics clearly identified? Are appropriate questions driving this research? For example, are they clear, specific, and answerable? Are they interconnected (if there is more than one)? Moreover, are such questions substantively relevant (that is, interesting and worthwhile) so as to justify the research effort? Is the relevance to some theoretical concern, or some professional or practical concern, made clear? Does it draw on relevant concepts from the relevant disciplinary literature? Next we can ask if the design of the study is appropriate to those research questions. In particular, has the choice of methodologies been justified? Then, are the data collection and data analysis instruments and procedures adequate and appropriate for the research questions? As Punch notes, a simplified model of research might stress:

- framing the research in terms of the research questions;
- determining what data are necessary to answer those questions;
- designing research to collect and analyze those data;
- using the data to answer the questions.

(1998: 41)

This summarizes the sorts of material elaborated in typical introductory texts on research design, highlighting the centrality of research questions. So a standard introductory textbook might urge that "[a]ll research starts from a *research problem*" (Giddens, 1989: 660). Then, for example, ". . . the experiment must address the question posed" (Stern and Lomax, 1997: 293). That says, in effect, the ways in which *data* are extracted from raw results connect with the questions one is asking. Such ideas might explain the claim that "[y]ou need to think about your data analysis before you begin designing research instruments" (Bryman, 2001: 236). Or, more bluntly, "[d]ifferent questions require different methods to answer them" (Punch, 1998: 19).

This concern with the research question – or, as I shall say, with the erotetic nature of research – is rarely taken seriously enough. The 'standard version' of such claims (say, those from Bryman or Punch) does not grant the full impact of implicit contextualization of the *research question* (and of research more generally), and especially the scope of the assumptions, or presuppositions, that giving due attention to the contextual character of that question may undermine. That my assumptions derive from a scientistic version of sports science may preclude my really asking, or answering, certain questions. Again, I cannot address higher-level choices if I assume that my subjects simply respond to stimuli, but never choose: in effect, behaving more or less like lab rats.

A more robust contextualism bears directly on the formulation of the research question. As is widely recognized, the same question can be asked in different forms of words: at its simplest, many research questions could be posed in English or in French. That point generalizes: at least for many research questions, the very same question (in some contexts) could be formulated in different forms of words.

Recognizing the contextual nature of our understanding also grants that the same form of words – here, the same question – can amount to something different in different contexts. Thus, the question "Why are you drunk?", asked by my wife, requires a different kind of answer than that provided by, say, my doctor: he notes my having X milligrams of alcohol per millilitre of blood – that explains my being drunk. But the kinds of answer appropriate for my wife would include, "I have been celebrating my promotion", "I have been drowning my sorrows at getting fired", or some such (McFee, 1992a: 60). That a question in the same form of words when asked by her requires a different kind of answer is another way of saying, in that context, the question amounts to something different.

Our erotetic conception of research exploits this insight. First, since questions are connected to answers, a different question requires a different (kind of) answer – and vice versa. So when a difference in *kind* of answer is called for in a particular context, we can rightly infer that a different question is asked (even if the same form of words is used).[1] Second, there may be no easy way to determine what is or is not the same context; and hence when we do or do not have the same (research) question asked.

This result is already fundamentally important, although that may not yet be obvious. At its simplest, then, the erotetic conception of research gives up the idea that one form of words is always exactly one question. As will discussed later, this concession has large implications for the proper use of multi-methods in research, at least for what must be investigated in 'validating' such methods. For the methods here amount to different ways of answering 'the' question; hence, they suggest different ways of *taking* that question. But can these two (or more) ways of taking the question be combined? Further, if they can, what are the *benefits* (if any), or drawbacks, in such combination?

Here, we should recall (chapter 1) the case where, rather than a research question, our researcher (concerned about her local leisure centre) offered a 'fishing trip' of methods; and that, common in sports science but not only there, where enthusiasm for a method ("I want to use the new force platform") replaces the question actually required for research. This can occur as readily when, say, his mentor inspires an apprentice-researcher with enthusiasm for ethnographic studies based on covert participant observation. Given the interest and vigour of the mentor's stories, this is the way to go! But our apprentice, having as yet no research question, has no basis for deciding the appropriateness of this set of methods, as against others.

Moreover, an argument for the impact of the nature of research subjects begins by recognizing the impact on the research *context* of human *agents* as subjects: that it makes a difference to how the research question is understood that the subjects are persons, as opposed to, say, animals (non-human animals);[2] parts of persons; and so on. For a question about a moral agent differs from one concerning a snail or (just) a hand, each requiring different *kinds* of answers (as our erotetic conception of research implies). Our apprentice ethnographer can justify his plans to use these methods only by showing that his research question conceptualizes the research subjects as persons – for such ethnography imports this assumption.

Yet *exactly* what scope has the difference identified here? Traditionally, it is presented as epistemological: for instance, "[q]ualitative research . . . aims to capture qualities that are not quantifiable such as feelings, thoughts, experiences, and so on" (Gratton and Jones, 2004: 22). This is certainly not wrong. If our concern is with the 'world' of some rugby players, even when the team's injury record is the ultimate focus, that is the world we must interrogate (Howe, 2004: 134–47). For that is the only site for the understanding we seek. But this difference is not restricted to the epistemological aspect. For a key difference between *that* research and *this* may be that, in one, the subjects were persons (viewed or treated as persons). When this is true, recognizing an erotetic difference acknowledges the impact of *this* sort of research subject. Then one can discuss with the players, noting that they "tended to be the most public about minor pains and injuries" (Howe, 2004: 141), rather than those which would have precluded playing. Hence, one tries to understand what pain and injury, common features of rugby players lives, meant to them. Yet what impact has such a recognition of one's subjects as persons? What is distinctive about such subjects? The answer, of course, reflects two related facts about these subjects: first, they are moral *subjects* – their moral status must be recognized. (In the last analysis, this is the impact of the Nuremberg Code and Helsinki Declaration (WMA, 2000), and other sets of legislation or regulation on research.) But, second, they are also moral *agents* – as, say, (human) glands, joints, muscles and nerves are not. So they can be asked about their position or response; and can give answers. Further, their answers can be taken seriously.

Making sense of the question: its relation to methods

Returning to our main thread, a connection has already been noted between the question asked and the methods suitable to answer it: that, as the question changes, so do the methods appropriate to answer it – and vice versa.[3] Then this comparatively straightforward connection of questions to methods means that a different *question* will require a different *method*. In that sense, ". . . all research findings are shaped by the circumstances of their production" (Bloor, 1997: 39).

Thus the methods used to answer a particular research question show how that question is conceptualized; or what question it is taken to be. If a question about the degree to which a player understands basketball can be fully answered by testing his ability to score with a lay-up shot, one sees how that question is regarded. (Here, the questioner might rightly be viewed as very confused about it.[4]) Again, that someone thinks an IQ test a suitable instrument to determine intelligence – or a standard 'creativity test' to determine creativity – shows how that issue is conceptualized (or what the *issue* is). For instance, that intelligence or creativity is not tied to specific media or specific context: hence the issue about intelligence or creativity would *not* be specific in these ways. Why? Suppose, say, creativity were always creative activity in some medium, such as music, painting or mathematics. Then questions about such creativity could scarcely be answered by determining one's ability to improve a teddybear, to make it more fun to play with (compare Cashdan and Whitehead, 1972: 84), where 'analysis' of the results consists simply in counting how many alternatives one produces – especially, were this part of *all* such inquiries into creativity. These unpromising cases illustrate simply the connection between question and methods.

Again, suppose that the right way to determine how (if at all) the religious beliefs of female long-distance runners contribute to their running involves interviewing them, getting them to include such commentary in training-diaries, and 'wiring them for sound' when they are running, having asked them to comment on their thoughts and feelings while running.[5] Clearly that concern with performance for female long-distance runners differs from that of someone whose method involves administering psychological tests, or someone who takes muscle biopsies. In each case, a different research question is being asked. That should be accepted even were that question presented in the same form of words (as the first two might share a formulation about motivation, perhaps).

Here, there are three complications. First, the same or different questions cannot be identified independently of whether or not the same methods are used for answers. In particular, having agreed both that the same form of words can amount to different research questions, and that the same research question can be formulated in different ways, simply addressing what sentences are used cannot determine what the research question really is. Then, second, we lack any clear idea of what counts as a single method here; and hence have no clear idea of a single question. Thus, was the research design for the religious beliefs of female long-distance runners using one method or three? Third, and relatedly, we have no clear subdivision between methods – what other kind of question (or questions) might warrant using the mixture of interview, directed training-diary, and recording while performing? Clearly the connection to religious belief is not fundamental here. So how do we know when we have similar-ish questions – sufficiently similar to use the same methods – and when not?

Luckily, these complications are not as damning as they may seem. First, and flowing from our contextualism (introduced in chapter 1, and to be elaborated later), we are much better at answering these questions in their context of occurrence than in the abstract. And general, abstract principles are not required here.

Rather, we have enough if we know how to go on in a particular context. Second, 'knowing how to go on' here is really knowing how to contribute to the debate around one's conclusions. For instance, I can argue that there is one unified topic here; and that my methods too form a unity – some over-arching term under which both fall ('ethnographic methods') will help, of course, although nothing is definitely resolved in that way. Someone who suspects that my methods do not, after all, cohere in this way can join in that debate. Moreover, such debates turn on whether these methods take the same presuppositions or make the same assumptions. If they do, that speaks to their being the same (or at least, compatible) methods. If not, are the differences in presuppositions or assumptions relevant differences in this context? If not, that too speaks for these being at least compatible methods. Thus, methods which assume that research subjects can only be treated 'in the third person' (as the Hawthorne subjects were treated: see chapter 3) presuppose something different from those that allow interchange (and especially conversation) between subjects and researchers. Interestingly, much of the standard classification of research methods is reproducible in roughly this way. Thus, designs presupposing that persons' answers are useful only when one has large numbers of them, to be treated statistically (the sort of things from which questionnaire designs begin), clearly differ from designs recognizing the importance of what *this* person says, as opposed to *that* person (as structured interview designs typically do). Both of these introduce different presuppositions from designs which consider what persons say in the contexts in which they normally act, rather than in response to formal processes of questioning.

There may be no universal way to identify the same research question, nor the same method, nor the unified methodology. But if these notions can be managed, or at least argued about, in our local context, we need not concern ourselves further with them here. Instead, disputes can be resolved by looking to how, in the local context, they are understood or debated. For a connection has been drawn to the debates over these matters (typically debates within academic disciplines). Or, if there is currently no such debate, to the need for such debates. Since an exceptionless or once-and-for-all account is not required, but only one for our specific context, there is no cause for concern.

Moreover, much of this attention to assumptions or presuppositions need not be explicit when drawing on established practices of the appropriate academic disciplines: they *may* have recognized when there are differences of assumption or presupposition – as indeed there will typically be *between* academic disciplines. In this sense, the sociologist sees sociological mankind, and asks sociological questions of it. In our case, of course, this would be that fragment of sociological mankind that is engaged in sport.

Two factors can profitably be added to this picture. First, one preferred way to identify issues here concerns the research subjects treatment as *persons* (chapter 1). So these offer a favoured set of presuppositions for many investigations into sport. If the questions are asked *of persons*, and the methods might with justice apply to persons (viewed as persons), the congruence here provides a starting point of debate, cohering with our emphasis on *talk* (broadly conceived:

see chapter 3). Second, if we are less good at recognizing whether two procedures *are* the same methods, we are a lot better at recognizing when they are *not*. (These points will be exemplified more fully in the discussion of triangulation later.)

Making sense of the question: its relation to context

But how is the erotetic nature of research to be explained? Ultimately, it follows from our *contextualism*, introduced in chapter 1 (and to be expanded in the Appendix). Here, a different set of examples highlights another aspect of this contextualism.

As before (chapter 1), this account acknowledges the contextual nature of truth-claims; that: "[t]he statements fit the facts always more or less loosely, in different ways on different occasions for different intents and purposes" (Austin, 1970: 130). There are only definite results as to truth when the circumstances of the describing somehow make one standard or another the right one for the purpose in hand: so truth essentially depends on the context in this way. This means both that no abstract resolution here, divorced from context, is possible and that there typically will be such a resolution once we take the details of the context into account – or, at least, there is room for debate towards such a resolution.

Reflection on two cases (suggested by Charles Travis) may help us understand the workings of this contextualism, and especially its conception of truth. Of course, "[t]o state something is to aim at truth" (2008: 3). And then: " [i]f we know that someone said such and such to be thus and so, we do, in some sense, know what he said (to be so)" (2008: 300).

That introduces our simplified cases. First, is it true that your shoes are under the bed if they jut out? Or if they are three floors down? In what context was it true? Or not? There seems no *one* answer here: rather, a context can be imagined in which a particular answer is appropriate. In that context, it would be true. (Or, at least, it would fail to be true only by being false!) So, if we are looking for your shoes, and I claim they are under the bed, you will be able to find them there, even if they jut out. So what I said on that occasion was true. If that was our concern, my saying the shoes were under the bed when they were three floors down would be saying something false. But when we are trying to hide the shoes – so that a visitor will not notice them, perhaps – I will be wrong to say they are under the bed. Since they jut out (where they might be seen), what I said was false. And a variety of occasions, or a variety of interests, can be imagined here. Equally, if I am trying to locate the geography of my apartment relative to yours, saying that your shoes (in your apartment, three floors below) are under the (my) bed will be true. Moreover, this will be what I said, on that occasion or that context. Here, the erotetic character is readily brought out for, in the first situation described earlier, we can imagine someone asking, "Where are your shoes?" when "Under the bed" answers that question truthfully. But we also recognize (as the second case) that, in the context of wanting the shoes hidden, replying that the shoes were under the bed would be false – they are jutting out. So this simplified case illustrates the question-and-answer structure of understanding.

Further, this need not be all-or-nothing, but can turn on matters of degree. Suppose, as our second case, I claim that I gave you a gold watch: how much of it must be gold, for what I said to be true? (And in what contexts?) Again, examples can readily be imagined here, ranging from needing a gold-coloured watch (when everyone else has silver-coloured ones) all the way through considering the different percentages of gold in the watch-case (with associated questions about the watch's being, or not being, gold), to the need to pay the ransom, when your watch – with its solid gold case – is especially useful. If I claimed to have given you a gold watch in that context, when all I provided was a gold-coloured watch, I would be speaking falsely. But when the ransom provides the occasion, perhaps I have something better than your gold watch (having a solid gold case): namely, a watch entirely made of gold (perhaps because touched by King Midas). This is perfect for paying the ransom! Moreover, I am glad to be rid of this object since it completely fails to keep time (gold is too soft for the workings). Indeed, it is such a disaster as a watch that, on another occasion, I truthfully deny that it was a watch at all.

In such simple examples, the mechanism behind the erotetic structure of the research question emerges, because we see how questions (or answers) can amount to something different in different situations. But once we are asking the question in the appropriate context, the answer can be true – and will be, if we are careful.

This idea can be hard to accept. It might seem that either the shoes are under the bed or they are not. Or that either it is or is not a gold watch. Faced with a similar case, Austin (1962: 143) remarks that "it would be pointless to insist on its truth or falsity", because it would be pointless to insist on either an exceptionless assertion or an exceptionless denial of the truth of the claim. Rather, any such assertions should reflect the context of the question. So the claim is not true without qualification nor false without qualification. In some given context, the claim will be (for instance) true: that, say, Lord Raglan was the Commander at the Battle of Alma and, despite some of his orders not getting through, the victory in a battle is conventionally ascribed to the Commander of the victorious side. So Lord Raglan won the battle of Alma. As I have just elaborated the context of the utterance, what was asserted about Lord Raglan (in that context) was true: Lord Raglan did win the battle of Alma. So that speaker spoke the truth, even though in a different context (faced with a question asked in the same form of words)[6] that Lord Raglan won the Battle of Alma might with justice be either disputed or denied – since the victory did not flow from Lord Raglan's orders. There is no internal contradiction here: what was claimed as *true* builds in (at least) the context described about the ascription of victory – in *that* context, this was the right thing to say. If, instead, the gap between Lord Raglan's orders and the conduct of the battle is stressed, a different context is produced; and hence a different enquiry. In that new context, the claim that Lord Raglan won the Battle of Alma might count as *false*: nothing said so far should preclude this!

This case illustrates the *point*, in some contexts, both of *asserting* this claim and of insisting – in that context – that the claim was true. But if this is correct, Austin's claim quoted earlier is at least over-emphatic if not actually an overstatement. For these claims, as then understood, are *true*. And there is no reason to deny that point. Austin (1962: 142) might agree, remarking that: "... in the case of stating truly or falsely, just as much as in the case of advising well or badly, the intents and purposes of the utterance and its context are important. ...". So that, in the context elaborated earlier for the claim about Lord Raglan, it *would* count as true. Hence in that context, or in another one could reliably assume, it would *not* be pointless to claim its truth.

This recognition of the fundamental place of the erotetic – and hence contextualist – helps contrast the claim here with another, with which it might otherwise be confused. For my claim is not that there are 'incompatible research traditions' and therefore one of them is wrong. Instead, there are, at best, two very different sets of concerns here: two erotetic contexts. If we grant that, and can identify the characteristics of each, we may work with the account of truth, understanding, and knowledge (and hence of research) appropriate to each. But I am insisting on my explanation here: this flows from the erotetic nature of research. Theorists of research who miss this are missing something important, which will typically mislead them. Suppose that one's research agenda was set by the concerns of the British Association of Sport and Exercise Sciences (BASES); and suppose that one's conception of research ethics were similarly dominated by VIC. Then, in practical terms, the prescriptions for ethical treatment of research subjects would be broadly in line with the suggestions of, say, McNamee *et al.* (2007). Making that point can explain why those ideas have merit in that context: namely, that the ideas reflect the practicalities of that context. But there are other contexts, and hence other concerns, too – using the central ideas of that book here could be problematic. That follows from the erotetic nature of research. Then the central features of these other contexts must be located. As urged in chapter 1, most fundamental here is that, in the 'sports sociology' (and also some 'sport psychology') tradition, one's subjects are people; and that interpersonal engagement is always moral in one way or another.

Of course, two points here are linked. First, all research is erotetic, with questions appropriately answered in its ways, in its contexts. Second, much sport research, in focusing on people in the contexts in which they act, must pay more attention to contextual matters than, say, laboratory-based sports science. And the contexts here will be the specificities of sport. This second thought therefore points in the direction of 'naturalistic' research, where possible.

Vignette: the confusion over 'multi-methods' and 'triangulation' in research

Recognizing the erotetic character of research raises serious issues for at least some research designs involving the mixing of methods. Much depends on: (a) which methods are chosen (since, the degree to which they share relevant assumptions or presuppositions provides a key debate); (b) which combinations of methods are chosen, and why; (c) what *justification* is offered for the multi-methods design (which may well overlap with point [b]).

As a hypothetical example, imagine a research design employs both postal questionnaires to collect a large volume of data about the use of local sports facilities by a particular community, and semi-structured interviews, explained by the researcher as 'trying to probe further' the reasons for the patterns of use of these facilities uncovered by the questionnaire. As imagined, the researcher takes the questionnaire to offer generality to the research conclusions, and the interviews to provide depth. Thus, she aims "to select the appropriate . . . methods that, in combination, will result in complementary data, and thereby reduce the possibility of unsubstantiated findings" (Olafson, 1991: 39–40). So far, of course, there need be nothing to criticize.

An explanation, once popular in social research, designed to explain the desirability of such mixing of methods, was that the combination permits *triangulation*.[7] So, what is *triangulation* in this context? A typical answer urges: "[t]riangulation may be defined as the use of two or more methods of data collection in the study of some aspect of human behavior" (Cohen and Manion, 1980: 269). This does not yet show *why* the multiplicity of methods is employed. But that will be crucial in any attempt to gauge the contributions of each.

As I imagine it, *triangulation* is explained as guaranteeing the soundness of the data, but also as making those data more realistic. As we will see, this justification can be read in either of two ways, corresponding to the two aspects just identified. Both 'readings' of *triangulation* fail to do justice to the *erotetic* character of social research,[8] by failing to recognize the connection between the *questions* a research design addresses (in principle) and the *answers* it can (therefore) possibly generate.

Since the argument here is quite complex, sketching it is useful, prior to presenting more detail, and also commenting as one goes along. The tension within the claims made for *triangulation* highlights how different questions within what can *seem* a single research design can thereby undermine it.

The first 'reading' explains triangulation as a way to produce *reliable* data: the results from one method reinforce those from the other (see Cook and Reinhardt, 1979: 23), typically by offering what is conceptualized as more data towards the same conclusion, as a way ". . . to enhance the validity of one's research" (Gratton and Jones, 2004: 114). This focus takes such reinforcing, or something similar, as a route to data soundness. But this is possible *only* if both methods address the same question. Yet the erotetic character of research makes this unlikely: that these are different ways of answering suggests there are subtly different questions here, especially when different presuppositions seem at work in each method. This can be called "triangulation between methods".

On our second reading, which could be called "triangulation within a method", triangulation creates a more realistic picture of the action or event by incorporating perspectives (as represented by, those different methods). But is there just one action or event here? The erotetic character of research speaks against this. And this second version, if correct, would not make the claim discussed more likely: instead, it aims at richness or more accuracy. That is, it focuses on quality of data rather than on soundness.

But our imaginary researcher might aim at both of these outcomes, explaining triangulation (and its achievements) in one way on one occasion and in the other way on another occasion. Thus Gratton and Jones (2004: 189) ask: "*Triangulation*: Have you used data from a range of methods to strengthen the validity of your claims?" Yet doing this undermines the term "triangulation" as a technical expression here. For neither explanation *could* offer what was, initially, required; further, both are internally flawed. Or so I urge.

To come to this as a conclusion – understanding what it shows us more generally – rather than as mere assertion requires moving more slowly. Here, the root-metaphor of *triangulation* is revealing, since the term "triangulation" in the research context is used metaphorically. What is its home? The idea derives from a technique used by sailors to locate their position when near to land.[9] In the simplest version, a bearing is taken on some fixed point (say, a church spire); a second bearing is taken from another fixed point (say, a lighthouse). Where the two bearings converge is the position of the yacht. (Imagine the bearings drawn as lines on a chart: they will cross where the yacht is – if the bearings themselves are accurate, a point we put aside.) This account of (literal) triangulation highlights its two key features: there are *two fixed points*, and there is the *convergence* of the bearings. If one takes only one bearing, and draws it on one's chart, one's yacht is *somewhere* along that line, but one does not know where.

Its appropriation into the metaphors of research seizes on both features from triangulation: first, that two fixed points (that is, two independent research methods) *seemed* more reliable than just one. Thus, discovering a pattern in one's interview data similar to that in one's questionnaire data made it seem more likely that the

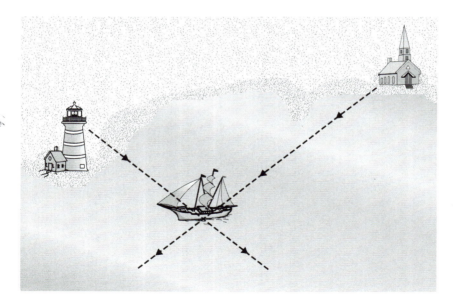

Figure 2.1 Triangulation at sea

pattern was genuine. In this sense, then, I spoke loosely of the results from one technique *reinforcing* those of the other. Given the similarity of results here, the pattern is less likely to be a figment of a particular technique. This, then, is one of the procedures called "triangulation"; and hence one basis for using triangulation as justification for claiming greater soundness to one's data. Thus: "[e]xclusive reliance on one method . . . may bias or distort the researcher's picture of the particular slice of reality he is investigating. He needs to be confident that the data generated are not simply artefacts of one specific method of collection (Cohen and Manion, 1980: 269).

Similar findings from different data-collection methods increase confidence in the quality of those data. Here, the different methods represent the *fixed points* (from the original use). (Discussed earlier as triangulation between methods.)

I first became aware of the idea of *triangulation* in research design in the context of educational research. That introduces the second use of the term. There, a concern was that classroom events as seen by, say, the teacher might look very different from how they looked to the pupil, or to a neutral observer. As Elliott (1976: 300) puts it, "[e]ach point of the triangle stands in a unique epistemological position". Hence taking account of such perspectives allowed one to recognize complexity: ". . . to map out, or explain more fully, the richness and complexity of human behaviour by studying it from more than one standpoint" (Cohen and Manion, 1980: 269). Here the data are *constructed* from the results of the different investigations. This represents the *convergence* (from the 'literal' use). We can readily imagine similar claims urged on behalf of, say, the team members and the coach of some sports team – to see what is really going on, we need all these perspectives. Thus: "[w]here triangulation is used in interpretive research to investigate different actors' viewpoints, the same method, e.g. accounts, will . . . produce different sets of data" (Cohen and Manion, 1980: 270).

There is no implication here that the data themselves are any sounder; rather, they better reflect the phenomena, for the object under investigation is a whole situation comprised by the *combination* of such viewpoints (Elliott, 1991: 31–32). (Discussed earlier as triangulation within a method.)

That identifies the two procedures both called "triangulation". But why *exactly* should either procedure be wanted? Any answer must relate to some virtue or strength in the research design. Here, there seem two candidates: first, 'fixed points' are provided by independently validated methods, offering increased soundness; second, 'unique intersection' is the idea that the methods address a single issue or question, offering complexity. To this debate, our erotetic conception of research adds, as a generalization, that asking a different (kind of) question requires different methods to answer; and, in using a different method, one asks a different question (at least typically).

When our researcher claims *triangulation* by urging that each method provides a 'fixed point' from which one and the same phenomenon can be viewed, she is combining the virtues of triangulation between methods (fixed points) with those of triangulation within a method (convergence on a single topic). But these cannot be combined: first, triangulation between methods has no guarantee of a unique intersection (a single problem); second, triangulation within a method has no fixed points (no independent methods). The first point follows directly from our erotetic conception of research, and we will return to it. The second warrants more commentary.

In elaboration, note that *triangulation* within a method aims, in effect, to overcome a limitation in (some) methods, especially those based on observations or accounts – we need the other perspectives precisely to overcome the deficiencies in our starting place. For example, at one time Elliott (1976) claimed the adding of perspectives as a way of improving 'quality' of data. For instance, replacing concern with *one* 'locational marker' (say, of a teacher's view of his role) with many "will give a much fuller picture" (Cohen and Manion, 1980: 271). Or as *investigator triangulation*, justifying "use of more than one observer (or participant) in a research setting" (Cohen and Manion, 1980: 274). But when the *quality* of data becomes the issue, appeal to triangulation imports another cause for concern (say, through the knowledge of *this* observer); and then using the term "triangulation" may obscure that fact by making us think of triangulation *between* methods.

Relevantly, Elliott (1991: 82) revised his position so that what the researcher gets, from what Elliott continues to call "triangulation", is not soundness in itself: it is just as reliable or unreliable as other collection of 'accounts' data, but is a factor in the *whole* phenomenon.

Where have we arrived? To summarize, my view thus far has three main elements:

- The term "triangulation" was/is used to describe two quite different procedures.
- The root-metaphor serves neither of these procedures – at least, not unambiguously.
- The metaphor can seem to apply by confusing/fudging the two quite different procedures.

Read one way (as triangulation between methods), it seems a plausible guarantee of the soundness of data, but only when just one question or topic or object is really under investigation. That requires a separate investigation into the relevant assumptions or presuppositions of the methods involved. Here, attempting to combine a questionnaire – with its statistical treatment of individual claims – with the particularity of semi-structured interviews, the presuppositions at least seem incompatible. (The debate should begin from the presumptions of different questions.) Read the other way (as triangulation within a method), if triangulation was actually involved in the construction of the 'object' of study, it offers no guarantee of the soundness of data.

At this point, it might be asked whether the options considered here exhaust the options: the answer is obviously, "no". But none of the others draws productively on the metaphor of *triangulation*. Further, appeal to 'triangulation' often acts as a placebo, replacing serious enquiry. For it might seem that achieving triangulation (understood as between methods) contributes to the soundness of my data. So those data may no longer be interrogated as to soundness.

What should be the methodological impact of this discussion of triangulation? If sound, the points made here apply to many multi-method enquiries, not just to those mentioning the word "triangulation" – although the issue also concerns the seductive power of that word/metaphor. At the least, we recognize an obligation on any researcher combining methods.

Might such an obligation be discharged? As we have seen, the use of multi-methods leads in two directions, as it were: when, say, my questionnaire data agrees with my interview data:

1 confidence in the status of each as 'quality data' increases; *but* this would only be justified when it is shown (or, anyway, suggested) that the issues converge, and
2 the questionnaire data is used as a basis for generalizing my findings from the interviews; but they will only generalize in so far as the data are congruent – hence, directed at roughly the same question.

Neither of these is *triangulation*; both require giving attention to the sameness of the question each method employs. This will be, and should be, a 'hard sell' to other researchers when the methods are far apart – that is, when their relevant pre-suppositions or assumptions are far apart.

In my imaginary research design, the researcher might reformulate her plans so that, say, the interviews constitute one phase, facilitating a second phase of questionnaires, or vice versa. (Call this "end-on multi-methods".) In a similar vein, some qualitative research might be imagined to facilitate quantitative research (say, it helps with background information on contexts and subjects, and aids with scale construction). But then, very clearly, the methods are not combined – they address different questions. In effect, this is a two-method research design because we have two-question design. Or, again, some quantitative research might facilitate qualitative research (for instance, by helping with choice of subjects, or even aiding with generality, by showing similar quantitative patterns elsewhere). But, again, the methods are not combined – they address different questions, so (again) this is a two-methods design.

The local moral from this investigation is that issues of methodological choice cannot be separated from those concerning both research question and research method(s). But that elaborates the erotetic character of research.

Conclusion

This chapter has explored and (partially) defended the erotetic character of research. Its starting point was the commonplace that an important element of the research process is the identification of the research question. But it offered a more robust (than usual) interpretation of what that involves. In doing so, it emphasized the importance for such research questions of the assumptions they make or the presuppositions imported. At its simplest, one cannot know what question is being asked without attention to such assumptions or presuppositions. Luckily, much of that attention takes place implicitly by, say, appeal to the practices of a particular discipline. Adherence to the ideas here would require rigorously checking that methods were appropriate to answer the research questions posed, and that questions themselves (when multiple) shared presuppositions sufficiently far for the same form of words to *really* generate the same question.

3 The issue of 'the qualitative' is not helpful

Researching sport is often researching people

Much social-scientific research in sport acquires its direction from its distinctive epistemological context. As we saw (chapter 2), the methods appropriately used in one's research are reciprocally related to what questions that research can address, structured as the answers to questions posed – at least, for qualitative research into social matters. Or, as I say, reflecting this question-and-answer structure, research is erotetic. Less commonly noted is that this fact is fundamental to the identification of central features of qualitative research here, by locating the features of the questions raised.

But what features have the questions raised? The most fundamental distinction here is not that between the qualitative and the quantitative, but rather between those research designs whose questions are answerable only in real world settings (to some degree or other) and those that can be addressed divorced from the context of the occurrence of the relevant behaviour. For the runner on the treadmill is not really running (as she might in her sport): at least, many crucial features are missing. Of course, cases form a broad spectrum rather than being sharply distinguished. Relatedly, research dealing with *persons* and actions must be contrasted with that dealing with (say) parts of persons, such as muscle fibres. For *persons*, not eyes, see what is going on; and persons are agents, making choices – where those choices inflect the world they inhabit. Nowhere is this more true than on the sports field, where the *actions* performed depend on the rules presently in play (McFee, 2004a: 15–16). And we have already defended broadly naturalistic research designs in sport by pointing out that, if sporting cultures provide a main focus, researchers will hope to investigate those cultures as they would have been were the research not taking place (chapter 1). And a key feature of such cultures will be the activities of moral agents. Any real-world research begins from these facts.

Research dealing with persons, in a real world situation, raises at least four kinds of difficulties:

- it is typically not repeatable – we cannot get exactly the same situation again;
- it is not a controlled situation;
- how the persons conceptualize the situation regularly alters that situation;

- there will be ethical issues, especially those associated with either covert research or research with covert aspects.

Although these points might seem familiar, my development of them may not. The first three concern primarily the epistemology of dealing with agents; the last with the ethics. This intimate connection in qualitative research between epistemological issues and ethical ones is not usually recognized. Let us then pursue the topics in that order.

First, dealing with persons, in the real world, is typically not repeatable. Since exactly the same situation rarely recurs, one cannot readily cancel out either what is common or what is different. The central difficulty here lies in identifying the situation's relevant aspects. As we saw in chapter 1, we could not even readily identify the relevant features in respect of one person (John Higgins, World Snooker Champion) with regard to a relatively closed skill, and one of which he is a master: namely, pocketing a snooker ball. For we cannot know what features of his state on Monday would have a bearing on his ability to pot that ball again on Tuesday. So we cannot check on, nor control for, such features. Yet that explanation can make the difficulty seem merely practical: that we could resolve it if only the situation were replicated. But that is impossible: the objection here is that *all* the features of that (other) situation cannot be replicated since there is no complete list of these features. There is no *all* here, no finite totality of relevant considerations. So such a replication makes no sense. Our failure to *assign* relevance actually masks the lack of a finite totality of candidate 'relevant' features. And this is true whether researching one person alone or many (such as a team or squad) in relation to one another: the relevant features still cannot be identified once-and-for-all in a context-independent way. This form of argument (and the recognition driving it) is fundamental here. Hence, this contextualism constrains qualitative research projects to begin from specific events in specific contexts.

Of course, a variety of contexts could be considered here. But our concern with subjects treated as persons, and with the social scientific investigation of such subjects in sporting contexts, tends to locate those subjects in the typical contexts of their actions. In this way, it tends towards the 'naturalistic' end of the continuum of research: if our concern is in this way with *sport in its context*, we must investigate the sport as it occurs.

Thus, second, why in researching in the real world of sport cannot one enter a controlled situation? As Harré and Secord (1976: 44) answer: "[t]he experimental set-up destroys the possibility of the study of the very features which are essential to social behaviour in its natural setting". In fact, a number of related illusions here concern the general idea of control-design methodologies. Even in laboratory work, the illusion of a controlled situation is achieved through *ceteris paribus* clauses: it is less a matter of ensuring that other things are equal as defining them as being equal. Yet our controlled experiment has no complete list, no finite totality, of these "other things" to keep equal. For instance, a classic double-blind design has the control group matched with the subject group – but for what features? Is gender important? (Usually, yes.) Is age important? (Usually, yes.) But what is not important? Each member of our experimental group differs in some respects from every member of the control group: so for which features are we to control? There is no theory-neutral way to resolve such issues. Then idealizations in qualitative (as in quantitative) research must be recognized. For instance, most deploy (implicitly or explicitly) the principle of total evidence that " in the application of inductive logic to a given knowledge situation, the total evidence available must be taken as the basis for determining degrees of confirmation" (Carnap, 1950: 211). This principle operates theoretically, to identify an idealization: " the requirement of total evidence . . . [compels] us to construct all applications of inductive logic in a fictitious simplified form" (Carnap, 1950: 208). That is, the 'fiction' is introduced of having all the relevant evidence – an assumption rarely visible, although always included, in quantitative research too!

But the principle also operates practically. That is, it offers a defeasible, grounded working practice, which justifies taking the evidence before us as all the relevant evidence. Of course, in a particular case, I may recognize that I lack some relevant fact. But that is not the example here: rather, the principle allows us to put aside the mere possibility of lacking evidence in a case with no independent reason to assume such a lack. So the mere possibility of lacking some relevant information alone cannot introduce scepticism, although of course on occasion (literally) our caution about our evidence is justified. As a quite general requirement for knowledge claims, this is not a place where research on persons is second-best.

Yet even this degree of control-design is typically unavailable to the qualitative researcher. Thus, the researcher engaged in oral history considers centrally the 'world' of his subjects: for example Alan Tomlinson's research into the golf-like game *knur and spel* (Tomlinson, 1992; 2005: 205–25). We cannot look to another group with which to compare them.

Third, the researcher in such a case tries to capture aspects of the subjects' conception of events – although, in the end, that conception must be subjected to the researcher's critical consideration. So the subject of the research cannot be detached from the context as that subject conceptualizes it. Further, the researcher's obligation here lies both in capturing that conceptualization and critiquing it (compare chapter 10). In the more extreme case, that so-and-so regards such-and-such an event as murder differentiates him/her from someone who regards that killing as manslaughter. What occurred cannot be decided unless both are recognized – but, equally, we must consider how best to conceptualize the event. Although the sporting case is typically less extreme, the point is exactly the same. Thus, a debate about drug-taking and the Olympics might suggest that athletes ". . . will seek out the next great 'thing' – a vitamin, a nutritional supplement, a training technique, a piece of training equipment, a new shoe, a drug" (Schmidt, 2007: M9). Now one issue is precisely whether or not the things on Schmidt's list are (or should be) in the same category. If drugs (such as anabolic steroids or human growth hormone) can, in good part, be conceptualized as no different – or not significantly different – from a new shoe, there is clearly no moral issue to be faced, except perhaps the partly practical one of giving fair access to the shoe (or the drug).[1] Rejecting that line of thinking involves that conceptualization of the activity being disputed. Further, there is no conception-free version for us to adopt – at least once it is conceded that the scale here must be that of human action. (Again, the comparison with murder makes the case neatly: the dagger was definitely between Jones's ribs, and caused his death; and Smith's hand was on the dagger – but that conception-neutral account alone cannot settle the question of whether or not Smith murdered Jones. For this might be an accident, or manslaughter.)

Suggesting in this way that naturalism – preserving the conceptions of the researched, in the context of that research – is a virtue here leads back to naturalistic or 'real world' research designs. In turn this reinforces the need for researchers to interact with the agents. The typical conceptualization of the method of controlled experimentation recognizes only the kinds of interaction with human subjects also possible with the subjects of physics or chemistry or even biology. That conceptualization of subjects has no place when dealing with persons. Indeed, it precludes precisely attention to that *talk* which is central to inter-personal exchanges. Thus one can ask one's subjects: hence the slogan that, for research purposes, human beings be treated as though they were persons (Harré, 1983) – that is, as agents operating in contexts. Dealing with human *events* in their contexts depends in particular on how those events are conceptualized by participants.

Researching people raises ethical issues

As noted earlier, researching people (as moral agents) raises ethical issues; especially those associated with either covert research or research with covert aspects. Yet it is easiest to begin from overt research: for (full) overtness requires that subjects (a) know that they are being researched; (b) know (and understand) the research protocol; (c) know any risks or dangers; and (d) know the fate of the data – say, its publication destination. So call this fully overt research (see chapter 8 for some elaboration). Moreover, overt research aims for the subjects' consent in that context: that is, informed consent should be endorsed as a goal for ethical conduct of fully overt research. (Of course, this must be genuine informed consent, not merely signing the form: the sort of thing McNamee *et al*. (2007: 72) rightly dismiss as mere "tick-box consent"!)

Yet that situation is not merely difficult to obtain, but a conceptual impossibility (see chapter 8). For one must be informed as to *all* the risks or dangers, *all* the features of the experimental protocol. But there is no *all* in either of these cases; no finite totality of what might be risks or dangers, nor of the features of the experimental design. Hence informed consent is, here, unobtainable in practice (even within human limits), but the conceptual flaws mean that the best that could be done cannot possibly guarantee ethical researching.

Most research into sport is not overt in this strong way: at least some aspect of my requirement for full overtness will be missing, often explained as the effect on data-production of the subjects knowing precisely what is being researched. Thus, informing the subjects in research considering the impact of different interventions into the subjects' adherence to programmes of mental training might be expected to impact on their behaviour: perhaps they take the mental training more seriously, knowing it is the research concern. At the least, one cannot be sure their behaviour remained unaffected. So such research cannot be successful if conceived as fully-overt: something must be kept from the subjects. As a result, a different conception of one's ethical treatment of subjects is required (see chapter 9). Here I merely sketch my conclusions, beginning with some comments on the general framework of the ethical treatment of subjects.

One difficulty for determining how to conduct research ethically concerns the nature and scope of ethics. In such discussions within philosophy, the nature and scope of moral philosophy remains contested. Here, two thoughts are useful. The first is a rule of thumb for ethical conduct: *behave as though those you are dealing with were your friends*. For we do not lie to our friends or otherwise deceive them (or, if we do, we have a good reason, mean no harm by it, and seek to rectify the situation as soon as possible); we do not seek to harm our friends in other ways – either physically or through affronts to their dignity or sense of self-worth; we do not expose them to ridicule; and so on. All this might be summarized as a version of the idea of respect for persons. My version is more positive (that one treats the others as friends, not merely fellow humans), and a little less abstract (since it offers some more content to the kinds of respect) – and therefore a little more helpful. But, of course, it still cannot tell a researcher how to act in a particular situation.

The second thought here (partially) explains why such exact advice cannot be given. It concerns a disputed feature of ethical thinking: its particularist character (see McFee, 2004a: 141–44). This is means, despite appearances to the contrary, there cannot be exceptionless principles for ethical conduct, applicable exceptionlessly to any situation:[2] rather, whatever can be urged must be applied in the particular situation in which one finds oneself. So a guideline which, in one situation, promoted ethical behaviour might, in another, promote actions of a morally reprehensible sort. For instance, that I borrowed a book from you is a reason to return it. But then I learn you stole the book from the library. Now I have no reason to return it to you; and (perhaps) reason not to. Moreover, we can readily agree: "[t]hat she wants power and he does not may be a reason to give the power to him rather than to her . . ." (Dancy, 2004: 75).

Such familiar cases embody the same reason functioning in diametrically opposed ways. Of course, such a particularist conception of the ethical needs supplementation and elaboration. And it remains contentious. But were such particularism granted, it would show both why we cannot offer exceptionless principles, say, for ethical conduct of research (namely, that we cannot offer exceptionless ethical principles anywhere else either!)[3] and what can be offered: namely, hints and reminders to be applied in this case, the case before us.

The place of *talk*

We have already recognized that *talk*, as I call it (following Harré, 1983), pervades human life. In this sense, it delimits much that is involved in treating *persons as persons* – as we might say, that would involve listening to them! And such listening typically involves giving due weight to what they say.

Some of the key features of *talk* as conceptualized here can be sketched. First, the most fundamental feature is the variety of *talk*: that is conversations, and questions, and orders and exclamations. Some will be what people say; some will be what they understand – and so might involve road-signs, traffic instructions, and the like. Indeed, there seems no clear outer limit to what counts as *talk*. As our general contextualism suggests (see chapters 1 and 2), *talk* can only be circumscribed in occasion-sensitive ways (if at all). Second, and also expansively, *talk* here typically includes far more than words spoken, heard or read: it encompasses the tones of voice, the bodily gestures and positions, the attentiveness of listening, and so on.

Third, such *talk* circumscribes the lives of persons by offering them the concepts and categories through which they understand; and (via yet more *talk*, in the form of education) the opportunity to modify such concepts and categories. Thus I learn to see; and, thereby, to contrast and compare: that the activity before me is football, connect and compare it to soccer, American grid-iron, Australian rules, and to rugby. Perhaps we cannot determine whether so-and-so was in control of the ball when he landed. But, because *talk* circumscribes our human world, we can discuss whether he was. Also, our knowledge of many of the rule-bound descriptions of sport (for example, the off-side rule in soccer or the leg-before-wicket rule in cricket) owes its place to such *talk*. Certainly another's understanding here cannot only be manifested in action: the actions must be rule-following (when they are) and not merely acting in accordance with the rule (see McFee, 2004a: 44–45). That would require our being told, in some way, and to some degree. In like manner, many explanations of events, sporting or otherwise, draw on *talk*.

Fourth, a key place within *talk* rests with what Searle (2008: 49) calls "Declaration", explained so that "[b]y definition, Declarations change reality by representing it as being so changed". Thus, I tell you that you are fired; in that way, I describe how the world now is – you used to work for me, but now you do not – and thereby make it so. Similarly, the umpire in cricket, or baseball, says, "You are out!" (for baseball, he is probably claiming, "You're out of here!"); and his saying that makes it so. Hence you are out. So *talk*, here, has the capacity to change the world. Again, the net effect is recognition of a power to *talk*. Too, research into understanding typically operates by giving a place to talk in these ways. In this sense, the expansive place of *talk* throughout human lives can be recognized. For that *talk* is partly constitutive of the social world in which it is located: and Declaration emphasizes one key aspect of that relationship. Then there can never be a recipe for dealing with *talk*, but only rules of thumb to see the relationship of this *talk* to the research question, in this context or that one.

Nevertheless, some central features of such *talk* can be highlighted. So, fifth, we recognize the centrality of assertion, of saying what one takes to be true. That is, *talk* allows us to claim that things are true. This part of *talk* is not more crucial than, say, the ritual formulae of words and gestures with which people greet one another. But, since (as we will see) research aims at knowledge-generation, it has a special resonance for us. When successful, the conclusions from research could be presented through such assertions. Here, these genuine assertions are contrasted with the same forms of words uttered as part of a play, or when teaching the language. Sixth, there are two senses in which – in such assertions – we must mean what we say. As Cavell (1969: 32) notes, what we say comprises what we mean (other things being equal); and our failing to mean what we say typically convicts us of some failure of moral seriousness – of lying, or frivolity ("I didn't mean it"), or self-deception.

This leads to our seventh insight here: that, in practice, we are fairly good at recognizing such failures – and especially lying – in other people, particularly those we know well. Such points should carry-over to our use of *talk* in the research context: then the possibility of being lied to in research contexts should not be especially worrying. As we do outside of that context, we can look for signs of lying, or for occasions when lying seems likely (say, where the answers are especially sensitive); and we will hope to know our research subjects (and the occasion) sufficiently well as to typically recognize lying or prevaricating, and such like.

Unsurprisingly, given this wide range of powers and capacities of *talk*, it offers much to the researcher addressing persons as subjects: this is, typically dealing with talkers. And many of our sporting questions will be answered through *talk*. Hence it is also unsurprising that our routes to understanding others' conceptualizations of sporting situations and events often begin from here.

A vivid portrayal of the power and complexity of *talk* is given by Colin Lyas, in a longish sketch of his relation to soccer:

> Suppose, because of my life history, I am *deeply* attached to that sport. . . . someone, equally passionately addicted, but brought up in a later age, might wonder why I support Ipswich and not some more fashionable club. Here the lack of understanding might be remedied by appealing to something in the other's life that illuminates this . . . [for example] homesickness for particular places associated with his or her upbringing, from which come the notions of allegiance to place. When we deal with someone who is equally passionate, but about a different sport, the task is easier. We can talk about the phenomenon of tribal allegiance, of terraces, wind, rain, friends at a match, characters, and so forth, and we simply understand that these, by accident of history, deflect into different sports.
>
> (1999: 94)

Here, perhaps the explanation works; perhaps it does not. But there is certainly a narrative to consider: its explanatory possibility draws on shared experiences and shared valuing, captured through the *talk*.

How does our concern with *talk* compare with that of, for instance, the ethologist? For, it might be urged, his interest too lies in inter-personal interaction, of which talk is one crucial aspect. A typical ethological investigation here (that by Morris, 1977)[4] involves studying people meeting in a park on Sunday afternoon; and, yes, there is *talk*. But only enough to greet a stranger, and (perhaps) to arrange stroller-priority on the path. The verbal interaction is highly attenuated. In contrast with the richness of conversations between friends, with common concerns and shared background knowledge, our ethologist is not really allowing genuine *talk* a place here. Hence he or she is not really treating the research subjects as (full) persons: too much of the life of persons is excluded in excluding in principle the full richness of *talk*. Indeed, our conception of treating one's research subjects as persons begins by not setting aside as 'evidence' in principle whatever that the subject might offer. And much of what people offer to one another comes as *talk*; or is shaped by *talk*. So this emphasis reflects the concern with persons as persons.

Two recipes for not really 'researching people'

Consider two cases (one practical, the second theoretical) that deviate from the injunctions urged here. First, the fact of being researched, once acknowledged, is widely recognized as potentially altering subjects' behaviour. This kind of reverse-effect even has a name (or, rather, lots of them). I do not doubt (or deny) the phenomenon: its cousin is familiar to all who have their teaching observed as part of peer-appraisal schemes – nothing is more calculated to make one teach badly! Oddly, though, the research-basis most often cited (if implicitly) for this claim is dubious, in ways revealing for us.

In psychology, this phenomenon of the research process impacting on the researched situation is often called "the Hawthorne effect", after research in the 1920s on female workers at the Western Electric Company's factory in Hawthorne, a suburb of Chicago,[5] concluding that ". . . merely asking people about some aspect of their lives changes their behaviour in that domain" (Breakwell *et al.*, 1995: 86). Further, this research is often read as indicating the effect of knowing that one is being researched. In reality, the outcome was arrived at by changing the work-setting of these women (say, raising the illumination) and then observing changes in their productivity. So any problems here did not arise because of *how* the subjects were talked to – or even *that* the subjects were talked to. Instead, the data-collection was simply in terms of some measure (of productivity) external to the activity. As Toulmin comments:

> the shortcoming . . . [of this work] resulted, not from the general fact that all . . . research [of this type] is flawed and unobjective as a result of the involvement of the workers, but from the fact that, in this particular study, . . . [the] researchers approach . . . was not *participatory enough*.
>
> (2001: 98; emphasis original)

For these workers might have had special reason to respond to changes in their environment, especially if they did not fully understand the context of the project. After all, these were "immigrant women recently arrived from Eastern Europe, some of whom as yet spoke little English" (Toulmin, 2001: 98). In particular, they might have feared for their jobs – and hence responded to what may well have seemed tacit suggestions by employers. That possibility was not seriously considered throughout the Hawthorne write-up: thus Gillespie (1991: 196) notes "the brisk rejection of economic motives as an explanation of the worker's behaviour". So the claim that the behaviour here demonstrates the effect of being researched seems tenuous: other explanations seem possible, even likely, especially in this case. What this case needed was precisely seeing these women as agents. So the failure, from our perspective, resides in how the subjects were regarded.

Our second, longer, case concerns methodological suggestions for what has been called "the new social psychology" (Ingham, 1990): suggestions issuing from major advocates of our commitment to *talk* as a research tool in social science. But this is precisely where this version is limited. Like us, Harré and Secord (1976: 6; emphasis original) speak directly of "treating people for *scientific purposes* as if they were human beings". Further, the direction suggested by the title of their chapter 6, "Why not ask them . . . ?", seems 'down our street'.[6] Then they write of "the idea of men as conscious social actors, capable of controlling their performances and commenting intelligently on them. . . ." (Harré and Secord, 1976: v). This too could describe my position: that persons should be treated as (moral) agents. But is that the right reading of the acting metaphor here? The term "actors" accepts a stronger, more literal, reading, an idea reinforced, by Harré and Secord (chapter 10), with stress on the "The Dramaturgical Standpoint" (Harré and Secord, 1976: 205). Here, the instruction is to "[t]reat the episode one is engaged in, whether as actor or audience, as a dramatic performance" (Harré and Secord, 1976: 205). Further, since "[t]he models [used to explain, or anyway characterize, episodes of human behaviour] are rituals, routines, games and entertainments" (Harré and Secord, 1976: 173), we are told to take the dramatic metaphor even more seriously, to "[r]econstruct the script, the stage directions, etc., . . . as if it were a play script in which rituals, games, routines and entertainments were simulated" (Harré and Secord, 1976: 205–6). Yet clearly this will be informative with respect to, say, sporting behaviour only if there is a useful comparison to be drawn here. But how can we know it is helpful?

Of course, Harré and Secord (1976: 184) stress the idea of a role; that is, of: "a set of actions a person of a particular type or category [for instance, a bridegroom] is expected to perform within the . . . structure of a certain kind of episode". Roles in this sense resemble the roles of actors. But the bridegroom here is not simulating bridegroom-behaviour (and, especially, not behaving according to some script), even if – for such formalized or ritualized activities – a script might be (or might have been) written. In that sense, our bridegroom, rather than acting the role, is *being* a bridegroom.

Harré and Secord recognize that using this dramaturgical standpoint suggests mere acting on the part of agents who, in reality, are actually fulfilling the role. Thus they quote from *Les Liaisons Dangereuses* a letter in which the central character ". . . describes how she trained herself as a social actress" (Harré and Secord, 1976: 210–11). In the letter in the novel, she says:

I saw that to feign love successfully one had only to join the talent of a comedian to the mind of an author. I practiced myself in both arts and perhaps with some success; but instead of seeking the vain applause of the theatre, I resolved to employ for my happiness what others sacrificed to vanity.

(1976: 211)

A dramaturgical model seems very appropriate here precisely because this is a case of feigning, or pretending. But this is precisely not a case of someone acting a certain way as the result of (here) *feeling* a certain way – that is, being in love.

So the comparison with drama imports a key factor absent for typical actions: namely, that the action does not actually reflect directly the desires, motivations and intentions of the agent – that she is just acting. But this cannot be true of typical actions, even if it is true of some.

More importantly, though, the model is flawed in assuming that one extant form of explanation is suitable here: typically, making sense of the variety of things people do requires many varied forms of explanation. And we usually have either no model for that explanation or, at least, no model preceding the action in its context. For, in our terminology, we expect the context (and the question as it occurs in that context) to bear directly on what question is being asked in that particular form of words; and hence on the appropriate ways of answering that question. So, if some (modified) dramaturgical standpoint is sometimes useful here, we would not expect that it always was!

Harré and Secord determine in advance the range of possible answers – and do so independently of the range of questions actually asked (say, about sport: see Marsh *et al.*, 1978); and hence of those potentially asked. In this sense, the investigation they describe is not genuinely erotetic. More centrally, the subjects are not treated as persons, but rather as actors!

The discussion of "Life on the Terraces" of the fans of a soccer club offers a practical example of the concrete strategies that Harré and Secord (1976: 296) sketch for conceptualizing research subjects. It begins from ". . . a large number of video-recordings of fans in the London Road end" (Marsh *et al.*, 1978: 61) of Oxford United Football Club. This permits categorization, first, of the roles groups of such fans adopt – characterized as, for example Rowdies or Town Boys, and identified by clothing as well as behaviour; and then of the careers of typical fans, where careers are understood ". . . as available structures in a youth culture for the establishment of self" (Marsh *et al.*, 1978: 64). Finally, there were social roles for individuals within the groups – such as Chant Leader, Aggro Leader, Nutter, Hooligan – which individuals might 'inhabit' either generally or as part of such a career. For these roles can be learned, and mastered. And doing so could even be a passport to another of the larger role-groupings. As might be expected from following the direction from Harré and Secord (1976), this social world is modeled dramaturgically. It seems a revealing way to understand this social context: certainly, it offers the reader insight into the social world of these sports fans. And similar insights, using similar categorization techniques, are revealing in Fleming (1995), in the analysis of children's participation in sport.

Now, there is a general suggestion here "that career structure can serve well in the explanation of social behaviour which might otherwise appear to have little rationality" (Marsh *et al.*, 1978: 82). But its origin is located, at best, in the specific comments of the subjects: that is, in the *talk* itself, without mediation of the dramaturgical model. So importing a predetermined model for such *talk* still seems a problematic way to characterize research with persons.

So this section has illustrated how the notion of *talk* is fundamental to our understanding of the requirement to research persons as persons by considering how that requirement might not be employed in our fashion. What has this told us about our picture of sport-research more generally?

A short argument for 'naturalistic' research into sport

No doubt *all* research is erotetic; that does not prescribe any particular directions for sport-related research. For all research questions will be made sense of, and answered, in their own contexts. But our general contextualism (ensuring that all research functions erotetically) connects with the specific contexts of sport in another way. For social-scientific research, in regarding research subjects as persons, investigates them in the context of their actions. For us, that typically means the context of the sporting event, or training situation, or so on. Questions that have arisen in particular contexts like those will be best investigated in their contexts, to the degree that is possible. For, in straying too far from that context, we (at least) run the risk of posing different questions.

Two practical points arise immediately. First, 'full' naturalism is likely to be impossible – almost all research will disrupt to some degree the context in which it takes place, even when trying assiduously not to do so. Hence any research design will involve some compromising of the goal of completely naturalistic research. Consider, for example, a design from the extremely 'naturalistic' end of the spectrum: ethnography. Still my discussion with one of the research subjects is artificial to the extent that my being there (with those topics to listen for, or slip into the conversation) is artificial: I am there as a researcher. Even if, in this context, my role is regular rather than artificial (say, I am driving the team's bus), I may still behave slightly differently. After all, I am concerned not to avoid exposure as a researcher, even were this to require no more than reminding others of what they have forgotten. So little, if any, research will be fully 'naturalistic'. Second, talk of a *spectrum of naturalism* is misleading: there is no single dimension of artificiality, nor any uncontentious way to determine the place along it of a particular research design. This is one reason why a sustained discussion of 'naturalism' is out of place here.

That said, the simplest way to arrive at the commitment to naturalism in our kind of social-scientific research into sport involves one aspect of such research (the data-collection aspect) as obviously directed at the conceptualization of the sport-related action by the research subjects. No doubt, as a researcher, I will want to go beyond how subjects conceptualize events; but my coming to them is partly to explore how *they* would explain those events – whether I am doing oral history into sports of the past (Tomlinson, 1992; 2005: 205–25), or ethnography into a culture of windsurfing (Wheaton, 2002), or participant-observations (and interviews) concerning the life-histories of top-class women's cricketers. Even when behaving more obviously as researchers (say, in interviews with sports-centre managers), if the subjects are regarded as persons – if the data are comprised of *talk* – our concern is with their conceptions of events, since those are what they can tell us. In fact, even asking a policymaker about policies (and especially about the impact of such policies) is asking for the conception of the policy, or whatever. Then, the real topic of this phase of the research here concerns such conceptions – what is sometimes put, over grandly, as 'how such-and-such person constructs reality'.[7]

Two related reasons explain why that same phase of research should be conducted in naturalistic settings (to the degree this is possible). First and most obviously, that is where the relevant *talk* takes place of its own accord. The lack of artificiality removes some difficulties (or some kinds of difficulties) – your subjects may not be lying to you as research subjects, but they may still be lying in ways friends can. Still, minimizing artificiality seems advantageous from that perspective. We can at least see what, say, the female cricketers purport to believe. Second, that (naturalistic) setting is typically what is being researched, either locally (the soccer club) or conceptually (the governance of soccer which takes place partly from this set of buildings). And being in the context to be researched may well offer insights to the researcher.

Of course, this baldest of sketches focuses on one phase of typical research, abstractly described. But it connects the understanding of sport-related questions to the *talk* that provides some of our data. To this extent, such research into sport aims to be as naturalistic as possible, although we have recognized the difficulties in maximizing such naturalism. And we have carefully said nothing about what methods best preserve such naturalism: that must be argued case by case.

Looking for qualitative research?

But why is my emphasis on 'research with persons (treated as persons) as subjects' more revealing than appeal to the qualitative/quantitative contrast? Because that contrast does not sufficiently highlight fundamental differences between two (or more) broad methodological strategies. This thought, while not strictly demonstrable, can be suggested in two ways. In this section, an informal trawl through recent copies of a major journal illustrates both the variety of work currently classified as qualitative; and perhaps casts doubt on the qualitative credentials of some of it (from our perspective): *The Sports Psychologist*[8] was chosen for this. The next section considers attempts to ensure the soundness of data from research with persons (viewed as persons): that is, where the data typically takes the form of *talk*; and suggests that strategies (effectively) quantifying one's data have a profound impact, transforming the nature of one's research.

First, we discuss our brief informal survey. Consider the following five articles from recent editions of *The Sports Psychologist*:

- "A Qualitative Investigation of Personal-Disclosure Mutual-Sharing Team Building Activity" (Dunn and Hart, 2004), which seeks to combine "subjective responses" (2004: 363) with "inductive qualitative data analysis technique" (2004: 369). These point away from our conception of person-directed research: for instance, reference here to the subjective is slightly dismissive of its value. And its aspirations towards an "inductive . . . *technique*" (emphasis original) suggest its model of soundness in research is a broadly scientistic one. While this article offers a good account of what the researchers did, it provides no justification (or any other sort of basis) for the elaborated descriptions of reading, thinking about, and discussing with others who had read and thought about them. In short, it takes for granted an epistemological stance, while simultaneously raising (implicit) questions as to the soundness of its data.

- "Self-Talk and Female Youth Soccer Performance" (Johnson *et al.*, 2004): here self-talk rapidly becomes "the ST treatment" (2004: 47) – that is to say, its connection with talk is broken, and it is treated as a technical idea; further, it is conceptualized explicitly as an "independent variable" (2004: 47). On the model here, then, variables will be classified, with a view to determining a dependent variable, controlling for other variables (or introducing a *ceteris paribus* clause), and treating the matter statistically. So, at the level of epistemological concepts, this is clearly not 'qualitative' in our sense.

- "Professional Women's Career Experiences in Sport Psychology: A Feminist Standpoint" (Draper *et al.*, 2005): despite the explicit commitment here to Feminism, the epistemology here is very traditional. Thus, the method included a "bracketing interview with a male colleague who was knowledgeable and experienced in qualitative interviewing . . . to unveil personal biases and assumptions . . . that could potentially influence the process of data collection and analysis" (2005: 35). But what conception of "bias" is deployed here? It seems like the commonsense misreading of bias – fueled by scientism – on which bias is not necessarily remediable (compare chapter 6). But, more important is that the "process of data collection and [especially] analysis" envisaged, and the ways it seeks to ensure the soundness of the data, returns us to conceptions of knowledge rooted in research in natural science.

- "A Qualitative Exploration of Psychological-Skills Use in Coaches" (Thelwell *et al.*, 2008) explicitly used "a predominantly content-analysis approach" (2008: 42) to analyse interviews via transcripts. That is to say, the occurrences of particular ideas were counted: its mind-style was therefore not our 'qualitative' one.

- "Reflective Practice for Sports Psychologists: Concepts, Models, Practical Implications, and Thoughts on Dissemination" (Anderson *et al.*, 2004) is the most methodologically sophisticated of the pieces – indeed, it has a specifically methodological agenda, and a precise epistemology, attempting to 'validate' the kind of craft-knowledge (or knowledge-in action) required by the concept of *reflective practice*. This is uncontentiously qualitative research in our sense.

These comments are meant simply to illustrate some of the variety within the field, rather than to present sustained critique of any of these pieces. I do not even claim them as typical. Moreover, I am not committed to the defence of every detail of my commentary. Further, and to repeat, these cases are offered only to illustrate some variety, not all of it; and certainly not as any kind of taxonomy of possibilities.

Even a cursory glance shows that, for articles purporting to be qualitative, only one uncontentiously treats its research subjects as persons (for the purpose of the research). So the epistemology either deployed or assumed by most of these pieces (through the qualitative/quantitative contrast) is not that argued for throughout this work.

Ways of trying to quantify *talk*?

Can ostensibly qualitative research designs acquire a quite different epistemological stance through the desire to make concrete – or, worse, to quantify – the *talk* that forms their natural data? It helps here to characterize quantitative research, sketching its virtues, since (as we will see) just these virtues can be sought for the data generated in non-numerical ways (and, perhaps, recorded in non-numerical ways – such as transcripts). The central thought is that quantitative data are numerical: information about the world in the form of numbers. But the world is not typically structured in the form of numbers: measurement (or similar) turns the information into numbers. So what are the virtues of measurement? Bryman rightly suggests the following:

- Measurement allows us to delineate *fine differences* between people in terms of the characteristic in question . . .;
- "Measurement gives us a constant device or yardstick for making such distinctions . . ." – giving consistency over time in our own research with respect to the work of other researchers;
- Measurement provides the basis for more precise estimates of the degree of relationship between concepts.

(2001: 66–67)

If data are quantitative, their analysis typically uses statistics. Here, statistics functions as a set of methods of enquiry: "statistics helps us to look for reliable regularities and associations among things 'in general' and 'in the long run'" (Rowntree, 1980: 16). For statistical techniques allow clarification that a relationship discovered could not have arisen by chance: that is what it means to say the relationship is *statistically significant*. Hence, statistical significance is not just significance – that is, importance. Those who do not recognize this technical use of the term can miss this point, reading "significant" instead in its everyday sense. Thus, an idiotic writer in the *Los Angeles Times* (2005: E14) claims that: "[a]lthough the findings were not yet, as one researcher put it, 'statistically significant', they were significant enough to the 70 patients in the study who had strokes or heart attacks, and to the 23 who died". Calling the reported result not statistically significant points out precisely that the study proved nothing – 'results' could have come about by chance! Hence there is no conclusion to be drawn.

Even granting these points, the ability to quantify one's data, and to treat them statistically, offers a powerful set of analytical tools. In particular, statistical treatment is widely recognized (in natural science) as providing methods to secure the so-called "holy trinity" (Sparkes, 1998: 365) of *validity*, *reliability*, and *generalizability* of measures (see chapters 1 and 4). But what can one do when these have no obvious application – when one's research data amounts largely to *talk*: to transcripts, and field notes of conversations, and the like?

Here, Lawrence Stenhouse (1978; 1980) proposed the construction of an analytic index as a useful tool in analysis. This indexing simply involved highlighting where, in one's transcripts or field-notes, such and such a concept occurred. Its methodological virtues included the need to read through the texts many times to determine the appropriate concepts to include in the list (thereby giving one great familiarity with one's data); and that one selected concepts, not words. So, for instance, one would recognize uses of terms such as "cash", "dosh", "bread", "ponies", "monkeys", "moola", "Semolians", and so on (as referring to money). Further, the occurrence of these terms were not obviously relevant occurrences of the concept – perhaps most obvious for "bread". That requires consideration, which could result in omitting items from one's index. (This accords with our contextualism: the same concepts need not be expressed in the same form of words; or vice versa.) So this kind of indexing produces a crude coding of the data, not itself an analysis of those data. Rather, it is preparation for the researcher's analysis – for her looking for patterns of similarity and difference, but also for key or revealing moments.

Such a procedure has some obvious disadvantages, especially from the perspective of the components of Sparkes's "trinity". In addition to being very time-consuming both to develop and to use, the Stenhousian analytic index was not easily mastered by researchers other than its constructor. That raised questions about its reliability, viewed as the possibility for other researchers to recognize one's data from one's raw results. And it was unclear just why those items were selected – raising questions about validity, understood as relating to the appropriateness of the items selected for one's index. In addition, the time-consuming character of the use of such an index militated against employing very long transcripts: even once 'coded', they were unmanageable: at the least, they could not show clearly the progress of data from source-evidence to conclusions.

One can only speculate on the impact here of the (sudden?) availability of considerable computer power. Certainly, the possibility of such power on the researcher's desk coincided with the development of software designed to facilitate the comparison and retrieval (the 'analysis') of such transcripts, field-notes and the like. The various programmes for so-called Computer-Assisted Qualitative Data Analysis are importantly different. But to highlight the fundamental conceptual problem here, I have selected for brief comment just one, choosing NUD*IST (Non-numerical Unstructured Data Indexing, Searching and Theorizing) partly since I have had direct experience of using it.[9] (I recognize that my complaints here repeat those of other researchers since the beginning: see, for example, Fielding and Lee, 1991: 6–10.)

Obviously, a task suitable for a computer will be done accurately and quickly by a computer (as compared with a researcher – even aided by his or her research assistants!). This facilitates the use of larger data sets. It might be objected that this would encourage analysis at a superficial level, followed by mechanical data 'crunching' procedures. Developers of NUD*IST (and Ethnograph) eagerly met objections of this kind. But that is not my objection.

The real question lies in whether that task is suitable for a computer. When the authors of NUD*IST claim that its use can transform qualitative analysis (Richards and Richards, 1991: 39), one should take very seriously the question about what is suitable for computerization. For their claim suggests that it is more than just computerizing a procedure like Stenhouse's – although Richards and Richards (1991: 50) recognize that NUD*IST will ". . . centre the research process around the index system".

Certainly, using such programmes makes public the procedures of researchers. As Richards and Richards (1991: 45) note, "[c]lerical tasks of qualitative research – data recording and indexing – are handled by NUD*IST by input into and exploration of separate text and index files". Then other researchers can (perhaps) track the moves from raw results, through true data, to conclusions.

With any such computer programme, as for Stenhouse's index, coding the raw data will always be time-consuming. Researchers must consider whether sample size, or perhaps another feature of the data, justifies the expenditure of time required to set it up. And avoid the obvious 'short-cut' of using words (or verbal expressions) as the method of coding – an error, in turn, facilitated by the word-search option in many word-processing packages. Since NUD*IST itself uses text-search procedures, great care is needed. Here, our contextual conception of understanding has a direct input: we know that no easy correspondence exists between forms of words and concepts, and that any coding must be of concepts. (And we have yet to address the Untypable: "the fleeting notes, doodles and marginalia within which insight is often captured" [Fielding and Lee, 1991: 8].) Indeed, although NUD*IST may additionally "deal with the analysis of photographs and other visual material" (Gratton and Jones, 2004: 225), it is centrally textual in the literal sense. Hence it is indeed another of the "variations on the code-and-retrieve theme" (Bryman, 2001: 406).[10]

Like most such programmes, NUD*IST allows for sections of the 'raw data' to be labelled, as a basis for retrieval, with no limit to the number of times a rich passage can be indexed in this way. Then giving the same category-label to another piece of text connects them. This, for instance, in a discussion by Burroughs-Lange and Lange (1993), the categories "research room", "in class", "support unit", "special school" all fell under the more general category "location". The resulting tree structures can then be understood taxonomically. In a similar vein, when investigating sports-psychological support services for elite women cricketers, a higher level indexing-item such as Goal Setting could be further divided into Cricket Goals and Fitness Training Goals. In effect, then, the potential within NUD*IST to both create and collapse categories may make less difficult both the process of identification of key concepts and the hierarchical organization of those concepts (through tree structures). In this way, NUD*IST seeks inter-code relationships, with a view to theory-building of a fairly traditional kind. And the hypothesis of relationships between this and that within the data can be tested rapidly. But it is the researcher who identifies the meaning-units.

However, the claim of NUD*IST (in its title) to be non-numerical is misleading. Perhaps that account is mathematically correct, but the programme is best at building-up rankings of the uses of particular concepts – thus facilitating the development of the hierarchical structures just referred to. That may not be strictly numerical, but suggests just the kinds of fixed segmentation of the world that 'numericalization' of data would imply. And its interface to the quantitative data-management programme SPSS (Statistical Package for Social Sciences) reinforces this idea.

Further, the conception of the development of theory deployed here looks fundamentally for higher orders of generality. (Of course, this was Sparkes's quest for generalizability, discussed earlier.) While the desire for greater generality can have its place within theory, this is not the only demand. Since our research is context-dependent, we must sometimes look for the best account of what went on here. In this, NUD*IST is structurally unhelpful: at best, it is only as helpful as paying close attention to one of Stenhouse's analytic indices – despite, say, its impressive speed of data-retrieval.

Our criticism here operates in two overlapping ways. First, programmes such as NUD*IST aim precisely to make *talk* more manageable. That moves us away from the human world; from *talk* as such. Second, they are 'numericalizing', even if not strictly numerical: they present the world to us in a way incompatible with the need to do justice to its human features; and especially its *talk*.

Of course, these brief remarks only point in a direction: they suggest that 'qualitative' researchers have good reason to be concerned about the epistemological credentials of such computerized tools, especially their compatibility with the assumptions and presuppositions of one's own research. For the danger lies in taking on "a culture of control, not just a tool" (Lyman, quoted Fielding and Lee, 1991: 7). So, at the least, one must plan to use, for example, NUD*IST, rather than coming to it as an analytic aid once the research is completed. Of course, both concerns will be intensified to the degree that a certain eclecticism is a characteristic of qualitative research, an eclecticism reflecting the occasion-specificity of topics, subjects and researchers, as well as technical matters. These all seem rightly to be at issue when one's research subjects are properly regarded as persons.

Similarly, Kari Fasting (2000: 153), using a different Computer-Assisted Qualitative Data Analysis package to analyze interviews with female recreational sportsplayers regarding how they experienced the female body, recognized that the "principles of qualitative content analysis" at work in the programme brought about "a reduction and abstraction of the content of a text". The question, as above, is whether such reduction and abstraction still leaves us with the context-full *talk* from which we began, and which was valued in the initial decision to conduct the research through these interviews.

Overall, this is a plea for care: were the aim really to quantify *talk* – or the epistemological assumptions tending in this direction given full rein (or were inescapable, once using the technology) – such tools would be incompatible with the conception of research developed here. Even if the programmes did not automatically militate in that direction, researchers' enthusiasm for the tool might tend that way. Here the danger of such a trend lies in its changing how the data were conceptualized: that would lead researchers away from the questions posed in the situation researched (thereby running counter to our erotetic emphasis). In giving up the attention to *talk* as such, it would no longer regard the subjects as persons.

A yet stronger point might be urged: that, where the researched are moral agents, they should not be regarded as (mere) subjects at all. Thus, to repeat, the code of conduct of the American Psychological Association (APA) no longer makes "reference to the term 'research subject' (except with reference to non-human animals)" (McNamee *et al.*, 2007: 74–75) – the parenthetical comment here reinforcing that the rationale for this omission lies precisely in (non-human) animals not being full moral agents.[11] But, as chapter 1 urges, these participants should not be conceptualized as co-contributors, or something similar. Doing that undermines the researcher's mastery over his/her research data (chapter 10): is she/he really the researcher anymore? This is an 'other side of the coin' mistake: in wishing to avoid down-playing the powers and capacities of subjects, it effectively over-rates them. That tendency should be rejected, while recognizing that something crucial is also missed if we regard the agential-subjects in such research as though they were the comparatively uncomplicated subjects of other research. Yet flourishing the 'qualitative-versus-quantitative' distinction encourages precisely this. It suggests only two situations need consideration, where the fundamental differentia are whether or not the data are segmental, and hence quantifiable. Suppose our concern is not quantitative, in that we are not counting (or anything similar): sets of radical contrasts could still be drawn between cases where the qualitative data grants agent-status to the participants (I would still call them "research subjects") and cases where that data simply reflects their responses typically from a third-person perspective – sometimes, as at Hawthorne, even treated in very crude behavioural terms. Of course, this is both important and complex. But it is a further reason why the qualitative-versus-quantitative contrast cannot bear too much (theoretical) weight.

Causality, stochastic causation, and the normativity of *talk*

In these ways, then, qualitative research discussed here centrally involves the perspective and the moral dimension of the persons who are its subjects. Then views that dismiss research involving persons as subjective (as 'anything goes', such that one can say what one likes) are perhaps the most importantly mistaken. For reference to people in the research context has sometimes seemed, mistakenly, to imply that there was no fact of the matter, but only the opinion of this person or that one.[12] By contrast, adherence to the ideas advocated here would involve selecting methods which relied on or prioritized *talk* – participant observation, auto-ethnography, or oral history – and recognized that *talk* as potentially informative of what another person or group saw as important.

One counter-argument offered denies there is a fact of the matter here by pointing out that different people might see the matter differently. Now, this claim is over-worked on most occasions. Those using it should reflect on the likelihood of its success as a defence for running a red traffic-signal ("But, judge, people see colours differently!") – the boring fact is that, in general, people do not see colours differently. Or when they do, sometimes that reflects standard regularities ("He's colour-blind!"); and sometimes differences in perception are explained by differences in knowledge and experience (as with the radiologists discussed briefly in chapter 5).

But occasionally something more profound is intended, contrasting the human case with that in science. The kinds of causality found in, say, much science do not depend on how an event is described. So that it seems that, if A causes B, then finding another description for A (say, C) will mean that C causes B also. So that, if the rainstorm causes the mudslide, and supposing that the description "sudden precipitation of water" picked out exactly the same event as "rainstorm", then the sudden precipitation too caused the mudslide.

This substitutability of descriptions does not necessarily follow, for instance, for claims involving human intentions. When *causality* amounts to the workings out of the causal (natural) laws, like those of science, is independent of the description under which the outcome is conceptualized. But not so agency. For example, I intend or plan to do something under one description: but might justifiably reject an account of what I intended under another description true of the outcome ("Yes, I intended to hit a six in the cricket match, but not to hit the biggest six ever on that ground, nor to break the pavilion clock" – even though all of these occurred.) What I did, and what I intended, reflect the description under which the action should be conceptualized.

First, the account here is normative, highlighting what ought or ought not to happen (say, as a result of choice), not what did. In this sense, action-descriptions differ from those describing regularities of behaviour: rule-governed activities provide the simplest examples. Thus, in playing chess, the issue is not whether the piece can be put on a particular square (it obviously can) but whether doing so is a legitimate move in chess. Moreover, simply placing a chess piece on a certain square, even when a legitimate move, can still be criticized. Perhaps I do not know the rules of chess, and am simply mirroring your moves: then my behaviour accords with a rule, without following it (McFee, 2004a: 44). Or perhaps my move, although legitimate, is a bad move – it will hasten my defeat! So here too the normative element must be distinguished from, say, a description of what people, or most people, do in this situation.

Second, the concepts and categories deployed are crucial here. These might differ between people, reflecting either differences in understanding or different concerns. Finding the correct description here is perspectival (and occasion-sensitive), reflecting the appropriate concepts and categories. But what is conceptual (because cultural) in these ways is a product of *talk*; it pervades the human world. For instance, we might grant a biological imperative on humans (as on non-human animals) to eat and to reproduce – among other such imperatives. Yet the forms in which these practices manifest themselves are not causal in any straightforward way: we do not simply take a bite from the first available food-source that passes, within grabbing range, across our field of vision. The causal basis here, if any, is well below the surface of typical human actions. Similarly, we do not simply have sex with the first object of sexual attraction within grabbing range (even putting aside cultural dimensions of attraction). Rather, what counts as food here, and how one prepares and eats it, is heavily cultural. We learn these 'facts'; and could (perhaps) discuss them. In like fashion, the elaborate 'rituals' involved in courtship among humans are poorly reflected when reduced even to causal imperatives of the sorts operative within the world of (other) primates. So an account of the (human) resources here must recognize how the object of desire (for food as for sex, or love) is necessarily the object as characterized or understood. In this sense, it is conceptual, even if we could not deploy the concepts discursively. That is, I would stress the cognitive dimension in the human versions of biological imperatives.

We are first-and-foremost agents: as Wittgenstein (1969 §402) put it (quoting Goethe), "in the beginning was the deed". Then rational explanation of my behaviour need not require a chain of thoughts that actually passed through my mind, either prior to or during my action. Rather, such explanations are typically constructed after the fact. So the immediacy of what is sometimes thought instinctive is just a red-herring. Instead, having recognized the dependence on *talk*, the degree of perspectivalism and occasion-sensitivity here can be plotted: less than the subjectivist hoped for (or his critic feared), but enough to rule out the sorts of laws beloved of scientism.

Of course, much here turns on what is or is not causal. As noted earlier, if causality is thought of in terms of the workings out of the causal (natural) laws of science, causality will be independent of the description under which the outcome is conceptualized. But, as we have seen, this is not true of intentional descriptions: *talk* – say, the expression of an intention – does not in general, say, merely correlate with the fulfillment of that intention. Rather, the agency in that relation between (here) intention and action is expressed by *talk*. Is this relation causal? Let us defer that question, for (in the end) it may turn on whether or not to call it "causal", once its features are recognized.

In effect, four key points about causality can be stated fairly bluntly here, deploying the argument against the assumption of finite totalities (from chapter 1). First, the general position for natural science assumes *causal necessity*: that if A causes B, and A occurs, then B (and only B) must occur – at least *ceteris paribus*. To rule out other occurrences, we must consider everything that might generate an alternative outcome. That imports the assumption of a finite totality of properties to consider, such that in principle we could consider them *all*. For natural science, this is generally made true by fiat.

But, second, this is not in general true for human events; and, in particular, human actions. So that, applied to human contexts as well as those of (natural) science, the claim that "A causes B" is not an exceptionless statement: it does not mean that in every circumstance A will be followed by B – unless we make it mean that (as we do in natural science). Rather, the claim is not exceptionless just because there are always cases which (if they occurred) could upset the outcome claimed or urged. But we cannot check for those since (among other things) we cannot enumerate them – they do not constitute a finite totality. Of course, a *ceteris paribus* clause puts that difficulty aside. But doing so gives the (false) impression of some finite list of features for consideration: we cannot even know what *cetera* we require to be *paria*.

To be clear, then, the project of natural science presupposes that there is a finite totality of properties to consider. Its *ceteris paribus* clause sets aside *all* those "other things" as equal, assuming that, in principle (although not in practice), we could identify that all. Hence, we could have considered all-minus-two, then all-minus-one . . . then, finally, *all!* But, for social science, different conceptualizations of an event (say, from different theoretical perspectives) may not always fit together. And questions about sport are, centrally, everyday ones, rather than something very technical. They have no clear, fixed relation to other concerns (and hence to other descriptions of human life). Rather, these might differ as questions and contexts differ.

Third, we recognize this in seeing how the descriptions under which human action are characterized, the perspective on them, is not invariant in the way that the causal account of them will be – as we have just noted.

Our fourth claim notes that some scientific causality admits of exceptions: the example from chapter 1 was the claim, "Smoking causes cancer". In granting that as true, we recognize it as offering the trend or tendency of so-called stochastic causation. But a scientism is inherent in traditional explanations of stochastic causation. This thought takes the causation as actually exceptionless if only we knew enough: that, roughly, it is smoking-plus-X (or smoking-minus-X) that causes cancer – where the "X" might stand for a large number of factors, including genetic dispositions. In this case, then, the causality (by smoking-plus-X) is actually exceptionless – it is only our ignorance of X that makes us treat the causality as (merely) stochastic, or statistical.

Now, what grounds this commitment to exceptionless causation? Why could we believe the causality here must be exceptionless? Perhaps for no reason other than thinking of it as scientific causation: that it is made so by fiat, as in general in natural science. Yet why should that follow? Instead, stochastic causation should not be taken as a kind of 'second-class' exceptionless causation ('exceptionless causation plus ignorance'). Instead, it too is causation which is not exceptionless. Once granting that possibility in this case, it becomes easier to concede it in sports research.

Part III
The place of truth

4   Research must aim at truth

Research is knowledge-generating

As urged in chapter 1, research is, by its nature, essentially knowledge-generating, at least in intention. So researchers should conceptualize their projects in terms of truth, since knowledge in this context is knowledge of what is true. No doubt the connection between research and truth might be exploited in many ways (for example, not *only* through hypothesis-generation). The argument *here* is only that our picture of research must safeguard truth, which seems a default position. For it would be odd to grant both that such-and-such was research and that it lacked any capacity to generate knowledge. Thus the argument here aims only at this conceptual point. Hence it contains few examples. A more convincing answer must await an elaborated actual account of truth, sketched in the next three chapters, which addresses more fully both proposed explanations of truth-denial and cases offering to show how my claims here might be rejected.

Why, short of general denial of the notion of truth (see chapters 6 and 7), should that default position be denied? The answer lies in a rejection of truth as the central concept here; such a rejection draws on what features of truth might be thought lacking. To understand and explore these, we can turn to the specific contrasts implicit in deploying the distinction between truth and something else.

But with what is truth here contrasted? Certainly, answerability to the world is fundamental for truth. Hence one contrast is with my wishing or wanting such-and-such. For truth (in this sense) depends on how things *are* in the world; what is true is not amenable to change simply by my choosing to do so. Similarly, truth will be contrasted with opinion. Suppose I know that it is not presently raining here (that this is true). And I have a view – an opinion – about whether or not it is currently raining in Seattle, although I do not know. If asked, I would assert that it is currently raining in Seattle: this is my opinion (philosophers sometimes call that, rather confusingly, my *belief*).[1] But I might be wrong. Yet for opinions of this kind, there is an answer as to their truth, if only we knew it. The truths here might with justice be called "empirical truths": roughly, truths about the world about us.

Sometimes identifying these as opinions just acknowledges that we do not know. In related cases, perhaps we can never know, for example, which of two sprinters would have won if . . . (say, if they ever competed against one another, or . . . over such-and-such distance . . .); and perhaps (now) we cannot find out (one or more is dead). For this kind of 'opinion', there seems a correct answer – just one we do not or cannot know. With such straightforwardly factual matters, what is at issue is just the variety of human ignorance. On such topics, only ignorance generates 'matters of opinion'. In the same vein, there is less diversity of view on many topics than is sometimes supposed: defusing the so-called 'matter of opinion' requires comparing like with like (McFee, 2004a: 94). Thus, the seemingly endless dispute over some moral question might be contrasted with the seeming agreement that, say, water boils at one hundred degrees Centigrade. The first are taken as matters of opinion; the second as matters of fact. But areas of agreement within morality can be found, if our cases are chosen carefully. For instance, no person who accepts that there are moral judgements urges that it is OK to torture innocent children. So, when simple enough cases are chosen, there is 'one answer' within morality. And, at the far reaches of science, issues (for example, the number of 'elementary particles') generate continued dispute, even among the knowledgeable – where the answer may be an 'aesthetic' matter! Thus, often, there is really no dispute not settled by careful attention to appropriate comparisons or to what each side is asking, on mature reflection, despite such-and such being set aside as a matter of opinion. And such resolutions are not confined to, say, scientific facts.

My finding out that something is so is fundamentally contrasted (in principle) with my making it so. At least superficially, research lies in the first of these camps.[2] Contrasting knowledge with mere opinion recognizes that truth, arrived at when one knows, has an evidence-base. But what counts as evidence? We must return to this topic.

Sometimes, reference to opinion is just politeness: "I agree to differ" means, roughly, "I will not be harsh with you tonight – despite your being mistaken". For these, the voicing of a matter of opinion aims to acknowledge kinds of tolerance for the views (or positions) of others. The ideal of tolerance is connected here; but it can be misread. With genuine differences in taste, belief [taken as credo], and so on, acknowledging the right to one's own opinion is endorsing the liberal virtue of tolerance. However, tolerance is a "reciprocal virtue" (Taylor *et al.*, 1994: 22). Thus when Bob Dylan sang that his liberal principles did not extend to letting arch-conservative presidential candidate Barry Goldwater move in next door, nor marry his daughter, we understand how Goldwater's own intolerance precludes his being granted the full extent of the tolerance of others.

Other cases where knowledge is contrasted with opinion should be importantly different from this one – but many are not. Much of what are dismissed as "matters of opinion" are *really* matters on which one should not have an opinion: for example, that soccer is a better game than rugby (or rugby than American football). Since there could never be answers (there are no agreed criteria for comparing), one cannot have a serious view about them – as opposed to what might be said in jest. Further, many profoundly-held commitments are not well treated as either knowledge (and hence truth) or belief: consider allegiance to sports teams. Someone who did not understand the culture of soccer might wonder why I did not support the (objectively) best team in the UK Premier League – which might be Manchester United, or Arsenal, or perhaps Chelsea. Do I not recognize these teams as better than the one I support? Of course, here drawing on the critic's allegiances (say, in basketball or baseball) makes similar points (compare Lyas, 1999: 94, quoted chapter 3). Yet, in general, we still want our conclusions from research into such topics to be true – to be things we knew as a result of conducting that research.

Some thoughts on evidence

In explaining empirical truth, evidence has a key role. But, what counts as evidence? No brief answer is possible, but five remarks are informative. First, evidence connects with perceptible features of the environment or situation: a simple thought might be that evidence is what is open to perception. Yet that thought imports a view of the kinds of things open to perception (see Travis, 2004: 247–48). But, second, human categories here go beyond that conception of evidence as, say, the sort of data a machine could record. To begin sketching this view of the perceptible, consider a multiple figure from psychology, such as the duck-rabbit or old woman-young woman (McFee, 2004a: 95): roughly the same patterns of light and shade fall on the retina of the person who sees only the young woman, only the old, or both aspects in the figure.

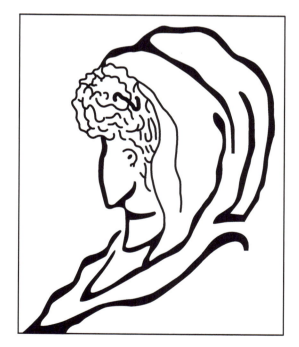

Figure 4.1 Young woman/old woman

But all these responses are answerable to the design. In our explanation, we say that, for the young woman, this line should be seen in such-and such way (This is the line of her cheek; this is a choker around her neck.) For the old woman, the viewer is invited to see that line in so-and-so way (This is her nose; this is her mouth.) Yet, however that figure is seen, some way of treating the lines composing it must be offered: the perceptible features that are these lines provide the evidence-base for any justifiable claim.

Thus genuine insights will be answerable to the state of the world. Or, at least, positions urged as insightful can be rejected when they are not answerable in this way. And that connects notions such as insightfulness back to truth, or something like it.

Third, and consonant with our general account, the focus is on what is perceptible *by persons*. But which concepts are involved in making that perceptual judgement? (How much do I need to know about football [soccer] to see off-side, even when it happens?) That is, we will recognize both that the perceptual process is theory-laden; and (therefore) that people can learn to deploy the relevant categories.

Fourth, the need to recognize the evidence here for what it is means that we can fail to do so. Multiple figures such as the old woman-young woman or the duck-rabbit highlight this topic too—we may be unable to see one aspect (say, the young woman), even though we try, and even though aided by others (McFee, 2004a: 94–95).

Fifth, since the perception of the evidence depends on one's concepts and categories, the nature of evidence is connected to the source of those concepts and categories, the matrix of disciplinary principles (Toulmin, 1972: 124)[3] within which we are working – roughly, the academic discipline: an economist can deploy economic evidence; a sociologist can use sociological evidence. So one learns how to understand evidence in acquiring mastery of these disciplinary matrices.

The constraints on data-soundness aim at knowledge-generation

Thus far, sketching some features of (empirical) truth, as they relate to evidence, has connected research with knowledge-generation. The point can be elaborated via the more fully worked case of numerical data. Consider, say, the *reliability* of a measure, understood broadly as the consistency of that measure (Bryman, 2001: 70), in terms of:

a   *stability* – can we be confident that there will be little fluctuation of the results over time (say, if we re-tested)?
b   *internal reliability* – are respondents' scores consistent, or do they lack internal coherence? If the latter, the indicators might not relate to the same thing.
c   *inter-observer consistency* – would other observers have arrived at roughly the same conclusions from those observations?

These topics indicate precisely the concern with *truth*: results that are true (reflecting a feature of the world) will not fluctuate over time. Hence such stability here is necessary for truth (once a single context is identified). That is, one cannot get truth without also getting stability of this kind. Similarly for the other characteristics: our 'scores' will be consistent across time for features independent of our wishes; and others will see what we see (once they are as well-trained and prepared as we are). These characteristics of sound quantitative research indeed aim towards truth,[4] correct also when considering 'qualitative' research designs.

Any analysis of qualitative research must show how the obligations for research soundness are met. Many procedures deployed in qualitative research reflect the same epistemic constraints as quantitative research. For instance, as noted in chapter 3, Carnap's principle of total evidence functions as a practical idealization in both qualitative and quantitative research designs. Hence no additional justification is needed. But what should be made of more traditional constraints? For instance, should the notions that Sparkes (1998: 365) calls a "holy trinity" be understood in the ways Sparkes offers? Well, conceding that he listed the correct understandings of these notions in this context effectively ties these notions to conceptions of research rejected here. For this account of, say, "validity" seems wedded to a scientistic epistemology – its reference to "a measure" can even sound quantitative!

So searching for, say, a gold standard of "content and construct validity" (see Punch, 1998: 100–2), on this understanding, is adopting our opponent's framework: we are not using these notions directly because he has used them up! Even when we search for another account of validity (that is, another way to meet this demand)[5] the agenda here might seem set by the scientistic epistemology.

The rationale for concern with validity or reliability here is, at root, a connection to the (possible) truth of the claims generated by the research. For whatever other notions achieve the same broad outcome for social research in 'real world' contexts, that outcome is both that the data should not be the invention of the researcher (something only he can see) and that it should reflect features of the situations – so that 'wishing does not make it so'.

So what is really being sought? Reflecting on the title of Andy Sparkes's book, *Telling Tales in Sport and Physical Activity* (2002), offers one insight: we need more than just tales, as comparison with (say) novels shows us. We do not comment on whether or not things in fact are as described in Jane Austen's novels, but we must for *research*. For just these features distinguish claims to truth from those of (mere) belief. So it cannot be (very) misleading to take the crucial features here as those associated with searching for truth.

The problem of scientism

Such a search can be explained by addressing the conception of truth, the access to data, and the nature of those data. In chapter 1, we identified scientism as involving both a valorization of a model of knowledge drawn from science, and the deployment of particular model of science (typically, a kind of inductivism: see chapter 5). Hence it bears on all aspects. The scientism here is not just the commitment to science as either the best or the only model of knowledge but it also takes a view of what activities are appropriate to data-gathering. Thus, in criticism of psycho-analytic psychology, we are reminded that "[i]t is very difficult to assess the validity of Freud's ideas" (Moxon, 2000: 7) since they do not lend themselves to laboratory experimentation. Hence, key features of natural science, viewed scientistically, will be controlled experimentation, measurement, hypothesis-testing (with contrastive null-hypotheses): these methods offer data, and others do not. Hence the dismissal as subjective of whatever is either not directly observable or involving persons' views of their world.[6]

Scientism of this kind also assumes that the practice of science (and hence scientific knowledge) is value-free: the researchers simply work-through the scientific method, as applied in this case. So they are not credited with a view (or perspective) that is relevant to the research findings in any way. Moreover, under such scientism, only the researchers are decision-makers here: if they recognize the rights of research subjects, it is only insofar as those rights will be safe-guarded by subjects signing a form offering 'informed consent' to the procedures. In addition to the "tick-box consent" (McNamee *et al.*, 2007: 72) mentality this may facilitate, such an attenuated conception of the possibilities of access to one's subjects cannot really recognize those subjects as persons, in ways that seem desirable when those subjects are confronted in 'real world' situations in sport (to the degree we can). For, since we can speak to human subjects, we can question our subjects in order to understand how they conceptualize the event.

Of course, some science – and even some good science – might be conducted on scientistic assumptions. But those assumptions simply do not mark out science from non-science; some of the best science has not had this character. (I would cite both Einstein and Darwin as examples here.)[7] Moreover, valuable enquiry can be conducted from quite different assumptions. And their impact will include both the nature of one's data and one's access to that data. Social-science researchers into sport are typically interested in matters occurring contextually: in this sporting event, or that team, or training regime. So our questions are typically contextual, for persons' actions (fully conceptualised) take place contextually: that is why we recognize that exploring our sportsplayers in the laboratory, or even in training, differs from an exploration, say, in the context of competition. The questions we wish to answer arise only in *this* context, not in *that* one (where the *this*, *that* will in turn be contextually explained). This, in turn, indicates something about the nature of data here. Indeed, it follows from, and explains, our emphasis on the place of *talk*. For *talk* is the primary mode of interaction between people. But one cannot always be fully naturalistic, since the original context did not contain a researcher! So, investigating the behaviour of sportspersons should be as contextual as possible: investigating the attitudes of runners, say, might be best done while they were running. If that proved too intrusive, in a case where questioning the runners is important, familiarity with such a context – and with the researcher – can make such a post-race conversation seem less unusual. The researcher's knowledge of both the context and the subject can be crucial, for asking questions that concern such runners, recognizing the occasions when lying or evasion are most likely, and so on.

In addition, the choice of methods responds to practical possibilities as well as to the topic selected, highlighting the issues of access. To give two related examples: investigating the 'black economy' of soccer (Sugden, 2002) suggests a covert, broadly ethnographic, design. Many activities here are of dubious legality – but, acting covertly (with a knowledgeable 'gatekeeper' perhaps), subjects may talk to me. If such methods are not available to someone concerned about the governance of international soccer (Sugden and Tomlinson, 1998), one might deploy interviews, trawling archives, and perhaps hoping for some 'whistle-blowing'. These may be my most realistic strategies – the ones least likely to disturb the context being investigated, but still likely to yield answers to my precise questions. As these cases illustrate, even similar-ish topics might require (or suggest) different research designs. No one set of strategies can be urged here, beyond the case-by-case examination of the research question, in the context of methods available to address it.

Such research aims to preserve the contexts to the degree that one can, since the context informs both what action is being performed (in line with our contextualism) and what question is being asked, given our erotetic conception of research. Yet what form should preservation of context, as characterized earlier, take? Well, experimentation on human subjects in their 'natural environments' – beloved by scientism – confronts two kinds of problem (mentioned in chapter 3). It is probably impossible, because the experiment would disturb the context. Recall from chapter 3 (Harré and Secord, 1972: 44) urging that: "[t]he experimental set-up destroys the possibility of the study of the very features which are essential to social behaviour in its natural setting". But this improbability is increased because, as we have suggested, precise contexts do not recur.

Moreover, an experimental intervention into the natural environments of sport (say, into what goes on in coaching sessions) is certainly not morally acceptable, since it would disrupt those environments without there being any direction to the intervention, nor any real justification for it. If we had a well-founded thesis about the effect of a particular intervention into that coaching situation, that might justify our doing it. But the justification would reside in the change: that it would be a change 'for the better' – we could not justify making such changes simply as research. For instance, it would be crazy to change a winning coaching formula just 'to see what would happen'; or just to provide evidence for some sociological thesis. As is often said, 'if it ain't broke, don't fix it': and this applies powerfully in research situations, where our intention is first-and-foremost to understand what is going on, and only later to change it (if we then want to, and if our understanding suggests some ways of doing so).

These are reasons, then, to embrace naturalistic research designs for researching sport – to the degree that is possible. If our sportsplayers are in some 'natural habitat', such as the locker-room, they may speak as they would were the researcher absent; or, at least, approximate that situation. But the issues are typically in the presuppositions of writers, not their explicit claims.

Truth about the social world

How is the concept *truth* to be understood in this context? And how is it to be ensured (in so far as we can)? As a first shot, such truth will be contrasted with my wishing or wanting – the truth will be independent of my desire for such-and-such to be true; and, unlike 'opinion', truth will have an evidence-base. But what counts as evidence can only be explained by recognizing its connections to perceptible features of the world around us, ultimately understood through the concepts and categories of some disciplinary matrix. Then the epistemological consequences are recognized: only social truth, human truth, would be useful here, which is not the kind always assumed or invoked in sports studies research, where the spectre of scientism looms large.

So the relevant conception of truth is one which is objective, humanly speaking. Only such human-sized truths can be explanatory of social events, such as sporting ones. Of course, more extreme examples illustrate the point most clearly. Thus, we need to understand the context of the Winter Olympics, the scoring system then in place in both pairs ice-skating and ice-dance, the issues of prestige and finance that surround skating, and no doubt other things, to get a clear view of the events at the Salt Lake City Winter Games of 2002, where one judge (Marie-Reine Le Gougne) "claimed that she was 'pressured' . . . to award her best marks" for a particular pair (McFee, 2004a: 98). What exactly happened? And how might it be explained? These two related questions require taking a view, based on our understanding of the matter, granting that our understanding is partial, and so on. But, having done so, we can offer a verdict on what occurred: say, that the scores were 'unsafe' in not necessarily reflecting the 'just deserts' of this pair, from Marie-Reine's knowledgeable and experienced viewpoint. And we can explain this failure to award the appropriate score by referring to the intervention of the person or group who applied this pressure. From the purely sporting point of view (if there is such a thing), this should lead to a re-thinking of the scoring system. And so on. My point, of course, is just to illustrate that every aspect of both description and explanation is suffused with the human and the personal – any more reductive conceptualization of the events would preclude researching this topic.

Of course, such a concern with truth is not undermined if one chooses to be incredulous about metanarratives – to adapt Lyotard's account of the postmodern (Lyotard, 1984: xxiii) – since such incredulity is compatible with truths of a more local kind. Even Lyotard (or Derrida) grants that there is such-and-such money in the bank account (that is, this is true), that one should wear one's seatbelt, and so on. No amount of incredulity will undermine such "simple truths" (Luntley, 1995: 110; see McFee, 2004a: 170); and hence cannot ground denying the concept of truth (Williams, 2002: 4–5; Dummett, 2004: 101). Further, incredulity is compatible with sometimes, on some occasions, *finding* such a metanarrative: in some contexts, natural science should be treated that way.

Then, someone claiming that there is no fact of the matter, or "no fixed standard, historical or contextual, on which to base our judgements" (Sparkes, 2002: 220), is importing that (opponent's) conception of what is required. Moreover,

adopting this view of Truth (and reasoning) has the consequence that there is little reliable reasoning and less truth around, especially when we move from natural
science to the human realm. And noting that absurdity reinforces our commitment to a human-sized truth.

Thinking about truth on a human scale requires at least four recognitions:

- that in 'real life', we recognize lying, although not reliably – still, we are better
  at doing so when we know well the person to whom we are speaking, and/or
  have mastery of the topic. Since we can often detect falsehood, there is in general no need for worry on this score (as parallels with lying, and such like, make
  plain);
- that this is a human matter, a matter for deliberation, argument. That is, our
  target is not some single resolution, but the possibility of a public debate on
  the topic;
- that very often serious research issues concerning the nature of sport from a
  person-sized perspective occur where the truth is a contested matter. For
  example, what did happen at the end of the Olympic basketball final in 1972?
  The dispute turns precisely on, say, how typical was the procedure actually
  employed to permit the competition to continue – in some places that procedure was widespread: but how widespread is widespread enough? And how big
  must a bad decision be to constitute a travesty of justice? (see McFee, 2004a:
  7–8);
- that general scepticism is not an option (doubt must be motivated, in the
  context).

The first three of these reflect points recognized previously, which the remainder
of the text fills out. But the fourth – in raising the spectre of scepticism – requires
immediate elaboration. For a consequence of our contextualism is that questions
occur, and answers are true (or false), only in contexts. Scepticism here attempts
to move from either the mere possibility that we are wrong on some topic to a general, abstracted doubting of our claims, or from a specific doubt to that same kind
of abstracted doubt. Thus, someone might ask whether a respondent's claims today
can be trusted, given that she might change her mind tomorrow. Or the fact that
one respondent lies to me *might* seem to taint the comments of all other respondents with unreliability. How can I be sure? (Both are worries the scientistic will
regularly raise when *talk* provides our data.) Yet these moves are unwarranted.
That someone *might* change her mind is irrelevant if there is no reason to suppose
she will: say, no basis (for instance, in the context) for taking today to be special.
With a context for doubt in this case, we therefore have reason to put a question-
mark over that testimony – in the second example, we have reason to doubt the
truthfulness of a key respondent. But that does nothing to undermine the testimony of other respondents. To doubt them, we need reasons in their cases, not
merely in the abstract.

Further, scepticism can turn from a worry into a theory of its own: a competitor
epistemology.[8] This move should be rejected. For, in reality, doubt must always be

grounded doubt – if we have no (specific) reason to suspect testimony to be flawed in this case, we have no basis for raising the possibility. Certainly, the fact that testimony is sometimes untrustworthy is beside the point, if we have no reason to be suspicious in this case.

Does its dependence on truth make my account a "realist tale", in a sense Sparkes (2002: 41) takes from Van Maanen, which is marked by "the almost complete absence of the author from most segments of the finished text"? The problem for answering lies in determining to what one is (or is not) committing oneself. First, Sparkes regularly treats realist tales and scientific ones in a similar way, since (for him) both are ". . . author-evacuated" (Sparkes, 2002: 51). But our account of truth in this and the next three chapters, taken together, shows that such evacuation is unnecessary – and perhaps even impossible – applied to the understanding of persons *as persons*. For that understanding requires the context of moral possibility. Second, the term "tale" is potentially misleading: all our research-narratives must be truth-seeking. That means the rejection of perspectivalism of the kind that does degenerate into relativism, a kind sometimes defended by appeal to a paradigm-relative epistemology.[9] But with that conception put aside (see chapters 6 and 7), insofar as it could apply in social investigation (and with it the term "paradigm", in this context), our account of truth generates truths in respect of the precise questions asked – at least in principle.

However, a good question here is: "Who needs to be convinced?" For, clearly, one will not win a debate like this with someone committed to scientism! But if the argument were compelling, what differences would that make?

For much qualitative research, these epistemological issues may have little direct 'bite': the data are sound, although the explanation of their soundness may be flawed. If so, elaborating the epistemology may be unnecessary. In this sense, using traditional methods and following a sound primer will typically produce reliable research results. But, first, not all methods (or techniques) could be sanctioned in this way. Thus, chapter 2 exposed flaws in many appeals to triangulation, which a primer might seem to permit or endorse. More challenging methods, such as auto-ethnography (compare Collinson and Hockey, 2004), will require more sophisticated defences. So there will be profound differences in the explanation of what is done; and sometimes this will impact on what is done, in ways some of the examples throughout this text may illustrate.

What exactly is being disputed? There may seem no hope of converting those who object to ascribing truth to the human realm. But even they might yet respond to reminders about such (human) facts as the size (or otherwise) of one's bank balance – if something there is true, might there not be other human truths? And might these not include truths about sport; not least that this team beat that one last Saturday? This is, in effect, an argument-by-examples for a conception of truth different than that with which they had been working.

So what should be made of the suggestion that we should be drawing distinctions here just because we should be "reading each of 'sports science' and 'sports sociology' in its own terms"? Their terms are still directed in some way at truth and knowledge-generation. If the point of these differences were to reflect differences in aspirations, one could ask if the aspirations were appropriate.[10] But even if the differences begin as merely 'styles of writing', views follow about the nature of truth – or, at least, of the relation of truth to various ways of writing. The connections between assertion, truth-claims, and the project of research explain why truth-claims about research conclusions will typically be presented via sets of assertions (structured into arguments), or will be translatable into such sets of assertions. If you think that, say, an uninterpreted drama could be your research results . . . well, I want to demonstrate you are wrong (see chapter 7). So my view here is clearly robust in this respect.

Still, that can seem like an argument for two conceptions of truth or 'two research traditions, each with its own conception of truth'. But this is wrong. For the truth here is just truth: always contextual, occasion-sensitive and perspectival to some degree. But, given different contexts (and especially different erotetic contexts), this bears differentially on the truths discovered. So we have an explanation of why many truths in natural science are exceptionless (namely, that we specify they shall be) while others, both inside natural science and without, are not: the assumption of a finite totality of things to be considered cannot be sustained in those cases (nor put aside by *ceteris paribus* clauses). And a major class of cases where there is no such totality will be those centrally involving humans in the normal contexts of the actions to be considered: here, within sport.

A central difficulty here, then, lies in putting aside conclusively the suggestion that there is real truth and also something which passes, in common parlance, for truth (but isn't quite truth really). That can only be done by thinking long and hard both about the range of what is true (and especially what is true though not exceptionlessly: see Appendix); and contrasting that with the range of what is not definitely true, but might still be a good conjecture or bet, and so on. Further, a strong explanation of the nature of truth (such as our occasion-sensitive, contextual account of understanding: see chapter 3) will be helpful.

Would presenting these considerations get through to a colleague, so as to modify her research practice? There may be no final answer, if all we have as 'evidence' are a few cryptic comments about qualitative methodology together with her data and results. But we can say more. For example, one marker here will be what kind of evidence that researcher permits or deploys: is it human-sized (as it should be)? While there may be no arrival at unanimity, a robust concern with truth on the part of researchers seems at least defensible in these ways.

Conclusion

The concern with truth is fundamental to research as such. For the goals of constraints on research (such a reliability) are best understood as striving for truth (or knowledge). But misconceptions over the nature of truth can obscure this fact. Here, concern with the exceptionlessness (or otherwise) of truth is crucial. Thus, one upshot of this chapter is that, even if one explains one's research project in terms other than truth (say, in terms of generating insight), answerability of that insight (or whatever) to the state of the world is still required. Without that, any (claimed) insight does not really connect with whatever situation actually occurred. Hence such other terms can still be understood, roughly, in terms of truth. At the centre of both ethical and epistemological issues for qualitative research into sport is the misconception that finite totalities of events, perspectives, features, situations, and so on, are to be surveyed. Hence one could, in principle, consider them *all* – then any research failing to consider them *all* is incomplete or defective for that reason. But, in the human world, there are no such finite totalities – there is never *all* in any of these cases. So it cannot be a criticism that *all* the factors have not been addressed.

Nor should qualitative researchers in sport be surprised to find this congruence between their epistemological obligations and their ethical ones, for both might plausibly derive from their position as persons in an inter-personal endeavour. For, of course, only persons (and not, say, body parts) have ethical obligations; but, equally, only persons can re-configure a situation by reconceptualizing it. That these two discussions have not moved hand-in-hand is a problem for the development of qualitative research (in general; and therefore into sport as one such case). Thus, some qualitative research which has been epistemologically sophisticated has drawn on a conception of the ethical which is inherently scientistic; and vice versa. One part of my plea here would be to explore these various interconnections, with chapter 10 offering one beginning.

5 Scientism is a bad model for truth (and natural science)

Introduction

We have suggested that a scientism prevalent in some writings on sport, and especially on sports science, offers a misguided epistemology for research into sport. Making good that claim requires clarifying the features of (natural) science[1] on this conception; and offering a contrastive account. Here, after an initial overview, in three stages: first, the most traditional or commonsensical account of science (inductivism) is briefly presented and rejected. As well as the putting aside of some misconceptions, this also clarifies a path taken by some writers here: having rejected inductivism as an account of science, they sought something more sophisticated. Many writers, for example, Neil Spurway (2004) and Tim Noakes (2004), used ideas found in Karl Popper's writings to castigate those who, when discussing the nature of science in an uninformed way, overstated the claims of scientific enquiry. Thus, without explicitly mentioning Popper, Noakes imports Popper's ideas when he writes, that "[s]cientists failed to observe the accepted scientific process which is to attempt the falsification of accepted wisdom" (2004: 146). For this reason, the second part involves a brief comparison of Popper's views with those of our preferred theorist, Thomas Kuhn. A major difficulty with Popper's view, given our concerns, is that his requirements for social science are the same as for natural science. That seems contrary to the outcomes of our reflections on both the erotetic character of research and the impact of using persons in human situations as research subjects. Since one feature of Kuhn's position is his different treatment of social science (as compared to natural science), that is our third topic, although its account somewhat overlaps the second.

Our treatment of Kuhn clarifies his use of a key technical term, "paradigm", introduced into the context of understanding science. But Kuhn's use of this term is widely misrepresented; and some of the misrepresentations cloud discussions of the epistemology of science. These will be discussed further in chapters 6 and 7.

While our concern with science here is partly intrinsic (to aid with sports science), its larger part is still driven by the need to avoid that scientism which both offers a view of scientific knowledge and takes that view as a model for (genuine) knowledge in general.

The failings of inductivism as an account of science

The scientistic position prioritizes those investigations where, it is claimed, truth and rationality on this conception are to be found: namely, in the practice of science, with both its implicit (and sometimes explicit) appeal to neutral facts and the universality implicit in the method of controlled experiment. Scientism inflates the (real) claims of science into a procedure, the scientific method, dismissing investigations which depart from the (assumed) features of this method. And so the clearest examples here are from those who dismiss work in sport-research as not scientific. In my favourite case, many sports psychologists claim, for instance, that "[i]t is very difficult to assess the validity of Freud's ideas" (Moxon, 2000: 7)[2] because these ideas do not lend themselves to laboratory experimentation, as though this were an index of the truth-relations of such ideas. It seems just obvious to such writers that what lacks this connection to empirical confirmation has no place in the pantheon of genuine sports or exercise science. So the public face of scientism includes passages informing us, without much comment, about the nature of scientific investigation and scientific truth.

But with what conception of science, and of the scientific method, are such theorists typically working? Many are certainly advocating a kind of inductivism, as the obvious account of science. So sketching the five main components this account of science very briefly is useful. First, it imagines the scientist making observations in her laboratory on Tuesday afternoon; and observing something. That is, it begins from particular observations, treated as unproblematic. Such observation supplies a secure basis, the facts, upon which scientific knowledge can be built.

So far, the account is inherently singular, talking about her laboratory on Tuesday afternoon. The second component is a gadget to generalize these particular observations: inductive generalization, to combine our singular claims into more general ones. Thus a typical (simplified) inductive argument, noticing that all the considerable number of swans observed in a wide variety of conditions had been white, might conclude that all swans are white. Or, conducting a similar experiment in Australia, noticing that 80 per cent of the swans observed were white, conclude that therefore 80 per cent of swans were white (or there was an 80 per cent chance of the next observed swan being white). Thus inductive generalizations go beyond the data of particular observations.

In the third component, laws and theories are compiled from these generalizations. The fourth component is then another logical mechanism, a kind of 'unpacking' of what was implicit in these laws and theories (together with the initial conditions) which then permits their use in predicting and explaining (fifth component). Thus, given Newton's laws but no application yet to the simple pendulum, scientists might 'unpack' a prediction of the behaviour of such a pendulum. Such unpacking (the fourth component) is (logical) deduction.

Chalmers (1999: 54) puts these components onto a helpful diagram (Figure 5.1), showing (1) facts acquired through observation being transformed (2) by induction to give (3) laws and theories which are 'unpacked' using (4) deduction to yield (5) predictions and explanations. This, then, is a simplified account of inductivism.

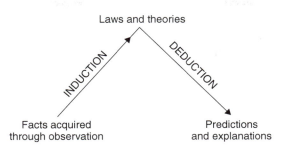

Figure 5.1 Chalmers' simplified account of inductivism

    The first three components provide our primary concerns here: the unproblematic facts provided by observation, the fact that theory arrives only with the third component (so the observations are theory-free), and the generalizing mechanism – induction. All three are contentious (as will be discussed later). But this models how science is often pictured – many scientists, whose experiments produce singular observed events, and whose work when added together permits generalizations about the behaviour of the phenomena under study. Taken together, these elements support a 'one right answer' conception of scientific truth (the facts are established simply by gawking at the phenomenon). They also provide a piecemeal view of scientists' activity, with scientific progress the culmination of many efforts; and readily lead to the 'science is value-free' picture for research ethics since, on it, facts are both simple and theory-free.

    As we will see, this view does not recognize the features of genuine science (as reflected in recent investigations of the philosophy of science). But, then, its adherents have not typically read (or understood) such philosophy of science.

    If the sports scientist (eager to prove his scientific credentials) simply adopts this conception, this tendency is exacerbated. For then modelling the notion of proof on the method of controlled experiment allows ideas not 'proven' in that sense to be dismissed as not scientific. Many defences of the scientific claims of sports science provide examples. Consider one potentially offered wholesale to beginners, an account of the nature of science (for students of sport and exercise science) such that a scientific approach "seeks to challenge existing knowledge through the collection of factual information" (Williams and James, 2001: 4). (Notice how the notion of *the factual* is not problematized here.) Further, in respect of theories, we are told that "[if] the theory does not apply to a certain situation, . . . [it] must be modified to account for that situation" (Williams and James, 2001: 4). That is, theories must operate exceptionlessly. And, we are told, "scientific theories are proposed in order to be rigorously tested" (Williams and James, 2001: 98) – note how "rigorously" slips in – while "[w]ithout an understanding of the principles of the scientific method, . . . it is difficult to consider data analysis" (Williams and James, 2001: 97).

As this case shows, my critique here concerns how the points are made (and what is insinuated) as well as the explicit claims. And, of course, the criticisms apply as well to any social-science researchers in sport research who defend this conception of scientific knowledge; and especially those regarding it as a model for knowledge.

Objections to inductivism become more accurate and more systematic when treated one at a time, beginning with criticism of inductive generalization. How is such a practice legitimated? As Chalmers (1999: 47) suggests, a *Principle of Induction* is typically appealed to: "If a large number of As have been observed under a wide variety of conditions and if all those observed As without exception possessed the property B, then all As have the property B". Here, taking "A" to be swans, and "B" the property of being white then produces the sort of argument sketched by Chalmers' *Principle of Induction*.

With Chalmers (1999), I offer two quick criticisms of this Principle. The first concerns its details: what counts as "large number", or "wide variety", in the Principle? In practice, one might appeal to, say, the smallest number of cases that would permit testing for statistical significance (to conclude that the relationship was not merely the product of chance). But inductivists cannot appeal to theory here to answer such a question (as one does in practice) because – for the inductivist – the Principle is what supports theory. So qualifications seeming sensible appear arbitrary within inductivism. The second criticism concerns the status of the Principle. Although supposed to warrant going beyond singular observational claims, the Principle clearly fails in practice (black swans lurk round the corner). Further, one must presuppose the Principle to establish it: claiming that "The Principle of Induction could be relied on in the past, so it can be relied on now" is itself an inductive argument.

Since, for these reasons, the Principle of Induction is not reliable, where does this leave the inductivist account of science? Discovering some other way of moving from the singularity of observations could preserve some answer of a broadly inductivist flavour. Undermining it fully requires not only demonstrating the flaws in its account of induction (as suggested here) but also exposing mistakes in its picture of generating facts through observation both passive and neutral. Understanding this mistake is one big reason for considering inductivism at all.

Our criticism of the inductivist picture of observation and of facts has three related components (again, following Chalmers, 1999): namely, that visual experiences are not determined by images on the retina, that observation presupposes theory, and that observation and experiment are guided by theory. Let us consider each in turn.

a *Visual experiences are not determined by images on the retina*

This entirely general thesis about observation (not about science as such) undermines the inductivist picture on which seeing is perfectly neutral. Two slogans present it neatly:

- "There's more to seeing than meets the eyeball" – two people with the same patterns of light and shade on their retinas can see different things.

This is exemplified in multiple figures from psychology (such as the *duck-rabbit* or the young woman-old woman).

- "Seeing is not just a matter of looking" – Chalmers (1999: 7–8) tells a story (from writings of Polanyi) concerning radiologists. When first one looks at X-rays, one sees only vague shapes, the radiologists' detailed comments on them seem like the widest fantasy. But, as one continues (and perhaps has features explained), one comes to see what is in the X-ray. But the changes are not in the patterns of light and shade on one's retina.

Further, all the observer has (direct) access to are his/her own experiences: that is, not to the retinal images or patterns of light and shade.

b *Observation presupposes theory* (and hence cannot neutrally ground it)

First, observation-statements are "theory-laden" (Hanson, 1958: 19). For example, in describing observations to others, we characterize them in terms of import-ing theory (for instance, talk about "oxygen" rather than "de-phlogisticated air"). In this sense, theories precede observations, contrary to the inductivist account. Second, observation-claims are as fallible as the theories they presuppose. Faced with an observation that conflicts with theory, the theory could be given up – equally, the observation could: for example, by claiming that it must be defective in some way. This regularly occurs when the science teacher, whose pupils present an experimental result different from that expected, asks, "where did you go wrong?" – their observation is not taken as refuting the established theory. Hence, observations cannot be a secure base for theory.

In these ways, then, that observation cannot be taken as *prior* to theory, as the inductivist assumed it was, counts heavily against the idea of (pre-theoretical) 'facts'.

c *Observation and experiment are guided by theory*

Three examples illustrate this point. First, the instruction "Observe, and write down your observations" is incoherent until some context for observation, or some question being addressed, is provided (Magee, 1973: 33). For what level of obser-vation is required? Do we mention every brick, or every molecule, or only "medium-sized dry goods"? There is no good answer here. (This, of course, reflects our commitment to the erotetic character of investigation.)

The second example is provided by Francis Bacon who, writing about heat, behaved as an inductivist should: he documented all the things that were hot; and his list included pepper. That, we should like to tell him, is a different kind of heat; but *theory* allows us to make the distinction. We rule out *on the basis of theory* appar-ently relevant observations; and are correct so to do. But an inductivist cannot say why.

The third case is a sad story. The Royal Society, the premier scientific society in the UK, was left – in someone's will – his life-long observations, which he hoped would provide data for scientific progress. But as these observations were not directed towards any problem (or set of them), nor guided by theory, they were use-less as observations for science. But, if inductivism were true, all observations would have exactly this character!

So observation is not the unproblematic matter our inductivists assumed. Recognizing the theory-laden character of observation in science (and the lack of effectiveness of the Principle of Induction) teaches us a lot about science: in particular, we identify ways of misunderstanding what goes on.

Once inductivism is demonstrated to present a mistaken view of science, that inductivist picture cannot be used in endorsing a conception of scientific truth or scientific method. Yet this is just what we find in the writings of some sports scientists, urging that the alternatives are "not proper or real or hard science" (McNamee *et al.*, 2007: 56). Indeed, this is how best to read consistently the claim that fundamental to scientific method is "the collection of factual information" (Williams and James, 2001: 4). Part of our target here lies in explaining and rejecting this account of the epistemology of science (and, with it, the view of scientific method it subtends). It is pernicious partly because it is assumed (or presupposed) as the account of 'the scientific method'. One must *reject* the search for the scientific method – as Kuhn does (discussed later) – rather than try to satisfy it.

Additionally (and the topic for the next chapter), rejecting inductivism cannot be a rejection of science (since it did not capture science). Yet that view of science is what postmodernist truth-deniers – in rejecting both science as such and its picture of truth – take themselves to be rejecting. In effect, they make three related mistakes.

First, they mistakenly regard inductivism as giving a correct account of the scientific method (if such a thing were possible); and then show that – on this conception – neither scientific truth nor scientific progress is possible. But, since we do not share that conception of science, we could perhaps join in these criticisms.

Second, they take rejection of inductivism to be rejection of both science and truth. But, of course, a different account of the epistemology of science would escape this criticism.

Third, they take rejection of a scientific conception of truth – which they read as roughly as implying 'one right answer' – to licence the 'no answers' or 'all arbitrary' conclusion. But this is clearly mistaken logic. That there is no single right answer is compatible with there being numerous answers, *all* acceptable (in their own context, on the appropriate occasion). So this is not a route to arbitrariness.

Where to next?

Let us return to our main thread. We have granted that erroneous views of science, or of what makes a theory or conclusion scientific, are very destructive both in the study of sport and in general. Part of the problem involves the nature of social scientific investigations of, say, sport. As I shall explain, with a better view of the scientific in place, social scientific enquiries do not (indeed, cannot) share the paradigm-relative structure sometimes assumed of them.

That said, the rest of this chapter is a brief excursus into the philosophy of science that might be deployed in the study of sport, urging the virtues of an account of the philosophy of science based on ideas from Thomas Kuhn. The argument is conducted strategically by contrasting such an account with Karl Popper's. So the chapter offers a fuller than is usual articulation of aspects of Popper's position. A related part of that argument defends briefly a distinctive epistemology for social scientific investigations; here, of sport.

Let us start, though, with natural science. Consider rehearsing four ways in which sports science, or exercise science, can and does go wrong through its deployment – or some such – of ideas from the philosophy of science. (The first three should be familiar by now.) The first is just:

By failing to deploy a philosophy of science

Of course, this is a failure just because some conception of science is always implicit (when not explicit) in claims to the scientificity of one's conclusions. So failing to deploy a philosophy of science is almost always deploying an implicit, and therefore not thought-through, philosophy of science. Certainly, it is galling (but not uncommon) to confront the sport scientist who denies any interest in the philosophy of science *and* simultaneously offers an account of science which is both fifty-years-old and refuted. (It is usually a kind of inductivism.)

The second area of mis-alignment follows from this one. In discussing the first, we recognized that some accounts of the nature of science, or of what is involved in being scientific, are obviously mistaken – and they *are*, some accounts having been conclusively refuted. Then one confuses oneself in our second way:

By deploying one of these obviously mistaken accounts

These two come together since, in practice, doing the first is almost always an implicit way of doing the second.

Scientism is the primary villain here, of course, understood as claiming that the only (or best) way to reason is embodied in the scientific method, on a certain understanding of science. Such scientism is visible in the assumption that no philosophy of science is needed to (say) investigate sport scientifically and in the assertion of obviously mistaken accounts of the nature of science. The scientistic conception lends itself naturally to an inductivist account both of the activities of scientists and of the products of theory.

As I said earlier (see chapter 1), rejecting the whole question of truth or of the scientific here (as some postmodernist theorists have done) is just a variant of this mistake, since it too imports a scientistic conception of what truth or knowledge would be like, if one could get it. To keep our list orderly, let us identify this as a third way to be mistaken:

By denying the public character (hence the truth-claims) of the scientific

This third way of going wrong is avoided by deploying Ramsey's Maxim (and is our topic in chapters 6 and 7). Here, then, I assume that we can both identify and put aside these three kinds of mistake, given our earlier arguments.

The fourth kind of mistake – to which most of the rest of the chapter is devoted

– is more subtle; and one might arrive at it through recognition of the previous three. It amounts to:

Adopting a mistaken (but not obviously mistaken) philosophy of science

Lest that formulation seem too cryptic, I will reformulate it as:

Giving too much credence to Popper

For a central thesis of this chapter is the damage one does to one's thinking by taking Karl Popper's work as an accurate account of science.[3]

So I will urge, first, that there are good reasons not to give much credence to Popper; second, that a Kuhnian view – once properly understood – is both more promising and more plausible than Popper's; and, third, that this conclusion is especially important in respect of social sciences, a fact obscured by a prevalent misreading of Kuhn. On Kuhn's view, social sciences do not function in the paradigm-relative way characteristic of natural sciences. But this is where Kuhn's jargon, and especially misguided talk of paradigms, is almost ubiquitous.

Not much of the discussion that follows draws from sport researches directly: rather, this is part of an investigation of how to (and, more especially, how not to) theorize one's study of sport.

Some Popperian failings

So, what is wrong with Popper? To decide, we first sketch his picture of science, at the centre of which is Popper's assertion that scientific claims, although not verifiable by observation and experiment, are falsifiable in these ways: as it were, that (while no amount of white swans can show us that *All swans are white*) one black swan shows us conclusively that it is *false* that *All swans are white*. For Popper, science is composed of bold conjectures, strongly falsifiable but not (yet?) falsified; and some alternatives to science (that is, some of what Popper dismisses as pseudosciences) were defective precisely in *not* being falsifiable, even in principle. Then, for Popper, science involves the making of bold conjectures, strongly falsifiable – and then strenuously attempting to falsify them – rather than on the build-up of piecemeal observations.

Suppose uninformed discussion within sports science of the nature of science has overstated the claims of scientific enquiry; further, suppose that overstating takes the form of an appeal to the scientific method (understood as piecemeal and cumulative: that is, as broadly in line with the inductivist conception discussed earlier). Confronting such an eventuality, Popper's falsificationist tendency seems to offer a useful direction. To the degree that Popper's account is insightful, such a defence of science is misguided: this theorist has not recognized the Popperian insight. In this way, deploying Popper's account seems to show that, after all, that theorist failed to understand the scientific method – contrary to his claims. The critical aspect here is surely one I would endorse.

But that way of proceeding has four related problems. First, paying attention to Popper in these ways suggests a strategy to would-be adherents of the scientific method: "align yourself with Popper, and you'll be all right". In addition to being mistaken advice, this embodies a huge danger. For instance, an Arkansas judge in 1982 dismissed the scientific credentials of 'Creation Science' on Popperian grounds. In that case, 'Creation Science' is set aside as neither falsifiable nor testable. But that makes clear exactly what then must be 'fixed'. So adherents of 'Creation Science' need only tinker with the descriptions of the methodologies on offer: once they meet Popper's test for science, their credentials need no more scrutiny. Instead, what should be urged in this case was that such views are false; that is, they have indeed been tested! Yet that move is precluded once the debate is transposed into one on the nature of science (see Laudan, 1982). (Although a very dangerous tendency, it is nothing like so dangerous applied to sport as in that case.)[4]

Second, the insight that appears to make Popper's ideas useful here is built on a mistake. The Popperian tenet is that sciences meet a demarcation-condition: they share a structure of falsifiability. But the condition here concerns all knowledge of an empirical kind, applying as much to history as to science; it is also a very weak condition indeed. Thus, it is either met by any plausible candidates to knowledge of the world around us or – if we interpret it so that it is not – it rules out as a science, say, astronomy (discussed later). So this tool is singularly unhelpful.

Of course, any theory which makes claims about how the world *is* must accommodate the possibility of the world turning out to be different. Hence, any discipline such as astrology need not be taken seriously if it claims that, however the world turns out, that was what was claimed or predicted (Chalmers, 1999: 63). So empirical knowledge must be falsifiable *in principle*. But, to recognize how weak this requirement is, suppose my theory of planetary motion includes among its predictions that such-and-such a planet should appear in so-and-so quadrant of the night sky on April Fool's Day – it is falsifiable because if the planet is not in that quadrant on that day, it would be wrong. But, since that theory is actually not wrong (let us suppose), there are never any such falsifying observations or instances. So all that is really claimed is that one can imagine a situation which, if it occurred, would mean we were wrong. This is so even though the falsifying situation never in fact arises: the theory still counts as falsifiable – still meets Popper's condition. This is not strong enough to be a demarcation-condition for science. For instance, this requirement is clearly met by, say, history. Thus, had Julius Caesar breakfasted on bacon and eggs on the day of his death, there could be evidence that he did. And hence the possibility of evidence that he did not. So any claims we make about Caesar's last breakfast are answerable to how the world was, and hence are falsifiable in principle, although (of course) not in practice. Such cases show us that Popper has not drawn a line of demarcation between science and non-science.

Here, some stronger requirement might be urged: that we need to do more than merely imagine such a falsifying instance. But what? If such an occurrence must actually be found, our astronomy too becomes unfalsifiable, because unfalsified. To cut a long story short, one either sticks with the weak idea of falsifiable in principle – but then more than just science is falsifiable; or one takes a stronger line – but then (as my example showed) astronomy, say, turns out not to be a science. And similar cases could be made for physics, chemistry or biology. So falsifiability in principle is all that could be demanded. Yet that criterion certainly admits history to the fold of the knowledge-generating.

Further, and third, although the history of science provides our test bed for accounts in the philosophy of science, Popper's ideas conflict with what happens in that history. As Chalmers (1999: 91–92) accurately puts it, Popper's position is ". . . inadequate on historical grounds", since the behaviour of real scientists does not match what it predicts as adherence to the scientific method. For Popper, a scientist faced with a falsifying instance should say, "Damn, I was mistaken all along", and try out another conjecture. But real scientists do not typically behave as Popper predicts: thus Clerk Maxwell recognized in his first paper that his account of electro-magnetic radiation has a consequence which conflicts with everyday experience (see Gamow, 1962: 112–14). Instead of providing a falsifying instance to Clerk Maxwell's theories, it was simply treated as an anomaly, to be addressed at a later date.

Moreover, for Popper, no claims in science are ever really true – as Popper (1985: 126) puts it: "As always, science is conjecture". Such conjectures are all 'hanging around' waiting to be falsified. Or, of theories, "they are merely *approximations* to what seems to be true: *they are not true*" (Popper, 1985: 120; emphasis original). This is the case even before we have specific tests or reasons for hesitancy.

As Chalmers (1999: 79) notes, others have been keen to 'correct' Popper on this point. But (mostly) Popper's own view is clear: "We are not interested in establishing scientific theories as secure, or certain, or probable. Conscious of our fallibility we are interested only in criticizing them and testing them, in the hope of finding out where we are mistaken" (Popper, 1963/1999: 310). So those not refuted remain 'on the books' as conjectures: it does not help to speak of "corroborations by severe tests" (Popper 1963/1999: 298), unless a positive logic of such corroborations would differ from confirmation, verification or probabilification. Of course, Popper sometimes seems to think that this alone offers a kind of confirmation. But, consistent with his own principles, he should not do so (discussed later).

Fourth, a consequence of treating the objections to practices in sports science *this* way is that the upshot of Kuhn's insight (discussed later) will be ignored. Yet Kuhn's work not only offers usable insights into natural science (or so I urge), it also highlights a key difference between natural and social sciences – one social scientists of sport have neglected at their peril. For they too have struggled to deal with critiques they might see as Popperian.

At the centre of all this discussion are two contrasts. The first is between natural and social science. For Popper, this is not really a contrast – both are at par, since both must meet the demarcation-condition for sciences. The second contrast is between theories that are true and those that are false (with the proviso that we may now take for true a theory later events lead us to revise). Again, for Popper, this contrast makes no sense, since (for him) truth in science is in principle unobtainable. I shall urge, with Kuhn, that natural and social science should be treated differently; and that, for both, our enquiries are aimed at truth. Further, having completed some investigation, and arrived at a conclusion (when we can), that conclusion should be regarded as true unless there is some reason (now) not to do so – that means that no weight need be given to the mere possibility of later refutation, if we have no specific reason for raising that possibility (discussed later). These Kuhnian insights (once granted) have a capacity to reshape the task for discussions of the epistemology of social science, by permitting the truth of our claims, but with the truth-bearing (or truth-generating) structures differing between the natural and social sciences. And that will be especially important if some theorists have made their peace with Popper, thinking they have an explanation of the scientific character of social thinking: they too must think again.

But why should anyone not agree with this view from the start? One explanation is that Kuhn was seen as, at least, a fellow-traveller of the kinds of relativism, and truth-denial, associated with postmodernist writing. For example, Chalmers (1999: 124–29) expressly contrasts Kuhnian views with objectivity and with realism; Sokal and Bricmont (1998: 67–73) treat Kuhn in the same breath as these post-whatever writers. Further, ideas from Kuhn have been offered in justification of, say, the claim that everything, including the physical world, is a social construct[5] – understood as a thesis to limit the claims to truth of the natural sciences. And philosophers who write against the pretensions of scientism in sports studies would want (rightly) to reject such relativism. So Kuhn's work might seem to offer too many 'hostages to fortune' to relativism, or postmodernism, or some such. In that sense, Kuhn is a victim of his own success: his work is taken up by those who wanted to oppose positivism, but who see no way to do so within a truth-regarding framework.

In such a climate, the quasi-scientism of Popper might be preferable to various postmodernist excesses. Luckily, that choice is not forced on us – or so I shall urge.

Kuhn's view of science

As I have said, Kuhn rightly takes social sciences to differ fundamentally from natural sciences; or, in his jargon, social sciences lack the paradigm-relative structure characteristic of the natural sciences. To elaborate that thought, a brief summary of Kuhn's position is needed. Put in an over-simplified way (as Kuhn recognized), that position takes mature natural science to proceed in two distinguishable phases. For the first, which Kuhn calls *normal science*, the activities of scientists are centrally a kind of unpacking of past insights. Thus, having already thought of forces in terms of masses undergoing accelerations, we ask how to make that out, say, in respect of the simple pendulum, and so on (Kuhn, 1970: 188; Kuhn, 2000: 169). In this sense, work in normal science is "firmly based upon one or more scientific achievements, achievements that some particular scientific community acknowledges for a time as supplying the foundation for its future practice" (Kuhn, 1970: 10). Such work then builds directly on the past achievements of that branch of science; in particular, on the theories taken for granted by it, and the view it adopts both of the constituents of the world and of their inter-connections. So that the practitioner of normal science "... has ... assimilated a time-tested and group-licenced way of seeing" (Kuhn, 1970: 189). Fundamental here is that this is a 'way of seeing' – contrasting, say, those who see oxygen being combined with other substances in combustion with those who 'see' phlogiston being given off (Kuhn, 1970: 53ff.). Here Kuhn introduces another (semi-)technical term: in normal science, there is one *paradigm* in place. Hence a paradigm is a time-tested and group-licenced way of seeing.

The normal science phase for any science is contrasted, for Kuhn, with a period of crisis and subsequent revolution. Just as the period of normal science is characterized by the presence of a single paradigm, the period of crisis or of revolution in science is characterized by the absence of a single paradigm. But the historical process in science means that periods of revolution lead to the establishment of a new normal science, which is then taught to succeeding generations as the obvious way for a scientist to see (his/her bit of) the world.

Now it is highly unlikely, on this view, that either sports science or exercise science will ever be in the revolutionary phase in its own right, because both sports science and exercise science involve unpacking – in this set of contexts – insights derived from the parent discipline of (say) physiology. So, in turn, they borrow concepts then 'validated' in the parent discipline of (in this case) physiology.[6]

Of course, Kuhn recognizes that this picture over-simplifies in many ways. First, we should consider, not "science" *tout court*, but this bit of science (so, not just *physics*, but some part of physics). Second, determining the exact history of any revolution is only achievable with the hindsight required for history. Indeed, as Kuhn (1987) recognizes in his most worked-through but least-read case, scientists whose work does initiate revolutions may not themselves see the work that way, at that time – most are aiming at reformation, not schism! Third, the anomalies thrown up by adherence to a paradigm are not themselves causes of a subsequent revolution, even if they are the occasion for it – anomalies can always be lived with. Thus, a consequence of James Clerk Maxwell's account of electro-magnetic radiation was that, every time one opens the oven, one should get a lethal dose of radiation. This clearly did not happen. But physicists, confident of the general usefulness of the theory, simply added an *ad hoc* modification at this point (the so-called "Maxwell's demon": Gamow, 1962: 112–14): they neither rejected the theory nor looked towards a change of paradigm – although it was the introduction of an Einsteinian paradigm here that finally made this *ad hoc* addition unnecessary! Fourth, the mere possibility of later 'correction' (via new theory) cannot introduce scepticism: we have reason to doubt our contemporary claims to scientific knowledge only if we presently have specific grounds for doubt.

Now our first key point, turning on Kuhn scholarship, is that normal science (central to Kuhn's account of science) makes no sense outside natural science – contrary both to what many commentators write, and to the widespread use of the term "paradigm" in social scientific contexts. As Kuhn (1970: viii) explains it: "the practice of astronomy, physics, chemistry or biology normally fails to evoke the controversies over fundamentals that today often seem endemic among, say, psychologists or sociologists". For that lack of controversy depends on the place of normal science. But Kuhn rightly recognizes such controversies as endemic for social science. Then the absence of a normal-science phase there explains why the theoretical claims of, say, one sociologist are always contested and disputed within the profession – Kuhn tells us to expect this; and this is what we find.[7] Hence Kuhn rightly takes social sciences to lack the paradigm-relative structure characteristic of the natural sciences, and therefore to differ fundamentally from natural sciences.[8]

What to make of Kuhn's view?

Anyone who takes Kuhn seriously enough to cite him (and his use of the term "paradigm")[9] – as, say, when Lew Hardy *et al.* (1996: 257) state that Kuhn "*defined* a scientific paradigm as a school of thought relative to the nature of knowledge and how one goes about studying the world" (emphasis mine) – should both seek to understand him, and also take seriously his own limitations of those ideas. As we have seen, doing so treats psychology and sociology differently from natural sciences. Further, taking Kuhn seriously in this way explains what we in fact find when looking at sociology or psychology: namely, a number of competing or contesting "ways of seeing" the social world – since their history never contains normal science-type phases, they employ no paradigms. Nor do we expect them to.

Suppose, then, we contrast the theoretical principles of science (such as Newton's principle of Universal Gravitation, Mendel's genetic Principle of Segregation) with its disciplinary principles (for example, that all physiological functions are to be explained in chemical terms) – it is the disciplinary ones which 'define' "the basic intellectual goals of a science, and give it a recognizable unity and continuity" (Toulmin, 1972: 124). They can also provide methodological unity. On this account, training in the social sciences requires only learning the disciplinary principles, as there are not (in the way there are for natural sciences during a period of normal science) theoretical principles accepted by all. Of course, in natural science both theoretical and disciplinary principles will be part of the paradigm, during the normal science phase. But it is this absence of a shared content (of theoretical principles) across the discipline that tells against the application of this picture to, say, sociology.

Granting Kuhn's picture requires us to act differently in prosecuting social scientific enquiries. Were Kuhn's account correct, we should have to consider how (if at all) these competing or contested "ways of seeing" the social world could be unified or accommodated – which would not make sense as a task were we convinced that talk of "competing paradigms" adequately characterized their inter-relations.

So Kuhn's view would be important *if right* – but is he right? Again Kuhn's own reasoning seems to me compelling; for the social world, we should expect a kind of perspective–dependence which follows from our seeing ourselves as agents, with concerns, reasons and interests, as well as recognizing the agency of others. For doing so is granting to others a 'take' on the world both potentially valuable (because truth-generating) and differing from one's own. First, we see events from our own perspective, both literally and metaphorically: "The view each of us has of the events through which we have lived is inevitably *incomplete* . . ." (Toulmin, 2001: 7; emphasis original). We only know some things, although we grant that others, if known, would be relevant. So we cannot take our perspective as the only one worth having. That will be especially true once other disciplines (or sub-disciplines) have different concerns from those of our sub-discipline.

Second, such perspectivalism, an inevitable consequence of our human limitations in space and time, cannot amount to a methodological flaw – as Toulmin (2001: 7) puts it, it is not "slanted". In particular, this perspectival emphasis does not produce bias: for bias is (necessarily) remediable, in principle (as when the essay-marking of the biased marker is contrasted with that of his unbiased colleague). However, this feature does show one way our 'take' on events is partial (you may stress events of which I am unaware); and hence some sense in which my account is incomplete.

Still, third, such incompleteness is typically not remediable by adding other perspectives, because there is no reason to think either that the perspectives are mutually consistent (and so on) or that there is some finite totality of such perspectives . . . if only it could be reached. Yet only then would one have *all* the perspectives on the events: only then would the idea of drawing up *all* the perspectives make sense.[10] That, in turn, is required for a single or unique theorization of those events. But we have recognized both why this is unlikely and why it should not be expected.

Moreover, the requirement for researching persons means that a participatory research style will often be the appropriate one in social science. And it will come as no surprise to find it regularly ignored, with scientism the order of the day. The method of controlled experiment, for example, seems especially inappropriate for dealing with human events in their contexts. For we can interact with human subjects in ways impossible for one's interaction with the subjects of physics or chemistry – or even biology. Persons often have aims, intentions, concerns and the like which, given the right opportunity, they can describe. Even when researchers cannot elaborate these concerns, they may glean them. Thus one can ask one's subjects. Hence the slogan that, for research purposes, human beings be treated as though they were persons: that is, as agents operating in contexts. Then experimentation on human subjects in their natural environments is probably impossible, both because the experiment would disturb the context, and because precise contexts do not recur. Further, it is certainly not morally acceptable, since it would disrupt those environments.

Of course, such a recognition brings its own problems. For how exactly should one's research subjects be addressed? Clearly, finding the appropriate attitude here may be crucial in constructing a research design both epistemologically rigorous and ethically sound. For instance, Alan Tomlinson (1997), discussing his own research towards the oral history of a sport, has characterized a process common to much covert research as involving first flattery and then betrayal. As Tomlinson (1997: 245) acknowledges, for some social research ". . . securing access is itself an entry into a relationship". That is the flattery part: subjects may only co-operate if they come to think of the researcher in a positive way – to that degree, regard him/her as a kind of friend. As Tomlinson (1997: 260) continues, the data thus generated were: "products of a social relationship that has been established by the researcher, and that relationship involves researcher knowledge which . . . I chose to reveal". That is (or, anyway, can be) the betrayal part: the decision as to what conclusions should be drawn from the research rests with the researcher. He/she cannot give it up without abrogating a responsibility implicit in one's commitment to "the very task of interpretation" (Tomlinson, 1997: 262). Indeed, this responsibility is what makes the relationship with subjects an *ethical* one: one where unethical behaviour is therefore (sadly) possible. Further, the betrayal aspect here is really an outcome of the researcher's role – of his/her task in making sense of the data. That is not something of which subjects could (nor should) have been informed, even if the researcher knew it prior to the research commencing. So, at least, it is not betrayal in respect of one's role as a research subject, even if one ends up feeling betrayed by the researcher's 'reading' of the data. But, of course, one cannot enter into this kind of debate until one recognizes it as a problem: that in turn requires giving serious consideration of research designs of this sort, rather than simply dismissing them (say, as not scientific).

The overall point, then, is that social science should be expected to exhibit exactly the perspectivalism it *does* exhibit: there are lots of ways in which our doings could (and should) be made sense of. Any of them may have strong adherents, with (some) good reasons. So there are various competing descriptions of what is (or might be) going on, with no guarantee that they can be integrated: there is no one set of concerns, no one way to draw up relevance. We see this in, say, the conflicting claims made for various ways to ground the study of sport – for instance, those Bill Morgan discusses eloquently in *Leftist Theories of Sport* (Morgan, 1994). Since the methods deployed and the concerns pursued are linked, any of these perspectives might be better served by this set of research methods rather than that set. We are not explaining this diversity if we talk of "competing paradigms": this simply tells us that there is a problem. So, Kuhn shows us that a different spin on 'perspectivalism' is needed. In this way, then, Kuhn's view here appears at least arguable.

Some critiques: Kuhn and others

Others might oppose this view by raising criticisms of Kuhn's picture of science. Consider two such revealing criticisms.[11] The first concerns Kuhn's appropriation of the term "paradigm": as Margaret Masterman (1972; see also McNamee, 2004: 12) noted, Kuhn used the term in a large number of ways. But is this really the criticism that it is sometimes supposed to be? Kuhn's own responses here are illuminating: he had not seen "paradigm" as a technical term when he used it so freely. As he confirms (2000: 298), he had taken it to mean a kind of extra special exemplar – what he saw as its central meaning prior to his use. But, faced with this criticism (which he welcomed: 2000: 300), Kuhn (1970: 182–87) highlighted two central ways in which he used the term: as disciplinary matrix and as shared example, with the second "thus a subset of the first" (1977: 294). And, as I have stressed earlier "[a] paradigm is what members of a scientific community, and they alone, share. Conversely, it is their possession of a common paradigm that constitutes a scientific community of a group of otherwise disparate men" (Kuhn, 1977: 294).

Further, Kuhn (2000: 34–35; also 1977: 319) moved on: he did not take the term "paradigm" to be doing the kind of work others – including followers – ascribed to it. Hence, more recently, his points have typically been made without this technical language. Once the central role of normal science for Kuhn's account is recognized, we also see that it is in that place that the idea of a paradigm functions more crucially. But then we also have a pretty clear sense for that term.

Second, Kuhn's work has been dismissed as "mob psychology" (1977: 321) rather than philosophy. This remark fails to notice that Kuhn is here commenting on a special kind of concept (also called "institutional concepts"),[12] not on all. And the appropriate use of such institutional concepts is regulated by a kind of "authoritative body" (Baker and Hacker 1984: 272–73). In that sense, it is (rightly) scientists – not everyone – who decide what is and what is not science; and also what is or is not good science. That is possible, of course, just because (by definition) these scientists share ". . . a time-tested and group-licenced way of see-ing" (Kuhn, 1970: 189 quoted earlier). Moreover, giving this role to normal sci-ence is not giving it to this or that particular scientist. For instance, Kuhn (1977: 321–25) urges that considerations for rational theory-choice in science[13] cannot involve just an appeal to the decisions of such-and-such a scientist, nor to any spe-cific group of them. Certainly, there is no counting of heads on Kuhn's account. So Kuhn's view recognizes a normative control on the sayings and doings of actual sci-entists – its regulation is genuine, even if within the paradigm.[14]

Equally, natural scientists sharing a paradigm do not (necessarily) agree across the board: there is still room for disagreement amongst them within the paradigm. They can prosecute that disagreement just because they share a *framework* for debate. Of course, since they are *within* 'normal science', they will not dispute the framework provided by the paradigm: that is, provided by the group-licenced and time-tested way of seeing into which their scientific education led them. But such a framework is not forever beyond dispute. Rather, engaging in that dispute is mov-ing outside of normal science. And, to repeat, these are considerations for natural sciences, such as physics or chemistry.

Earlier I suggested, with Kuhn, that we should expect to treat natural and social science differently; but that, for both, we should regard the conclusions reached as true unless we had some reason (now) not to do so. Of course (to repeat from chapter 3), this is an idealization, deploying the principle of total evidence: "in the application of inductive logic to a given knowledge situation, the total evi-dence available must be taken as the basis for determining degrees of confirmation (Carnap, 1950: 211). This principle operates theoretically to identify the "ideal-ization" (shared with qualitative research) that one has all the relevant evidence (Carnap, 1950: 208). But, practically, it also grounds a defeasible working practice:

that the evidence before us is all that is relevant, unless there is a specific reason to think otherwise. So the mere possibility of lacking some relevant information cannot introduce scepticism. That means that we need give no weight to the mere possibility of later refutation, unless we have specific reason now for raising that possibility, where reflecting on history does not count.

With this proviso, then, our account permits the *truth* of our claims: that is one departure from Popperianism. On our account, truth-bearing (or truth-generating) structures will be different in the natural and social sciences. Further, recognizing that the social sciences differ in these ways from natural sciences will preclude using one as a gold standard for truth in the other. If this is so, it revises radically the epistemology of the sciences of sport, in contrast to that a Popperian would endorse.

The question of postmodernism

Of course, one can deny the scientism of much writing on natural science without rejecting its commitments to the possibility of truth. Here, as in (chapter 1), I draw on Ramsey's Maxim, that ". . . wherever there is a violent and persistent philosophical dispute there is likely to be a false assumption shared by both parties" (Bambrough 1969: 10). This strategy, therefore, undermines *both* of a pair of standard oppositions by rejecting an assumption both share. For both scientistic and postmodern accounts of scientific 'knowledge' assume a view of Truth (with a capital "T"), and a corresponding view of reasoning or rationality, that treats truth as universal and trans-historical, and reasoning as the application of exceptionless general principles. Then what is true will be so exceptionlessly and trans-historically: and what is *not* will not be Truth. Of course, each version responds differently to these assumed views. As two sides of the same coin, these positions share a set of misconceptions. So the outcome of rejecting the misconceptions will not be simply a 'middle way'. Instead, a view of a *principled search for truth* need not commit itself to either of the two mistaken conceptions.

Moreover, granting that most claims (especially in social science) are essentially contested, with no 'one right answer', is not necessarily accepting that there is no truth even about the social. For we recognize the different contexts provided by, say, different concerns (McFee, 2004a: 175–76): that my doctor asking if I can play football on Saturday is looking at different factors – and hence likely to get a different answer – than the friend who voices a question in the same words. The doctor's concern may be with my recovery from knee surgery, the friend's about whether I can afford the new kit. And another friend might be worried that I have a prior obligation. These are different issues. So we cannot expect just *one* answer. But, in its place, each answer is right (and complete). Hence my position (and Kuhn's) does not offer comfort to those who deny a place or role for truth, although granting a certain incredulity towards metanarratives.

As an appropriate example: it was reported to me that, at one of its meetings, the British Sociological Association agreed that Norbert Elias's concept of the *civilizing process* was a metanarrative, where that seemed to mean a *correct* metanarrative. This (apocryphal?) example brings out three points. First, one might doubt that there was such agreement in the sociological community. (After all, I know a few Professors of Sociology!) But, second, even supposing this happened, what would be its force? Certainly, it would not function as, say, a comparable gathering of physicists aiming to resolve some nomenclature in string theory. For this imagined agreement would place the idea of a civilizing process as an over-arching theoretical structure in all cases: that it applied in all cases of social explanation, while other explanations (say, in terms of structure/functions, or of gender) only had a place when helpful. But neither of these claims seems true. Surely there will continue to be sociologists grounding their work in other metanarratives (Marxists, or post-colonial theorists, say), and theorists whose pluralism suggests looking to what theoretical structure is most felicitous, faced with the issue at hand. That is just to grant that there is no single shared background in sociology of the kind shared in physics during a phase of normal science; which, in turn, is a way of saying that there can be no normal science – and hence no paradigms – in sociology. And these points are urged earlier.

Then, third, the very features of human life (and social scientific enquiry) that speak against its having normal science phases also speak against the assumption of a general, over-arching theory of the kind suggested by the term "metanarrative". Here we must go carefully. That we are incredulous about metanarratives does not mean we will never find one. It only means that we should not begin by assuming there will be one, in any field of enquiry. Moreover, having failed to find the background conditions for such a metanarrative in a particular domain, despite a rigorous investigation, we can justify criticizing putative metanarratives: "Yes, such-and-such is certainly a metanarrative, but that is just what is wrong with it!" To repeat a point made earlier, it is precisely the *lack* of a paradigm-relative structure for the social sciences that makes this a plausible starting point. Then this is one (desirable) flexibility produced, as a by-product, from accepting Kuhn's account of science.

A last look at Popper?

My treatment of Popper might seem unjust: certainly, considerations of brevity have left it fairly cursory here. It may help those engaged with the philosophy of science to clarify, without greatly expanding, five points of my criticism.

First, on the place of *falsifiability*: for Popper, science is marked out by its use of falsifiability – in effect, this uses a four-fold classification:

i   the unfalsifiable (because true by definition) which make no claim about the world;
ii the falsifiable in principle, but falsified;
iii the falsifiable in principle, but [as yet] unfalsified;
iv the unfalsifiable which [appear to] make claims about the world.

Popper urges that only kind (iii) has any place in current science: in particular, (iv) is the error to be avoided. Now, we can agree that only (iii) is informative; and that kind (iv) is problematic. But, on my view, falsifiability (in principle) is a criterion with respect to all claims of empirical knowledge and that follows from the need for, say, history to 'confront the world' as much as physics (where both might be contrasted with, say, astrology: see Chalmers, 1999: 63–65). For historical or sociological truths, as much as scientific ones, need just this 'confrontation with the world'.

Second, what is the status of observations (say) that, for Popper, make up falsifying instances? Popper's view assumes that falsifying instances are themselves clear: but, in science, observations are always theory-laden, and can therefore be rejected if the embedded theory is rejected. Suppose I investigate the strange ability of bats to fly in a dark cave without bashing into the walls. Someone tells me that it has nothing to do with the hearing of the bats, but I find a falsifying instance of this claim. Such an instance must be correct – which means that, in asserting it, I will be asserting what is true. Do I know these things? Do I know that, say, bats fitted with ear-baffles, flying in the dark, bump into the walls of the cave? And, of course, my claim to know this may not survive the theoretical change in how the concepts are deployed (given that my observations are theory-laden, and that the theory in question – with which the observations are 'laden' – is theory in science). As Chalmers (1999: 87) notes, "[t]he falsificationists themselves insist that the observation statements that constitute the basis of science are theory-dependent and fallible". So no observation can be *simply* falsifying, even in Popper's own terms. But now the structure Popper offered for science is much less clear.

Third, for Popper, all experiments become crucial experiments, which determine the life or death of the theory in question. For instance, perhaps "[t]he findings of Michelson and Morley gave a verdict of death to the theory of the ether" (Zukav, 1979: 152). Yet, for the falsificationist, all experiments function in this way[15] – the experiments either falsify the theory at issue or they do not. But this is not how, as a matter of fact, scientists always respond to experiments seeming to contradict their theories: sometimes the right response is to recognize the distinctive character of this experiment or this situation, while this should not be dismissed as giving-in to the *ad hoc*. Popper wrote:

> I can therefore gladly admit that falsificationists like myself much prefer an attempt to solve an interesting problem with a bold conjecture, *even (and especially) if it soon turns out to be false*, to any recital of a sequence of irrelevant truisms. We prefer this because we believe that this is the way in which we can learn from our mistakes; and that in finding that our conjecture was false we shall have learned much about the truth, and shall have got nearer to the truth.
>
> (1963/1999: 313; emphasis original)

But the contrast between taking falsification seriously and reciting irrelevant truisms does not exhaust the alternatives. So a less dogmatic view should be taken of the scientists' activities.

Fourth, Popper is sometimes clear that his theory precludes the possibility of scientific truth. Since science is composed of bold, unfalsified conjectures, we cannot know the truth of any of them: indeed, it makes no sense to speak of coming to know them. For Popper introduces the idea of falsifiability as an alternative to putting weight on verification, since (for him) no claim can be conclusively verified. But then appealing to truths here, or to what we know, would just reinstate verification. Also, the idea of scientific 'truths' not available to us in principle make no sense of science as an enquiry. Then, Popper makes clear that science is simply a 'structure', with no further claims to truth:

> The empirical basis of objective science has thus nothing 'absolute' about it. Science does not rest upon solid bedrock. The bold structure of its theories rise, as it were, above a swamp. It is like a building erected on piles. The piles are driven down from above into the swamp, but not down to any natural or 'given' base; and if we stop driving the piles deeper, it is not because we have reached firm ground. We simply stop when we are satisfied that the piles are firm enough to carry the structure, at least for the time being.
>
> (1968: 111)

At other times, though, Popper (1963/1999: 313) writes as though (on his view) science can get "nearer to the truth": yet how, by his own lights, can we get nearer to something not possible? So (for Popper) there can be no scientific truths, both because science is composed of unfalsifed conjectures rather than claims known to be true and because one cannot approach what is in principle unavailable.[16] (To see this point, notice that probability only makes sense in a world where – in principle – it could be maximal: that is, a world with certainty. In a similar way, the thought of moving towards something builds in the possibility in principle of arrival.)

Fifth, whatever is said about scientific truths, there can clearly be truths at the human level: truths about how much money (or how big an overdraft) is in my bank account. Those truths are surely investigable; and of the character needed to sort out truths about sporting activities. If Popper's view cannot accommodate the rational, truth-generating study of such matters (whether we call the study "scientific" or not), it must fail as an account of the nature of human understanding.

My treatment of Popper still remains perfunctory: my main aim was to speak for Kuhn, and to elaborate his conception of science; and, in particular, the impact of his account on the social-scientific study of (say) sport. But doing so requires some consideration of alternatives. The remarks on Popper highlight some of these.[17]

Thoughts for sport

These points about the philosophy of science should be clear enough, despite the brevity the treatment. But why should any of that matter for the study of sport? It would be sufficient here to offer a warning in a hypothetical mode: if anyone attempts to point our colleagues in sports science away from positivism by suggesting Popper, he/she will be the subject of these considerations. And Spurway (2004: 34–35) is one clear example here.[18] But that topic could seem to acquire a greater urgency when Jim Parry (2004: 27) writes that, faced with falsificationism: "[w]e should learn from this, says Popper, that what we call knowledge is necessarily provisional". Of course, Parry does not say that Popper is right. But if his target is those who read other texts carelessly, he must suspect that his claim too will be misread or misunderstood – say, quoted without the "says Popper", as the right way to consider knowledge. Or when Mike McNamee (2004: 17) writes of a tendency ". . . to celebrate the moves that were made by Popper in destabilizing logical positivism. . . .". This could sound like a blanket endorsement of Popper; it is not. But to find McNamee's warning against "lionizing" Popper, we must read on. But many may not read on that far (that is, to the end of the sentence!).

As these last quotations make plain, these writers are not in fact advocating Popperian ideas in ways I regard as dangerous. Both are making some positive comments, while using Popper's thought negatively, against the scientism of others. But such guarded comments are not the usual fare here. Nor are all writers as careful as these two. If these two were typical, perhaps I need not have worried so much.

As far as discussion of sport goes, should one introduce Popper at all? Those who most need the 'destabilization of logical positivism' may take too much from Popper; they might even take from him the thought that there is no (genuine) knowledge in this area – knowledge claims should be regarded as provisional. Further, Popper stresses a continuity between natural and social science at precisely the point where (for Kuhn and me at least) it is most promising to draw a contrast.

Of course, it might seem to some that scientistic conceptions of the project of sport science and exercise science were dead-and-gone; and even the strategic deployment of Popper is on the wane. So am I seeking to initiate a debate that has already taken place? First, that is not my experience of the scientific study of sport and exercise (as I have encountered it around the world). And, second, the explanation may reside in the relative youth of sports science as a discipline: they are still looking for validation! So, even if a parallel to the argument of this chapter would be unnecessary in mainstream sociology or politics, that does nothing to undermine its importance in this field.

Ideas from the philosophy of science as such are not here contested, despite the reservations voiced about Popper. For a more subtle account of Popper might be forthcoming within the philosophy of science. Rather our concern is with the application of such ideas. So, for instance, my advocacy of Kuhn does more than import, into the philosophy of sport (and especially of sports science), ideas taken-for-granted from philosophy of science. This procedure is itself problematic (compare McFee, 2004b). But that is not my criticism here. Rather, my fear is that Popper's philosophy of science may come to seem obvious to some writers on sport research (and especially sports-science research), so that they think (again) that there is nothing left to discuss about the nature of scientific truth, scientific knowledge, or the scientific method. I assume that – on the basis of the argument here – we are opposed to such an outcome.

Conclusion

In conclusion, and to connect this discussion clearly to the next, let us review again what (for me) we have learned from a Kuhnian account of science. Here, three features make it a revealing account of science in this context:

1   its rejection of a 'linear development' conception of scientific progress – we do not need to see a single pattern of *improvement* in the history of science (once we are looking at it with the detachment of philosophy). Hence, we do not need to assume a single 'right answer', which science either has or towards which it is aiming;

2   its clarifying the relation of natural science to social science. There is a fundamental difference between social and natural science; and it reflects how they depend on their pasts. In particular, social science should not assume the possibility of a "normal science" phase: if we wanted to explain that fact, we could point to the implausibility of a finite totality of conditions to be considered;

3   its introducing the term "paradigm" into this discourse, as a means to achieve the previous two points. For the paradigm is what is shared by practitioners in a normal-science phase. And the contrast to linear development (from the philosophers' perspective, if not from the practitioners) is the radical change from one normal science phase to another that accompanies a paradigm shift. Equally, social sciences differ from natural sciences in lacking this paradigm-relative structure and so lacking the normal science phase. But, as we will see, that has proved problematic when it has been misunderstood (see chapter 6).

We have already noted that one dimension of our strategy against postmodernism deploys Ramsey's Maxim; another will recognize the (typical) scholarly failings when it comes to the notion of a paradigm.

6   Postmodernism and truth-denial as a kind of scientism

Introduction

We have seen that much sports science implicitly endorses scientism – exemplified by adherence to a commonsense view, inductivism, as a model for scientific knowledge or the scientific method. Such a scientistic conception does no justice to the reality of natural-scientific knowledge. But we appealed to Ramsey's Maxim because those postmodernists who reject both science (on this conception) and the account of truth it deploys (or, at least, implies) also take this picture of scientific knowledge as definitive of the epistemology of natural science. Against such a position, in chapter 5, we highlighted three misconceptions (here repeated): First, the truth-deniers mistakenly regard inductivism as giving a correct account of *the scientific method* (were such a thing possible); and then show that, on this conception, neither scientific truth nor scientific 'progress' is possible. Second, they take rejection of inductivism to be rejection of both science and truth. But a different account of the epistemology of science, such as that from Kuhn sketched in chapter 5, would escape this criticism. Third, they take rejection of a scientific conception of truth – which they read as roughly as implying 'one right answer' – to licence the 'no answers' or 'all arbitrary' conclusion. But that conclusion cannot follow from granting the previous claims. Instead, there being no *single* right answer is compatible with there being numerous answers all acceptable, in their own contexts on an appropriate occasion. So this is not a route to arbitrariness.

Thus, viewed simply as a discussion of pictures of research that are truth-denying, this chapter would be redundant: we have already concluded, in chapter 4, that genuine research must aim at truth. And we have used Ramsey's Maxim, in chapter 5, to identify a misplaced assumption about the nature of truth here, one which generates scientism. Truth was not the universal and transhistorical notion that scientistic thinkers assumed (not Truth with a capital "t"). Rejecting that conception of truth permits us to acknowledge one insight from scientism – that truth is a goal of research – while rejecting the thought that doing so commits us to there always being 'one right answer'.

So this chapter is the counterpart of the previous one. It moves us forward in three ways. First, it allows us to identify the insight from truth-denial: namely, that there is the possibility of diversity here. In this way, it permits us to say more about how truth should be conceptualized: or, as I shall say, about our perspectivalism. Doing so distinguishes it from the relativism of the truth-deniers. Second, it clarifies one reason offered in defence of truth-denial: namely, a picture on which stresses the place of competing paradigms. For a clear account of Kuhn's idea of normal science, discussed in chapter 5, shows us why social sciences lack a paradigm-relative structure. This sets up a fuller discussion of truth-denial in sport, in chapter 7.

As this chapter shows, the insight behind such truth-denial (the insight of perspectivalism) can be productively incorporated into an account of truth which, having learned from natural science, recognizes the distinctiveness of the social world. A broadly Kuhnian account of natural science (and hence, of truth in natural science) was offered. Therefore this chapter first highlights the flaws in a relativist position, before dismissing a use of Kuhn's account of paradigms to ground such relativism. This allows us to show more clearly the contours of the epistemological stance this text develops.

Truth-denial, science, and relativism

Surely science is among the most problematic of concepts for truth-deniers: what will they say? A typical postmodern discussion of scientific truth urges that, if truth and rationality require this universality and neutrality, then – finding little of either about – the search for truth or for reason can be dismissed as unrealistic, as (say) a commitment to what Lyotard (1984: xxiii) calls metanarratives. Instead, we should recognize a 'postmodern condition' reflected in the absence of such metanarratives.

Theses such as Lyotard's appear to commit postmodernists to an attack on the concept of truth. With no metanarratives, no overarching explanatory frameworks, the model of knowledge based on the (supposed) qualities of scientific knowledge is undermined if science is just one narrative among many, with no further claim to authority.

The argument, for the Lyotardian, begins from a general (and agreed) characteristic of science: the inherently changeable nature of the truths of science, in a world where theories can change. Once we reject the assumptions behind some scientific theory, we are one step from disputing the theory itself. If successful, this argument only shows the limitations of scientific knowledge as our model. But this argument might seem to show more: namely, that science offers just one way of describing, explaining, or (more generally) talking about the world. A typical version[1] here urges that "[o]nly descriptions of the world can be true or false" (Rorty, 1989: 5). Then science is just one such description, among many. So "... it is difficult to think of the world as deciding between ..." (Rorty, 1989: 5) alternative descriptions of events. Instead, we must recognize "... that there is nothing 'beneath' socialization or prior to history" (Rorty, 1989: xiii). Hence "[t]ruth cannot be out there ... because sentences cannot so exist, or be out there" (Rorty, 1989: 5). That is tantamount to claiming that there is no truth. For suppose that, in this way, language is all we can get – yet, as Quine (1986: 10) notes, "... truth should hinge on reality, not language: sentences are language". This might seem to speak against the application of the idea of truth here, in just the ways Rorty implies.[2] And this conception has been applied to the study of sport (for example, by Terry Roberts, 1998: see especially p. 248).

Yet the resultant, relativist view has self-refuting consequences. For when our relativist urges that all truth is relative to, say, time or place or culture (and hence that two persons in genuine disagreement might both be right), is his comment true or not? If it is true, but only relativistically, perhaps it does not apply in this context, or to the sporting claim we are considering. Certainly, I have little reason to take it seriously. But if he claims his relativist thesis is true in some more universal way, then he is not (after all) a full-blooded relativist. Hence either relativism is false (since at least the truth of relativism is not relativistic) or we have no reason to believe relativism applies to us. Neither is an attractive proposition (see McFee, 1992a: 301–9; McFee, 2004a:167–71). And we risk falling into ". . . the trap of concluding that all rational argument is mere rationalization and then proceeding to *argue rationally* for this position" (Putnam, 1981: 161; emphasis original).

Even the first element of this 'trap' is problematic: suppose I claim to attend philosophy conferences to disseminate my wisdom (such as it is), but this is a rationalization – I really come to conferences hoping to meet attractive women. While my rationalization does not give the real reason for my behaviour, there *is* a real reason.

But, as Putnam identifies, one cannot justify rationally one's accusation that *all* rational argument is mere rationalization: for, by its own lights, any putative justification should be dismissed as mere rationalization. That the position is so easily put aside must make its attractions (if any) doubtful. As Putnam urges, one should tell such relativists, "Well, relativism is not true-for-me" (see McFee, 1992a: 303–4). The relativist who remains unconcerned has, in effect, just begged the question against his opponent.

A more realistic reading of the objection here argues, not that there is no rational argument (which, as we saw, precludes one saying why), but that rational argument is different than is sometimes supposed. But now the protagonist's position depends on accurately capturing how I regard logical or rational argument: if he or she is wrong about this, the objection by-passes my position. Thus, one cannot actually hold (or accept) a relativist position: like round squares, genuinely relativist positions lack internal consistency.

Yet the limitation of this point to genuine relativists is often missed. For example, the scientistic perspective takes anyone who disputes the scientistic conception of truth to really be rejecting truth as such: for example, Kuhn is regularly dismissed as a relativist (compare Chalmers, 1999: 129; 193) despite his contrary protestations that his theory does not prioritize "mob psychology" (Kuhn, 1977: 321). Similarly, having granted Kuhn's concerns with the conceptual, we cannot readily dismiss him as a sociologist of knowledge (since the issues he addresses cannot now be empirical), as some theorists of 'the social character of knowledge' have sought to do.

Paradigms again

In chapter 5, a Kuhnian perspectivalism about social science stressed that our doings might be made sense of in lots of ways. Any of them may find strong adherents, with (some) good reasons. So various competing descriptions of what is (or might be) going on offers no guarantee of their being integrated: there is no *one* set of concerns, no one way to draw up relevance. Since the methods deployed and the concerns pursued are linked, any of these perspectives might be better served by *this* set of research methods rather than *that* set. Then, given our contextualism, quite often one set of perspectives and methods will be preferred in a context or on an occasion. When this occurs, the results derived can be true. So our perspectivalism is not truth-denying. Moreover, such perspectivalism offered the beginning of an account of human truth, suggesting its central place in social scientific thinking, to be elaborated later.

Still, this perspectivalism might seem to readily collapse into a self-refuting relativism (discussed earlier), on which no view can be dismissed as false,[3] a tendency sometimes supported by appeal to truth or knowledge as paradigm-relative. Then, with each view supposedly relying on the framework provided by a paradigm, views dependent on two different paradigms can 'pass one another by'.

Then, Kuhn is right to take social sciences as differing fundamentally from natural sciences; or, in his jargon, as lacking the paradigm-relative structure characteristic of the natural sciences. As we saw Kuhn explain it, the idea of normal science (central to Kuhn's account) makes no sense outside natural science.[4] This is contrary to what many commentators write, and contrary to the widespread use of the term "paradigm" in social scientific contexts. Thus even Harré and Secord (1976: 19) describe their attempt to clarify the epistemology of social research they endorse by claiming they ". . . are trying to bring a paradigm shift into focus", explicitly citing Kuhn.

Of course, the notion of a *paradigm* is even deployed by the scientistic end of sports psychology. Thus, Hardy *et al.* (1996: 257) state that "Kuhn (1962) *defined* a scientific paradigm as a school of thought relative to the nature of knowledge and how one goes about studying the world" (emphasis mine). But this obscures the fact that, for Kuhn, there is typically only one paradigm in place in (an area of) science – that being a prerequisite for normal science!

The situation is not much improved elsewhere. Thus, in a crucial text, Sparkes (1992: 12) claims that "[a]t a most fundamental level different paradigms provide particular sets of lenses for seeing the world and making sense of it in different ways". But, if true, this cannot be Kuhn's sense of the term "paradigm", since for him paradigm-conflict always resolves with the formation of a new normal science. Thus, for Kuhn, one or other of these "lenses" would ultimately be rejected; and not just by its practitioners. Instead, one of these lenses might, in favoured circumstances, form the basis for a new normal science. Hence the 'lens' metaphor seems an unhelpful one, since one can deploy a number of lenses, perhaps for different purposes. Yet what does the term "paradigm" mean, if not what Kuhn means by it?

At the least, we are owed an account making plain why we should accept some of the claims here. On the Kuhnian picture, the diversity Sparkes mentions only makes sense during the moment of revolutionary science – which is always a temporary moment. But, rather than offer the necessary elaboration of the term "paradigm", the discussion continues as though we all understood what a paradigm (in this sense) was.[5]

Then, later, we are told "that all researchers make assumptions of some kind or other in relation to issues of ontology, epistemology, human nature, and methodology" (Sparkes, 1992: 14). That seems satisfactory as far as it goes (although I would be more guarded about that "all", since sometimes researchers' assumptions are nothing like as clear as this). Then we are told "that these assumptions tend to cluster within the framework of particular paradigms" (Sparkes, 1992: 14). Similarly, in Sparkes' introduction to the volume, there is reference to ". . . the research emanating from any given paradigm" (Sparkes, 1992: 2), as though it is a kind of ground for such blooming. If the point of such claims is just that "assumptions" about methodology (the sort that are implicit in one's methodological decisions and practices) reflect "assumptions" about epistemology – such as those implicit in one's methodological practices – that will be a truism for any researcher who is consistent. But it certainly puts the *demand* for such consistency very obliquely.

Moreover, as Sparkes (1989: 139) rightly notes: ". . . calls for methodological pluralism, in which methods can be mixed and matched irrespective of paradigmatic stance, become highly questionable since this implies that theoretical perspectives can also be integrated". This issue for pluralism arises just as predicted. The erotetic character of research explains what exactly is problematic here – ensuring convergence onto a single question or topic requires matching presuppositions or assumptions (as highlighted in the discussion of mixing methods, in chapter 2). For methods cannot be separated from their background assumptions. But we mislead ourselves if reference to (Kuhnian) paradigms[6] (or "paradigmatic stance") is then used to characterize either that process of assumption-dependence or the difficulties it generates for combining social-scientific research methods.

Sparkes doubtless feels that the issue is not, after all, a scholarly one (at least from his perspective): instead, it should have some substantial 'bite'. Well, consider the claim that ". . . the uniqueness of a paradigm comes in the particular perspectives of those who use the techniques [of data-gathering]" (Sparkes, 1992: 16). This seems to support only a relativistic reading:[7] that paradigms are unique, depending on a distinctive perspective of the researcher. Contrast this with the idea, implicit here, that a perspective is something we can (and typically will) share – so nothing *unique* there. Or that the point of deploying techniques of data-gathering is precisely that these techniques are shared, reflecting a research community. Then the reason for suspicion of the paradigms-talk becomes clear. Cut loose from Kuhn's use of the term, it can be offered in a scientistic context or a relativist one. And can seem to support either.

Certainly, the central thought here follows contours similar to the postmodernist discussion of scientific truth: that your discussion of football hooliganism (say) is not a competitor to mine, especially if our research designs are radically different ("representing different paradigms"); they can happily co-exist. Indeed, they should do so, since there can be no tribunal of appeal to select one or prefer one. But is there no limit to such harmoniousness?

Here, truth-deniers might stress that (say) research in sports physiology and in sports sociology offers different pictures of the world, which cannot (typically) be combined. Of course, that is often correct. But from this it does not follow that they pursue different kinds of truth (see chapter 4), nor that they have really given up searching for truths – although adopting the scientistic view of truth might suggest either of these. And, if no sport-based examples have been provided, there is reference to key theorists here; and the errors are typically in the assumptions, not the detail, of the research.

Rejecting scientistic thinking seems to amount both to the rejection of truth and to the adoption of some relativistic alternative – no doubt under the banner of postmodernism – with reference to *incommensurable paradigms* as one explanation. But neither of these inferences is inevitable. Instead, rejecting scientism is rejecting only its conception of truth, not truth as such; similarly, accepting a perspectival account in one version, as here, does not lead one to relativism. Both the scientistic endorsement of this conception of truth and reasoning and its postmodern rejection assume the correctness of that very conception: for both, this is what Truth requires. This, then, Ramsey's Maxim enjoins us to dispute.

Perspectivalism without paradigms

So we need an alternative conceptualization to the scientistic one sketched earlier of what it is for some (research) claim to be true. For that scientistic conception imagines that truth-claims are always independent of researchers, but this cannot be correct, if weight must be given to how the event should be conceptualized. Here, it is crucial, first, that we see events from our own perspective, both literally and metaphorically. For we only know some things – although we grant that others, if known, would be relevant. Second, such perspectivalism is an inevitable consequence of our human limitations in space and time: again (from chapter 5), "[t]he view each of us has of the events through which we have lived is inevitably *incomplete* . . ." (Toulmin, 2001: 7). Our 'take' on events is partial: you may stress events of which I was unaware. But these facts, had I known them, might have altered my judgement. So my account is incomplete. Then, third, sometimes these facts could be pointed out to me. Thus approaching the truth might seem to require adding your perspective to mine, and so on, thereby removing this 'incompleteness'. But this is a mistaken understanding of the nature of the incompleteness. It is typically not remediable by the addition of other perspectives, because we have no reason to think either that the perspectives are mutually consistent (and so on) or that there is some finite totality of such perspectives, if only it could be reached. Yet only then would one have a complete account by having *all* the perspectives on the events, another misplaced commitment to a finite totality. Since this is impossible, it is not really incompleteness at all. As such, it cannot amount to a methodological flaw: as Toulmin (2001: 7) puts it, research is not "... *slanted*".

We saw in chapter 4 that the relevant conception of truth is one which is objective, humanly speaking. Only such human-sized truths can be explanatory of social events, such as sporting ones. Such truth will be contrasted with my wishing or wanting – the truth will be independent of my desire for such-and-such to be true; and, unlike opinion, truth will have an evidence-base. So we have recognized the epistemological consequences: only social truth, human truth, would be useful here.

But what are the other characteristics of this conception of truth in social matters? Well, truth is reliable – not self-indulgent in ways rejected earlier. Further, whether or not some claim here is true, as opposed to false, will be arguable – using respectable methods, and such like. That is one reason why, when investigating sport (as when pursuing other truths in the social realm), we draw on the concepts and techniques of academic disciplines. For they represent standard ways to understand both what questions to ask, and what methods to use to resolve (or answer) those questions. As Tomlinson (1997: 262) grants, "[i]n the messy world of social science research at least, the integrity of the project should be at the forefront of the researcher's consideration". Of course, that traditional conception of questions or answers may still be rejected, replacing them with others. For truth here is erotetic – it involves finding the appropriate question and its corresponding answer.

For that reason, however, we cannot reasonably expect such an account to be articulated simply: say, as truth is correspondence to reality – which is not so much false as unhelpful. As we have seen and as for example Steven Ward (1997: 773) correctly identifies, in postmodernism there is a rejection of "... the notion that scientific truth can ever transcend the local semantic processes ...". This Ward (1997: 774; see also chapter 3) characterizes as "standpoint epistemology", on which "... all knowledge is localised perspective and all interpretations are mediated by and can be reduced to the linguistic or social characteristics of the groups which produce them". But Ward would align the views developed here with those he criticizes. Such a case "... is both overstated and oversimplified" (Sugden, 2004: 205), since Ward (1997: 781) characterizes it as "... war between the realists and the relativists". But there is not one single "war" here: our perspectivalism is not what Ward castigates.

Nor does Ward's rejection of relativism collapse our case into his. For there are constraints here, even if they are neither abstract nor exceptionless. As Sugden and Tomlinson (2002: 17) recognize, "... if local voices are to make a contribution to this shared understanding, ... such perspectives must themselves be re-evaluated through the metalanguage of social science". As Sugden and Tomlinson (2002: 16) paraphrase Marx, "... people make history, but how they make history is to some extent determined by what tools and raw materials they can get access to and the range of imagined possibilities that existing economic, political and cultural circumstances suggest". This draws explicitly the connections to the disciplines. For they imply guidelines for our dealing with the concepts of truth and rationality. But those dealings will be occasion-specific, taking place in particular contexts. So the contextual nature of truth-claims (McFee, 2004a: 47–52) must be re-affirmed. As Austin (1970: 130) notes: "[t]he statements fit the facts always more or less loosely, in different ways on different occasions for different intents and purposes". As we saw, there is only a definite result as to truth when the circumstances of the describing somehow make one standard or another the right one for the purpose in hand: so truth essentially depends on the context in this way. For instance, in some scenarios a hovercraft with oil-drums lashed to the deck counts as a tanker in the harbour (Travis, 2008: 235–36: see chapter 1). This was not true in other scenarios: "That's no oil tanker!" Again, there are problematic or disputable cases: this hovercraft is a welcome sight, but is it truly a tanker? At a particular moment, in which of these three worlds do we find ourselves? Once we know in which of the worlds we are, the truth (or otherwise) of the claim about the tanker is perfectly determinate.[8] So contextualism cannot undermine truth. But where does it leave us?

First, we retain our commitment to simple truths: that is, ". . . to the idea that things go on independently of our thinking of them" (Luntley, 1995: 107) – say, to the colour of post boxes and cars, as well as the reality of pain, depression and love. Postmodernists in fact accept such truths, at least through their actions. For why else ". . . do they wear seat-belts in their cars, go to the dentist when they have a toothache, or go to the bank manager for a loan" (Luntley, 1995: 107)? Recognizing in this way the social character of these facts puts more soberly some attractions of postmodernism, while retaining the notion of truth.

Second, due weight is given to reasoning that stresses the appeal to concrete cases rather than to abstract principles. For example, plotting an Olympic tradition involves a narrative which *defines* our thinking as appropriate by linking it to concrete events in Olympic history, concrete instances. Thus, "Olympism" is understood only by reference to what has happened previously as Olympism – although some such reference (as with revolutionaries) proceeds through denial. Indeed, fundamental here is the idea that searching for truth is the search for a *narrative*, where that is contrasted with merely the stories others might tell, since our narrative is constrained in the ways we have been describing. In line with the points mentioned earlier, we might stress again the importance of a ". . . narrative with a personal perspective" (Toulmin, 2001: 7).

But does this idea of a *narrative* here not resemble the tales and stories we put aside in chapter 4? As we said, true stories[9] are what is wanted. Yet, once turning to specific methods, the criterion for truth here reflects our erotetic conception of research. Thus, suppose we have settled on an auto-ethnographic research design. Since ethnographic researchers aim to ". . . directly capture the lived experience of those they are researching" (Collinson and Hockey, 2004: 191), the data of auto-ethnography here consists fundamentally of a self-directed narrative by the author. But what is its interest? Centrally, the focus within sport research will be on ". . . feeling as an embodied form of consciousness" (Collinson and Hockey, 2004: 190); and my narrative, once reflected upon, will offer those events in that social context which are (literally) memorable for me, presented in those evocative terms. For this kind of focus was selected in selecting auto-ethnography as one's investigative method, whether as distance runner or Olympic rower (compare Collinson and Hockey, 2004: 188). Then the aim is to be true to my feelings, reactions, or memories. So I must be satisfied with the narrative, once written-through reflectively – and where we can report my dissatisfaction with how a certain point is expressed. For our topic here is *my* responses, or someone else's; and my remembering it strongly[10] after the fact indicates that this captures "[s]port's ability to invoke powerful emotions in people" (Carter, 2008: 15).

An investigation of "... baseball as it is experienced in Cuba" (Carter, 2008: viii) might also be called a narrative or, better, many – to include, for instance, "... how Cubans create or engage in specific narrative practices found within baseball" (Carter, 2008: xiii). In ways strongly similar to the auto-ethnography case, the truth-conditions for such narratives cannot be detached from the perspective of the participants for "[b]aseball embodies Cuban's notions of themselves" (Carter, 2008: 3) – an account which misses this would be false, and one that captures it, to whatever degree, is true to that degree.

A third point concerning truth recognizes that our judgments are located historically. So what counts as possible *now* (and hence as true or false) depends in part on the concepts available *now*. Persons from an earlier time could not deny some assertion since, to them, the assertion would make no sense. Consider two cases here:

(i) "In such-and-such a house is presently being born the greatest physicist of the twentieth century."

Suppose both that I am pointing to Einstein's birth-place, at his birth-time, and that Einstein is the greatest physicist of the twentieth century; this judgment requires hindsight, because only the passage of time proves it true (or false).

(ii) "The creator of the theory of relativity is presently being born in the house."

This makes no sense: the expression "theory of relativity" requires later conceptual events even to be meaningful. More than mere hindsight is required to assert it. In this second case, then, assertions and denials at different times can be incommensurable in the strict sense of being unable to be put into one-to-one correspondence.[11]

Fourth, the sceptical 'threat' to scientific knowledge is treated historically. Of course later science may take for granted what is presently denied. For some cases, I presently have reason for hesitancy about particular scientific claims: these are doubtful by today's science. Other cases attempt to produce scepticism about present science from the mere possibility of a (future) change of view, which treats truth (and science) ahistorically, contrary to our current picture. Instead, there is no basis for unjustified (or unmotivated) doubt.

So, nothing I have said is an attack on science, for at least three related reasons:

- I recognize the genuine insights of science;
- denying scientism is not rejecting science; and
- scientific claims necessarily involve theoretical conceptions from their very

beginning. That is, the theory-laden character of science is granted – for example, in observation.

Three main related points defend this conclusion here: first, the general connection of observation to theory (Hanson, 1958: 19; 54–58; Chalmers, 1999: 5–9); second, concerning the need for concrete cases drawn from real science: thus, how does this reflect (say) the dispute between Lavoisier and Priestley (Kuhn, 1970: 53–57; 79–80)?; and third, the sense in which 'narratives' of science (say, the history of twentieth-century physics) are best written with hindsight (Kuhn, 1987: 349–70).

Finally, the suggested contextualizing and concretizing of truth takes the contexts for investigation of people as human contexts. Giving weight to human concepts involves discovering and exploring them in appropriate ways.[12] Then some place must be given to asking people, and discussing with them (although without granting that they are always right): the agent's view of a particular action is stressed, relating that behaviour more specifically to aspects of the context of (social) action. Thus, a referee or umpire might ask: "Is he in control of the ball?" (McFee, 2004a: 103), reflecting a key kind of question in a sport-related case. For, in order that it be a "fair catch" in American football, the receiving player must not only land with his feet in bounds, but must also be in control of the ball. This question will be answered in its context. There is no specific grip on the ball, nor degree of pressure, that will decide the matter uncontentiously. So no abstract answer can be given for all cases.

The aspirations of qualitative research fit well such a contextual or perspectival account of truth. For example, an ethnographic investigation will draw on the questions or issues as they arise in *this* context: what is going on *here*? Since the *here* of this research will typically be different from the *here* of other investigations (and since the questions that drive each will also be contextual) it makes no sense to expect just one answer. For different answers, or questions answered by different methods, will typically require different answers (as we have seen). And any answer to a question indexicalised to that location or that debate (to here and now, say) may have no purchase in another location or another debate.

Confidence in our 'answers'?

How much confidence can we have in the 'answers' put forward? First, the contrast with quantitative research[13] does not provide a sound conception of dependable research – and especially not one illuminating the questions with which one was originally concerned (given the erotetic nature of research). So how do we get that confidence in qualitative research? We do this indirectly, from reliable methods, and from theory – and this is equally true of other methods.

Then Sparkes' "holy trinity" (see chapter 4) is in no better hands when applied to, say, quantitative methods. There too we deal mostly with incompleteness. Even laboratory work only achieves the illusion of a 'controlled' situation through *ceteris paribus* clauses: we do not so much ensure that 'other things are equal' as assert that they are equal and then proceed 'as if' they were. For natural science, this amounts, roughly, to *defining* these "other things" as equal, via our *ceteris paribus* clause. Yet, as we acknowledged in chapter 3, here there is no complete list, no finite totality, of these "other things" to keep equal even in our controlled experiment. Thus a classic double-blind design matches control group and subject group – but for what features? Here we can replicate those questions. Hence, is gender important? (Usually, yes.) Is age important? (Usually, yes.) But what is not important? Since each member of our experimental group differs in some respects from every member of the control group, for which features should we control? Our conclusion is that such issues cannot be resolved in a theory-neutral way. Yet this is a quite general requirement for knowledge-claims, not a place where research on persons is second-best.

Moreover, this is often not the situation in which we find ourselves: the methods deployed may be new or unformed, the theory may be emergent. And that may seem more likely when we turn to new sets of questions. So we cannot simply depend on past successes to provide this confidence; and especially when, as qualitative researchers, we begin by rejecting (as misconceived) a well-established research tradition.

Since truth here is perspectival, a big issue will be: Does the researcher's perspective colour the data generated? The worry here is not *bias* as such, because bias is *essentially* remediable – as when the essay-marking of the biased marker is contrasted with that of his *unbiased* colleague. So a biased judgement is always one which does not award 'one's just deserts' – which implies that there *are* such 'just deserts' in this case. Instead, the worry is that the researcher's perspective, his/her conceptualization of the field of enquiry or of the methods appropriate to it, imports a misconception which precludes a clear view of the desired topic – as an initial commitment to the phlogiston theory guarantees that one can never recognize oxygen, or an initial racism militates against a clear view of colonialism.

In fact, there can be no guarantee here: one's perspective could turn out to be destructive in just this way. At best, one can strive to make that unlikely. Then ways to avoid one's perspective playing a role include:

(a) attention to the methods and/or the procedures of the relevant academic discipline: these typically provide a detachment from one's own preoccupations with the topic;

(b) recognizing the flexibility of methods applied in a different context then selecting the appropriate methods for the context is recognizing the ("objective") features of the situation;

(c) allowing a reasonable time span for research – this will typically mean a longer time span than was first thought (especially in ethnography: the importance of ". . . getting to know you");

(d) considering the quality of data (say, as revealing, rather than just true/false) and also the quality of the commentary and/or discussion surrounding it; the quality of the argument will not depend on the researcher's place within it.

Further, our debates regularly concern what questions must be asked. For, while research cannot be value-free, researchers should avoid simply importing without thought any values or concerns (and especially their own). Hence they should ". . . exhibit *reflexivity* about the part played by such factors" (Bryman, 2001: 23; emphasis original).[14] Thus a *reflexivity* about theoretical and conceptual assumptions guards against that "technical rationality" (Schön, 1983: 165) on which the ends (or issues) are all decided, and debate is only about means of achieving them.

So our research must be about persons (in contrast to the reduction to parts or features of persons); it must give weight to persons' knowledge or understanding, without being swamped by it (compare the practice of checking back with respondents – as researcher, one listens to what they say, but ultimately makes one's own decision as to how the data they provide should be analyzed); since qualitative research is essentially erotetic, it must draw the connection between issue identified and method selected to address it (finding the same words is not enough); it must draw on the academic discipline (for detachment, theory, argument).

The epistemology of qualitative research into sport should be viewed as erotetic: that is, as involving conceptions of knowledge appropriate to the questions being asked or the issues being raised. A primary constraint here is the need for attention to context; and hence for the behaviours (better, the actions)[15] for study being located in their natural context, to the degree that this is possible. This may seem to preclude any preference for one research design over another. In the abstract, it does. But, in any context, there will typically be more we can say. Hence, although one cannot have favoured styles of research-method (one must always choose those appropriate to the question asked), embedded ethnography or participant observation (say) will typically meet the naturalistic constraint better than, for instance, a semi-structured interview. And the freedom to intervene in a naturalistic way (given by ethnography) makes it a more powerful tool, where it is appropriate. Thus, the erotetic approach does allow us to compare research methods, but only in context; and only when both methods meet the constraints of the methodology in this context (not the usual case).

Conclusion

The domination of much research into sport by scientistic conceptions of the nature of research applies to those places where a direct appeal is made to scientificity – say, in sports science – but also to those rejecting such a direct appeal. As we saw, one scientistic tradition sees truth (often with a capital "T") as universal and transhistorical (a conception rejected here). But postmodernist opponents of such 'scientistic' thinking share this view of Truth (and reasoning): truth is again treated as universal and transhistorical, and reasoning as the application of exceptionless general principles. Then what is true will be so exceptionlessly and transhistorically: and what is not will not be Truth. Our example, from chapter 1, was the claim by Krüger (2004) that, because the final result of Leni Riefenstahl's *Olympia* was a selection, none of it could possibly be *true*, since any claim to truth could be contested using material not selected. Thus, many of those who do not see themselves as 'looking across' at the epistemology of natural science – that is, many "feminist poststructuralists, phenomenologists, various kinds of ethnographers, autoethnographers" (to use a list from the publisher's referee) – still explain their own epistemological stance in explicit contrast to that in natural science. So many who claim to reject this scientistic conception either fail to do so or (in casting their epistemology as a rejection of truth) implicitly endorse a scientistic view of truth. And that is 'looking across': one's own conception is cast as "not this".

What follows from the "not this" rejection of that view of truth? It may seem a rejection of the place of truth in research. Thus, when encouraged to look for ". . . *alternative* and legitimate ways for qualitative researchers to represent their findings" (Sparkes, 2002: 3; emphasis mine), we should begin by asking, "Alternative to what?" If the *contrast* were with a knowledge-generating intention, or with aiming at truth, that would not be a suitable direction for someone wanting to conduct research (in our sense).

Gestures in the direction of truth-denial are suggested precisely because truth-telling can seem a limited goal when the model for truth-telling comes from truth in natural science, on one view. At the most extreme, it might be claimed that: "[p]ostmodernism suspects all truth claims as masking and serving particular interests in local, cultural and political struggles " (Richardson, 2000: 928).

This may just be endorsing Lyotard's "incredulity about metanarratives" (Lyotard, 1984: xxiii): that is, not just assuming there will be a single, over-arching explanation – and perhaps not expecting one. But if, with Sparkes (2002: 23), this positions attempts ". . . to dismantle distinctions between fact and fiction", it attacks the applicability of the concept *truth* in this context. For, as we have seen, "truth" accompanies "fact": hence researching any topic must retain a distinction between what is true ("facts of the matter") and what is invented. Conceptually, two features here must be recognized for research. First, it requires getting right these ". . . distinctions between fact and fiction", such that what passes for truth is indeed true, in context. For then, if successful, one's research arrives at such truth. Second, it requires recognizing the scope of what can be true. In particular, all claims involving the human world should not be dismissed as *possibly* true: no doubt my having an overdraft requires the human construction of the banking system; no doubt it deploys concepts (centrally, "overdraft") that make no sense outside of human activities and decisions. There would not be any overdrafts if there were no people! But that does not make these notions fictional. Nor does it allow the question of whether I have an overdraft to depend simply on what people say. For what those people say can, in context, be *true*.

In failing to acknowledge these features, many who see themselves as having moved on from a scientistic epistemological stance have not really done so. (This fact is less often noted; and still less taken to heart.) Hence these issues can persist even when aiming (and claiming) to challenge the prevalent scientism.

Here discussion of Krüger's claims about the 1936 Olympic Games might reappear. For, recall (from chapter 1), Krüger (2004: 35) urged that the question ". . . were there any original Games?" required a "no" answer because there could never be a single account of those Games which was *the truth*, but only competing accounts with no tribunal to arbitrate between them. But, first, this worry might be practical, not conceptual: if our evidence is ". . . only those official pictures from inside the arenas that the Nazis want us to have" (Krüger, 2004: 35), we may not be able to arrive at the truth. But that does not mean there is *no* truth. Second, we accept that different people might have different concerns about that Games, and hence different perspectives on them. Exploiting our *erotetic* conception of knowledge, we can grant the truth of each as an answer to its question, without requiring a single, unified account. Third, despite his explicit commitment to the perspective of "the postmodernist", Krüger's aspirations are in the direction suggested in this text: he comments that ". . . we still have a hard time distinguishing between fact and fiction" (Krüger, 2004: 35) – but that implies that we might so distinguish. That in turn implies just the contrast between fact and fiction which seemed to be denied. In this respect, Krüger (2004) behaves exactly as predicted before: his situation illustrates that trying to be a consistent relativist is indeed self-contradictory.

So we have seen both how postmodernist accounts might fail to allow such comparison as this, and how such a failure flows from a kind of implicit scientism – like their scientist opponents, postmodernist theorists of sport share a misguided view of what truth would be like. This is what is put aside by Ramsey's Maxim.

7 Truth-denial is not just a style of writing

Introduction

In this chapter, we identify and reject some claims in favour of truth-denial offered by some of its most ardent advocates in the field of sport research, by focusing on an extreme example. Since these truth-deniers regularly align themselves with postmodernism, that will be one preferred description of their position. At its heart, though, their claim is that the truth-directed claims I endorse are simply one way, among many, of presenting one's research. So there are reasons for a perspectivalist to prefer this position. Then we consider such a position in perhaps its most extreme form, as the claim that one can both conduct and present one's research through a dramatic medium: this is, as ethnodrama.

Faced with postmodernist truth-deniers, we should again point out that they do not (at least typically) deny truths throughout their lives: they too have bank balances, and such like. In part, we have already presented that argument as expressing a dissatisfaction (which we share) with truth on a scientistic account. Of course, when postmodernists claim that their plan just involves locating more revealing ways to present research-findings, we can recognize that doing so often still permits (eventually) the 'translation' of those findings into assertions. But that will not satisfy those wanting more, as Richardson (later) seems to.

Where does the contextual, particularist and perspectival character of truth urged throughout this text leave those who are about to plan, prepare and execute research projects into aspects of sport? Since many of the situations of interest in researching sport are only manifest in actions performed (and made sense of) in precise contexts, how does one explore such situations?

The limits of research?

To pose this question sharply, in the context of postmodernist research strategies, with their attendant rejections of truth, consider perhaps the most extreme version here. It treats as unjustified the kinds of truth-telling to which, of its nature, presentation in prose seems to commit us. Instead, that is just one mode of presentation among others. Thus the author's mouthpiece, Professor Z, claims: "Prose . . . is not the only way to represent sociological understanding. Another possible way is through poetic presentation. Poetry touches us where we live, in our bodies, and invites us to experience reflexivity and the transformational process of self-creation" (Richardson, 1996: 8). Anyone taking seriously this injunction will surely count as a truth-denier, since he/she will not be presenting the audience with claims designed for truth-assessment.

What forms might such a presentation take? Well, one concern will be to make vivid the social world – here of sport. And, to repeat, many of the situations of interest in researching sport are only manifest in actions performed (and made sense of) in precise contexts. So how does one explore such situations?

At this point, an extreme version might dispute the connection to 'facts of the matter' of such presentations. After all, need the cases they capture be real situations? Or can they be hypothetical, or something similar? And here the research potential of, for instance, role-playing is granted. But then one's answers are not, or need not be, *true*. Stressing the fictional character of (say) one's data is one implicit way to truth-denial, although without mentioning it directly: one's research presentation lacks that crucial connection to knowledge-generation, and to truth. So, in addition to their intrinsic interest, questions about the place of the fictional in research also interrogate the precise role of truth in the research process, thereby casting an indirect light on our perspectival account of social truth.

The obvious starting place, then, is a research-use of role-play, but also attempts to go beyond it. In effect, there are two related topics here, pulling in opposite directions. One concerns the deployment of fiction as such. But can such investigations (still) generate knowledge if they deploy fiction? Here the question does not, of course, concern the use of covert research methods but when, say, we recognize the novels of Jane Austen as *fictions* – the characters and situations are 'made up' – but still regard them as *true*. And hence might see the learning of such truths as a process akin to research.

The other direction for deploying the fictional urges, with Laurel Richardson (2000: 993), that "[p]oetry is . . . a practical and powerful method for analyzing social worlds". So this stresses both analytical and presentational dimensions of the research. Hence some 'investigations' seem to endorse fictional methods, and even truth-irrelevant methods, of deploying and presenting research into social situations. For example, Richardson writes as though poetry were a suitable way to present her research findings: that it is an alternative to prose.

But we cannot begin from the thought that "[p]rose . . . is *simply* a literary technique, a convention, and not the sole legitimate carrier of knowledge" (Richardson, 2001: 877; emphasis mine). In particular, the "simply" gives entirely the wrong impression, since the assertions of prose have a direct connection to the presupposition of truth-speaking (given that we must mean what we say).[1] Hence what identifies continuous text as prose is precisely what ensures that prose has an unchallengeable legitimacy here – whatever may also be achieved through drama, poetry, and such like. That we can lie merely reflects this fact. And this is also the reason that *fictions* should not be dismissed as *lies*.

Indeed, Richardson's own claims specifically suggest presentation of her results through an expressive literary form, poetry. That the findings can be reflected by poetry must reflect something of their epistemological status. For her, "poetic representation is a viable method for seeing beyond social scientific conventions and discursive practices, and therefore should be of interest to those concerned with epistemological issues and challenges" (Richardson, 2001: 877). So this plea is for the force of poetry as insight-generating here. It seems to refer to a kind of writing best suited to presenting data, broached later. Moreover, this direction for sport research seems explicitly endorsed for research into sport and exercise when one is "committed to recognizing and fostering the growing use in sport and exercise sciences of alternative forms of representation, such as autoethnography, ethnodrama and ethnographically creative non-fiction . . . (Smith and Gilbourne, 2009: 1).

However, researchers might then ". . . turn their ethnographic field notes into performances" (Sparkes, 2002: 127), such that ethnographic drama (or ethnodrama) is "a way of shaping an experience without losing the experience" (Richardson, 2000: 934: quoted Sparkes, 2002: 129). Here, we will imagine in particular the ethnodrama option mentioned earlier.[2] Then the claims of ethnodrama are sometimes offered in relation to presenting data but sometimes to generating it (considered in later sections). This case offers an extreme, and hence perspicuous, perspective on truth-denial. It also embraces an explanation typical of such truth-denial; and one regularly offered by major theorists here. But we can first address the general question of the fictional before turning specifically to the claims of such an ethnodrama-based research design.

Fiction, knowledge-generation and research

Fictions are regularly and rightly claimed to offer insight, understanding, knowledge: that there is a sense in which the fictions are *true*, but with no explanation of how or why. Sometimes that may not matter. Using a motley collection of ill-matched theory may make good pragmatic sense. Yet the concern in philosophy is typically with justification even when it is granted that such-and-such works. So we might agree that there is insight into one's situation to be got from fictions, from (say) the novels of Jane Austen, without knowing how: that, in turn, poses a problem. For clearly we get no factual information about Miss Emma Woodhouse – there was no such person (at least, in the relevant sense). And the action is all stage-managed. How can there be insight available there? What occurs is entirely designed by Austen. Whatever is correct about such cases (which at least portray social organizations at a particular time), how can science fiction, for instance, be insight-generating? Yet we surely recognize that it is.

A red herring here will be claims by artists to 'research'. As Picasso wrote to Kahnweiller: "I can hardly understand the importance given to the word *research* in connection with modern painting . . . to search means nothing in painting. To *find* is the thing . . .".[3] At issue is the degree to which the basis of artists' decisions on how to proceed is research. That process is not really knowledge-generating, if we think of the knowledge as independent of the artworks later produced or attempted. Compare the kind of 'product development' which takes place in the Research and Development sections of large companies: as we have already noted, R&D, in this sense, is not research.

Let us consider a case: it might well be illuminating to ask what we would have done faced with the predicament in, say, the film *Sophie's Choice* (McFee, 2000: 125–26). Then the insight comes from the case as we observe it: its fictional status is neither here nor there. But we consider such cases, we do not create them. Thus their features are determinate independent of our wishes, desires or inclinations. It would be odd to view this kind of 'finding out' as research.

Nevertheless, something can be learned from such films, as from the plays of Shakespeare or the novels of Jane Austen. But what? Again, that Jane Austen or Shakespeare presented considerable amounts of material manifesting understanding of the human mind does not make either of them psychologists. What they were doing was informal, non-disciplinary: so, not research – however informative it turned out to be.

The literature offers the beginnings of an answer concerning truth from fiction. As given in a reliable summary, those relevant for us are:[4]

- as ". . . a source of categorial understanding" (Davies, 2001: 270–71);
- as ". . . a source of affective knowledge, knowledge as to what it is like to be in a particular circumstance" (Davies, 2001: 271).

These come together since the categories one deploys have a significant bearing on "what it is like to be in a particular circumstance", as these concepts shape how our actions should be understood – our actions being *intentional* under such concepts (in the jargon). Yet, even with these explanations before us, are we sure what fictions offer?

As Martha Nussbaum (1990: 38; emphasis original) stresses, here there is "the need for fine-tuned *concreteness* in ethical attention and judgement". Then concrete cases (say, in novels) offer the specificities, and attendant diversity, sketching key elements of "the priority of the particular" (Nussbaum, 1990: 37). That can make one dissatisfied with simple answers about what one should do. As Gilbert Ryle (1990: 289) put it: "To the employer of a hundred crayons the dichotomy 'Chalk or Charcoal' has no appeal". Having given attention to the full complexity of a case, we will not readily dragoon our conceptual discriminations into a couple of simple camps: "given the copious, specific and plastic vocabulary of . . . [many critics], it then becomes a hopeless as well as a repellent task to split it up into . . . a platoon of sheep-terms for angelic and goat-terms for satanic powers, impulses and propensities (Ryle, 1990: 289).

Equally, we must be clear what is and what is not of relevance, and confident that we are not ignorant of some key facts. Fictional cases meeting these constraints might deploy (again) a "principle of total evidence" (Carnap, 1950: 211–12): everything that counts will be told to the reader or viewer.

As this point is both complex and important, let me repeat it more bluntly: my argument has been that fictional works can offer concrete, specific cases (rather than mere abstractions) and that such cases are complete (at least in principle) in ways that real cases may not be – since real cases may confront our ignorance as to what is going on. In this way, then, we might benefit from the confrontation with the fictional, benefit in our understanding of 'what is going on' or 'how the world is working': that is to say, in our grasp of what is true.

Might a case in its full specificity ultimately be too specific, lacking the generality that might make it useful in our lives? In the nursery rhyme: "Jack and Jill need water . . . but the hill is slippery. I say that Jack ought not to go up the hill, but you disagree" (Gibbard, 2002: 52). The issue between us is not ". . . what to do in your case or in mine, but somehow in Jack's, in Jack's shoes" (Gibbard, 2002: 52).

Still, the issue cannot simply concern the here and now, or there would be no point in speculating on what Jack should have done – even by Jack! "Why . . . should Jack rethink his decision, when the moving finger has writ and he can't unbreak his crown?" (Gibbard, 2002: 52). Clearly, somehow present consideration bears on future cases. But we will never be in precisely that situation: nor could we be – we are not Jack. Yet neither can Jack, at least if he has the capacity to remember (and perhaps profit from) his past. What is learned from thinking about Jack's case, and his decisions, may be brought to bear on our (rather different) cases, and our decisions. But, since these cases *are* different, what is learned needs to be applied in this new situation. We grant that, somehow, we manage this in practice (see McFee 2004a: 142–44). So this issue need not perplex us in theory, however problematic it becomes in practice.

But some practical problems, as they might be encountered in sports research, are worthy of comment. For, to the degree that, say, one captured something fundamental in an ethnography of Cuban baseball, one's techniques – and, indeed presentation – turn centrally on one's specific relations with specific Cubans: in this case, to one's gatekeepers, guides, informants, sources and the like. Or, putting it more bluntly, to the Cubans with whom one has dealt. Yet why should any of that account be more generally informative? The answer includes a number of aspects. Like the 'Jack and Jill' story, we can see further than those data, to learn – for the future – from the present narrative. For one ascribes to those individuals as research participants no direct individual characteristics: indeed, anonymizing them will be fundamental to one's process, so that one can have ". . . provided pseudonyms for all of . . . [one's participants] irrespective of their expressed wishes to be identified" (Carter, 2008: x). So what one draws from them cannot depend on their particular authority as experts – this is not like interviewing the President of the IOC about Olympic matters! Except, in this sort of case, they are experts in virtue of being typical participants in the sporting community under consideration. Or, better, participants with broadly characteristic features, views, and attitudes. No doubt many had characteristics, irrelevant to their position here, which did not intersect with the research protocol. Only a careful consideration both of the case and of one's questions in respect of it can resolve which features of particular individuals or contexts should be stressed. These, then, cannot be treated in the abstract. When we turn to the particular context, then treated case-by-case, all the sources drawn on by the academic disciplines at issue are potentially available here. So dismissing the practical issue really just endorses the resources of disciplines; and denies the possibility of giving productive context-free accounts.

However, this was a slight detour from the central concerns of the discussion that focused on the issue of *fictionality* – which showed how a consideration of fictional cases can offer insight in research, by playing a role in conceptual development. This is already quite a gain; but is it a recipe for ethnodrama as research? I shall urge that it is not.

What about poetry?

It seemed that Richardson's aforementioned account gave some special place to poetry. One might take the vividness of its presentation of ideas, feelings and responses as central here – perhaps also virtues to be stressed for auto-ethnography (see Collinson and Hockey, 2004: 190). But my thought throughout is that what cannot be knowledge-generating cannot, for that reason, be research – whatever else it is, and however valuable it is. Further, not just anything could count as knowledge-generating, even when we learn from it. Suppose R. G. Collingwood (1938: 336) was right to claim that, in *The Wasteland*, T. S. Eliot shows "... his audience, at risk of their displeasure, the secrets of their own hearts", a revelation needed because "... no community altogether knows its own heart" (Collingwood, 1938: 336). This certainly describes, and partly explains, our coming to understand, which can only happen if the insight the artwork embodies is genuine. But reading Eliot is not research into the human condition (for us); nor was writing it for Eliot – although, through writing it, he may have come to recognize what he thought, or felt.

The impact of such points is often missed. Thus, for example, Richardson may acknowledge:

> that her poetic presentation, as a text that violates conventions and destabilises traditional forms of judgement, is defined as an act of heresy in sociological terms by her audience at the conference *because* it violates their sense of safety and security.
>
> (Sparkes, 2002: 197; emphasis mine)

But the disbelief of the audience – I imagine it accompanied by sharp intakes of breath – has a different source all together. So her "because" is misplaced. Rather, their disbelief is justified by the impossibility of her poem being either a satisfactory *presentation* of research data or an *analytic tool* in respect of it. As we have seen, this follows partly from the knowledge-related status of (genuine) research and partly from the art-status of poetry as of drama. That conference audience was entitled not only to *expect* but to *receive* a consideration of research data and conclusions plus, perhaps, some methodological reflections. It is unclear how the meeting of these legitimate expectations is permitted on this conception of research.

Moreover, this feeling of misrepresentation should be intensified if the audience learns that, for Richardson (2000: 936), "[l]ike wet clay, the material can be shaped". For this metaphor highlights (and seems to concede) exactly the practical difficulties for finding something solid from qualitative data: that there are stories to be told. Are there not features or patterns to be discovered, or made sense of, in the material? Just this sense of discovery, rather than creation, is fundamental to the distinction between the researcher and, say, the poet or novelist, imposing different constraints on each. The researcher requires something to discuss with other researchers, with the possibility of moving forward a joint research project. Since one cannot move one's poem forward, its presentation simply occludes genuine research efforts.

Interestingly, Tom Carter (2008: 146–49), in his account of baseball in Cuba, describes two poems as "poetic examples" of strongly felt positions, or narratives, which offer ". . . an organic critique of contemporary social situations on the island" (Carter, 2008: 146). But these are neither the product nor the presentation of research. Insofar as we classify them as insightful, we are referring to the insight they offer into fundamental aspects of the experience of sport-related social groupings who endorse them. And, although not research themselves, they might be starting points for research!

Vignette – ethnodrama: making fictions as research?

Let us draw together some earlier recognitions. All sides (at least, all the sides considered here) grant that I may come to understand better what I have been doing, what I have been feeling – and, especially, what others have been doing to me! – by writing a testament or by role-playing. That understanding might then be brought back to the actual situation, with the possibility of a change to how I behave. So it might amount to *action*. And, even when it does not, it might amount to a change in how I conceptualize what I do: this too is a change in what action I perform (although in a more subtle way), since there is a change in the way behaviour *should* be characterized (even when it is not). This in turn highlights the subtle inter-play between understanding the situation in which one finds oneself and changing that situation. But these procedures might have a place, say, in investigating craft-knowledge. Of course, the testament written or the role-playing must be true to my feelings on the one hand and true to the situation on the other. If it simply reflects my feelings, it may just manifest my paranoia, or some such. At the least, nothing there is revealing about the situation. So my role-play must grow from what I do know: say, from my actual experience as sports psychologist with a football team. Equally, my craft-knowledge cannot be reflected if the perspective is not at least partially mine. For the relevant case investigates those values that hold in place my habits of behaviour.

Given the credentials of procedures of this kind, one might seek to do more. Then drama might seem to take these possibilities further: to offer the (naturalistic?) opportunity – given that we need concrete cases to study – of *making* such concrete cases, and hence tailoring them specifically to our needs. Thus, for researchers turning ". . . their ethnographic field notes into performances" (Sparkes, 2002: 127), the resultant dramatic forms might be the ". . . most powerful way for ethnography to recover yet interrogate the meanings of lived experience" (Denzin, 1997: 94: quoted Sparkes, 2002: 129). But its research credentials must be addressed: can I learn something new? Can my coming to learn it be research?

Dealing with practices or activities, the claims of role-playing seem strong. But any use of drama must go beyond these: that is, ethnodrama must be more than simply extended role-playing, not least because the needs of staging typically preclude the 'time-out' discussions of success and failure characteristic of much role-play.[5] So where does that leave drama?

Any reply must show why the outcome *is research*: this means justifying its epistemological status as knowledge-generating. Further, one's case here must not be overstated. Whatever an ethnodrama offers must be justified by the features of that form, and from how it is conceptualized. Central here will be its capacity to offer insight, at least potentially.

As our thinking about films and novels illustrates, that insight might arise from applying to one's own situation ideas learned in respect of the different situation portrayed in the artwork – or, better, one might see one's own situation through concepts grasped (or modified) through one's encounter with the artworks. The net effect is that the insight comes from seeing one's own world in a new light. Thus, to repeat, the claim that one has a drama – even an ethnodrama – must go beyond simply the recognition of the force of, say, role-playing in the investigation of professional practice. For one is implicitly claiming that the characters in this ethnodrama are doing more than simply role-play, since their context is provided by fieldwork into, for instance, the roles of the sport psychologist in a football club – these reflect our researchers' field-notes in ways designed to yield insight. But in what ways?

Again, comparison with role-play is suggestive, since role-play can yield insight. When it does, it can provide insight for both participants and audience: the participants begin to notice or to recognize features of their own lives that they had previously seen differently. Similarly, role-play can reveal to audience members elements that they too had seen differently in their own lives – things they had not noticed, even when they had observed their co-workers, say. In both these cases, the spontaneity is important, if slightly differently: the participants learn something about their situations by confronting values in ways they previously had not – and, obviously, that makes no sense if this were not the first time for this precise confrontation. Equally, the audience members have something made vivid for them as the participants come to realize . . . as the scales fall from their eyes, as it were. Clearly, this is only insight-producing if it occurs. (Or, more exactly, the other case – where a pre-arranged insight is presented – is precisely the one from the other arts.)

By contrast, the case for a drama here is problematic: as Sparkes (2002: 127) describes it, recall, researchers create the ethnodrama by turning "their ethnographic field notes into performances". In this sense, what they have observed in working as, say, a sports psychologist with a football club becomes the speeches, and similar, of the play. Perhaps, for dramatic effect, discussion of a dilemma between an inexperienced sports psychologist and his mentor/guru makes more vivid what was actually interior dialogue. So there are concerns with presentation, with the resultant dramatic forms.

As imagined here, the actors know what they are going to do or say prior to the performance, as with more traditional drama – surely the default position. So no new insight or understanding is available to them: they have played the part before, rehearsed, and such like, so that any insight could have arrived for them before tonight. *Hamlet* cannot be a 'who-done-it?' for Hamlet! Only the audience is open to insight this evening. But here too no *new* insight is possible, since there is (in one sense) no spontaneity – or, if there is, this will be contingent (and not necessarily revealing). Of course, the audience may come to grasp something. Yet that is best understood on the model from other arts, where something previously known is now presented.

Three further points help put aside misunderstanding: first, I am not assuming that all performances are indistinguishable – indeed (see, for example, McFee, 1992a: 108–9), I have recognized the importance of this *not* being so. Yet they are all performances of the *same* play: and that fact must be given due weight. Second, actors may come to some new insight into a character as a result of a particular performance: I am sure they do. But how likely is that tonight? – surely they cannot *always* have such insights, every single performance. And is this genuine insight? (As director, I would want a say in what the actors did! And in determining its appropriateness.) Third, the role of improvisation raises two different cases: (a) there may be improvisation in the construction of a play – as of a film or dance – but, once the work is 'set', that aspect disappears; or (b) there may be improvised passages in works. These resemble the role-playing cases discussed earlier. Of course, on a particular night, they may fall very flat. When they do, there is little or no insight gained. Indeed, genuine role-play may have more chance of success here (success in generating understanding), since the participants really are engaging in the activity, if at another time, rather than merely acting it.

Stressing the role of spontaneity here suggests a parallel with a more traditional research problem offered to students, when the tutor has already completed that research – already 'knows the answer', as it were. This might be part of research-training: but, in a clear sense, this cannot (really) be research. That is the point I am deploying here.

My coming to learn such-and-such in order to put it into the play, and then taking it forward, has twin criteria for success: first, in the success of the insight: have I genuinely seen something about my situation? Then, second, is success in 'translating' my revised understanding into action – although, of course, these are not two stages or processes, but merely the positive formulation of two failure conditions. For I cannot gain genuine understanding if I misrepresent the situation.

Success here would leave the role of the play itself obscure: the learning went into its composition, and grew from there. Even if we imagine – as for some improvisation – that the process is on-going, how exactly does it fit into the model of knowledge or understanding? For clearly the outcome of the play is the play, not action in the site of one's professional practice.

Moreover, while the actions of dancers or actors may embody the knowledge-in-action or craft-knowledge of their crafts (dancer, actor), they cannot embody it for any craft-knowledge portrayed or depicted: say, as sports psychologist in the ethnodrama envisioned earlier. (The mistaken view here is roughly that of expecting a TV surgeon – say, from *ER* or *Holby City* – to be able to remove your appendix. Some actors, and even comedians such as Harry Hill, turn out to be doctors too, but this would simply be a fortuitous accident.) Actors viewed solely as actors lack the craft-knowledge of crafts portrayed, hence their behaviour cannot instantiate it. Of course, an actor might portray or depict such knowledge. But, in this respect, the behaviour is a *ringer* for a genuine action (compare Travis, 2004: 248): the criteria for success here are set by the activity portrayed or depicted – by the degree to which the portrayal or depiction is successful. But, for genuine agents, there are no criteria for success independent of successes and failures within the profession or practice.

So, as here, the question, "research by whom?" is a powerful tool. For, bluntly, the drama cannot be research for the audience, merely a pedagogical tool. Although presented to them as enlightening or insightful, the knowledge is generated prior to their involvement. And making (or composing) the drama cannot amount to the generation of knowledge either – the insight is at best exemplified through the drama.

Presenting one's results through drama?

Might drama then be used to present the results of one's research: that is, "... in terms of disseminating ... [a researcher's] findings" (Sparkes, 2002: 145)? There seem to be at least three related problems here, clustering around the criteria for success.

First, a successful drama will be successful by whatever are the appropriate dramatic criteria, suitable for the genre, and so on. The research report has accuracy as a goal – for which some elegance might be sacrificed – while, for the play, the very notion of accuracy makes no sense. A play which, say, misrepresents the detail of the battle of Waterloo is unrealistic, not inaccurate. Even the worst excesses here (such as the dreadful film *Braveheart*) only become inaccurate when someone begins (mistakenly) attributing historical veracity to them. But such ideas have no bearing on its accuracy as a presentation of the research findings or conclusions. So these constraints pull in opposite directions – the better the play, the less successful as a research report!

Second, the contribution of actors to the dramatic impact must be given due weight: if they are not to be classified as co-authors (which would not do for, say, the evaluation of one's personal research record for a new post or a promotion; or for one's PhD), the dramatic presentation cannot depend on them. One might as well read the play. But now the advantage of depicting one's results through drama is obscure. For instance, even though Plato's works begin as dialogues, they eventually turn into monologues, punctuated with, "Yes, O Socrates". Then any virtues from the dialogue-form are lost.

Third, the need for an evaluation of one's research findings requires that those results be accompanied by accounts of how they were arrived at: again, this is not readily accommodated within a dramatic form.

Moreover, if one has already produced the results in some more sober form – say, a research report or academic paper – again, the virtues of the dramatic presentation are unclear. This sober presentation would be needed (at least roughly) to assess the accuracy (to the research findings) of one's dramatic representation. Thus, someone claiming that, say, a poetic presentation ". . . may actually better represent the speaker than the practice of quoting snippets of prose" (Richardson, 2000: 933) should be asked the sense given to the term "better". It cannot really be as a better poem. Instead, research criteria – accuracy especially – are to the fore.

Finally, a strength of, say, *King Lear* is precisely that it is amenable to many 'readings', and hence can stimulate debates among adherents of disparate readings. (One might contrast this with, say, the didacticism of a company's training film, where one position only is pushed.) Of course, the debate around a genuine work of drama might lead to conclusions arguable in terms of the dramatic work, but with the possibility of a single, conclusive reading seeming unlikely – especially for the best drama! If this is a characteristic of drama, we see (again) how unsuitable drama (even ethnodramatic representations say, of coaching) is as a vehicle to present one's research results – and for precisely the reason that makes it valuable as a means to stimulate discussion, reconsideration . . .

For these reasons, then, the project of presenting (or exemplifying) one's research results dramatically looks unpromising. Attempted justifications of certain procedures as knowledge-generating in ways consonant with their being research are unconvincing, precisely because the fundamental connection between research and truth is severed. And the objections here are not to particular methods, such as ethnodrama, but rather, first, to the uses to which these methods are put and, second, to the understanding of these methods – understood as their relation to the project of knowledge-generation.

But this sets (or clarifies) a research agenda. We have seen how the fact of being researcher and researched engenders no (special) logical difficulties – whatever practicalities it raises. Further, the particularity of events must be understood contextually, so that the limits of generalizability can be plotted (case-by-case). The novels and films (say) have a role in instantiating concrete cases – in offering "fine-tuned *concreteness*" (in the expression from Nussbaum, 1990: 38). If this gives us ground for exploring how the investigation of the context through drama can be knowledge-generating (if it can), this is now a focused task. And one where we know that saying "Well, it works" is not saying enough.

Drawing on Ramsey's Maxim, the insight behind postmodernist thinking was a contextual, perspectival account of truth, but one still retaining the concept *truth* in a robust form. Its virtues were illustrated through an implicit contrast with a view (drawn from key theorists from the literature) which sets aside the notion of truth, both by dealing in fictions, and by offering dramatic presentation as a method either of generating or of presenting one's research data. And our critique of the truth-denial of (some) postmodernism has highlighted the self-refuting character of central kinds of relativism.

Another vignette: a place for action research into sport?

To end more positively, I should sketch an account applicable to sport which is arguably insightful *because* it deploys the epistemology endorsed here. In fact, more can be done: we can also use this account to ground our view of that epistemology. For a commonly suggested constraint on theory is that it should explain what had previously seemed obscure: that, as Kuhn (1977: 325) notes, "[a] theory should be fruitful of new research findings". That is, a fruitful theory should explain more than simply those elements that were its explicit topic or from which it began. That is just what this case offers. So, as a version of this idea, this chapter concludes with a case where endorsing the model of research into sport urged here allows explanation of a surprising omission from the pantheon of sport-related research.

In researching sport, a concern might arise with professions (in the sense in which doctoring and lawyering are professions) associated with sport – I imagine coaching to be such a profession. So what conception of knowledge appropriately engages with the knowledge embodied in the activities of such professions? And how should such knowledge be investigated?

Miraculous as it may seem, answers to both these questions can be treated in a related way. For a concept of professional knowledge as *reflective practice* has been developed by Donald Schön to deal specifically with this case. Moreover, I have urged (McFee, 1993; McFee, 1994/2004: 181–92) that action research is best understood as research into reflective practice; and various writers have suggested that action-research offers a practical and persuasive model for knowledge or understanding of sport.

But this conception of practical knowledge does not in fact seem to have provided an effective protocol for research into sport. First, the nature of an epistemology of professional practice is not well-understood; and, second, appropriate understanding seems to conflict with the requirement for knowledge-generation in research. For practical knowledge is not readily reported. Of course, the epistemology defended here makes plain that this second worry is unnecessary. So, in this section and the next, I first sketch briefly my preferred version of the theory behind such action-research drawing on its conception of knowledge (an account of the reflective practitioner by Schön 1983; 1987), then comment on some reasons why – as explained by the account of research developed here – this procedure has failed to take off.

Schön's argument is *against* the claim that all the kinds of intelligent activity essential to a *profession*[6] like (say) teaching are either simply propositional, or merely skills (like knowing how to ride a bike): as Schön (1987: vii) says, ". . . competent practitioners usually know more than they can say". But a typical form of explanation might be, "I just do that", or "It is natural for me", since these are action-patterns that one has acquired. The explanation of them lies (no doubt) in the values that hold them in place. But these would not typically be theorized nor would one typically be aware of them directly when one was acting. Yet, crucially, this point is about what professionals can readily explain or say, not what they know. Rather, the professional who "knows how to go on" in the profession has another kind of knowledge ("knowing-in-action": 1987: 23): he or she "goes on" with various actions. As Schön urges, saying that is not claiming that no knowledge or understanding is at work here – instead, we recognize "reflection-in-action" (1987: 29).

This position is not suggesting that a distinctive *kind* of thinking or reflecting is operative here – there is just a certain kind of acting; but it is intelligent acting, as indicated by the flexibility the practitioner displays when unusual events occur. (In this sense, a reflective practitioner is not really someone who *reflects*.) Then, the connection to practice (and to good practice) is clear: one cannot ask, "How does reflection relate to practice?", since the practice is in the account of the reflection from the beginning. Thus action is not ". . . only a kind of implementation" (Schön, 1983: 165) of ideas detached from that action. Further, this is an account of what makes a reflective practitioner: these practitioners do "reflection-in-action", rather than simply responding in habit-laden or rote ways. All who have supervised student-teachers will be familiar with crude examples of this point: visiting a well-delivered class one day and then, the next day, finding that student teaching precisely the same material in precisely the same manner with a radically different group of pupils. Of course, this student may grow into reflective practice: he or she is not there yet, at least on the basis of these lessons. But, moreover, there is no guarantee that this model fits *all* cases of craft-knowledge – hence it may not suit all action research, even that into 'the professions'. On this, we must just 'taste it and see'.

As we have noted, for Schön, the reflective practitioner is not someone who is both reflective and a practitioner. In the technical language of philosophy, the adjective "reflective" functions attributively, rather than predicatively. The expression "beautiful dancer" is ambiguous in precisely this respect: in one sense, a beautiful dancer is a person who is beautiful and also a dancer – the predicative use – while (in another) it is someone who dances beautifully. In this second use – the attributive one – the terms "beautiful" and "dancer" cannot be ". . . split" (Sibley, 2001: 156). So Darcy Bussell (who is both beautiful and dances beautifully) is, as it were, a beautiful, beautiful dancer! Just as the expression "beautiful dancer" (in its attributive use) cannot be split, so the expression "reflective practitioner" (in Schön's use) picks out someone who practices reflectively, rather than some who acts and reflects.

So this is not (attributively) a property of some practitioners, but rather a clarification of what is involved in being a practitioner at all, in some full sense of the word (contrast: "he's not really a teacher anymore, although he still draws the salary: he's just going through the motions"). Thus, in Schön's sense of "reflective", there cannot be unreflective teachers. Rather, those who fail (wholly or to some degree) to be reflective practitioners fail (to that degree) to really do the job. Schön is characterizing what effective professionals do, allowing us to explain why some are not effective, or not fully effective, or not effective in some aspect of their professional lives.

Moreover, Schön's book *Educating the Reflective Practitioner* (1987) describes examples, not of reflective practice, but of *acquisition* of the craft-knowledge that would allow someone – at a later date – to do reflection-in-action. This is fundamental to thinking about our own practice: one needs to learn reflection-in-action, not learn to 'reflect at leisure'. In this way, Schön's work is an introductory foray into the epistemology of professional practice. I have merely stated his conclusions here, not argued for them.

Still, this conception meets our picture of the epistemology appropriate for qualitative research, locating the knowledge of the practitioner as embodied in his or her (intelligent and responsive) actions; and one mode of access here will be through discussion with the practitioners. Interestingly, another aspect of our access to such knowledge will be through the practitioner's responding to new situations – the capacity for *reflection-in-action* which (as we saw) marks him or her out as a reflective practitioner. And one research tool, to investigate such reflection-in-action, will be precisely the interventions action research requires. So our example is appropriately contextual and builds-in an appropriate conception of knowledge (and truth).

Why there is not more action research into sport

But why has such an epistemology of professional practice not proved rewarding for sports research? From my perspective, the explanation cannot be a lack of models for the practical operation of, say, the action-research cycle: Kurt Lewin's initial work on the topic sketched one version clearly. Another is clear in Elliott's primer for action research in education (Elliott, 1991: 70–72), highlighting self-reflective spirals of planning, observing, and reconsidering – with the next planning phase inflected by the previous reconsideration. Nor does the explanation of the failure of this model to take hold in sports studies lie in the time taken to implement the successive cycles of action research – although this can prove too long for even the average PhD! The failure cannot be assigned simply to the need for repeated intervention, although this might be problematic if the researcher's role involved, say, coaching a sports team (Why change a winning formula? Why persevere with a losing one?). Nor, even, does it depend on the fact that many occupations in the field of sport are not, after all, professions in the relevant sense – although, of course, that is one consideration. That is to say, the explanation does not lie in the details of action-research models at all.

Rather the primary issues derive from the sorts of confusions that have been our topic throughout this work: that is, from the heart of Schön's epistemology of practice. For the issues turn on its difference from scientistic models; and can sometimes be seen in the researches actually undertaken, highlighting their differences from that actually required. First, there are investigations about how to make one's practice more reflective (see Edwards, 1999); but (as we saw) that would separate the practice from the reflection – instead, there may be places where training in reflective practice must be removed from the workplace (for a non-sport example, see Putnam, 1996). Moreover, just this sort of issue was raised when a particular model was proposed for deployment in sport – its traditional epistemology of practice left its action-research credentials suspect (at least arguably: see Evans *et al.*, 2000a; Gilbourne, 2000; Evans *et al.*, 2000b), in that it still detached the psychological practices from the activities. Or, as we might say, the reflection was separated from the practice. But how else can one proceed? After all, we want to consider what occurs as more than just a sequence of activities – to see them as thoughtful actions, actions embodying knowledge or understanding.

Second, the desire for intervention central to action research designs typically fails some (supposed) test of generality: the contextual, perspectival nature of the knowledge or understanding here leaves open the question of whether whatever we do in this situation takes us further in other situations. Perhaps sports psychology should accept that its research is local, or contextual (McFee, 2004c). That is, perhaps a case-study approach is required, of the sort action research supports. But that seems to run counter to at least some aspirations of at least some sports psychologists.

Relatedly, the intervention itself must be recognized as an input from one person (or group) to another person (or group): that is, not as, say, a 'magic bullet' that will inevitably resolve the situation (if only we find the right bullet). Such a strictly causal model has no role in interpersonal affairs. Even statistical (or stochastic) causation – of the kind where, say, smoking causes cancer, but not exceptionlessly – misconceives what could happen, partly by failing to recognize that we are here dealing with the specifics of this situation: the person under consideration might be the very one for whom the well-documented trend does not hold.

Third, action-research designs are importantly different from others in having, as one might think, action as their outcome: we do not hope simply that research will lead to understanding, but rather require that it suggest alternative action, finding a kind of validation in the action being successful. In this way, the chief explanatory mode is a species of 'inference to the best explanation' as practised by a great many medical practitioners (and perfected by the title character in TV's *House*): if these pills make you better, then you probably had such-and-such a condition! So intervention can function as a tool of validation. But this feature does not lend itself to the production of knowledge in sports psychology – or, rather, it is such a feature, but only once one's conception of knowledge is revised (to incorporate knowing-in-action).

These last features make sense of knowledge as perspectival, and contextual, in ways urged earlier; and, given Schön's focus on the practical, exploit the specifics of this kind of practical knowledge from professions. For the idea of reflection-in-action grants that the action done thoughtfully differs from the same action done without thought – but the difference is not, of course, the addition of (parallel) thought. A useful comparison is with a pianist's performance dismissed as "merely technical": it differs from an expressive performance; and that difference is reflected in our conceptualization of it. (Indeed, that it was even a candidate for the category of the expressive is revealing here.) Moreover, while the differences between the merely technical performance and the expressive one will certainly be fine differences, differences of shading (at least typically), they are not – as is sometimes urged – imperceptible. We certainly perceived these differences, as our differential account of each performance illustrates. What is true of each requires human judgement to determine; but, if done carefully, that determination shows what is *true* of the case.

To review, we have recognized in this example both the force of our demand for a recognition of the research epistemology appropriate to qualitative research (and, in this case, to the specifics of qualitative research into professions) and the problems that arise for those attempting research in such areas, but without such a conception of knowledge. For it is precisely this lack which bedevils action research into sport.

Conclusion

The upshot, then, is that we have both supported an account of the embodiment of knowledge within action that should be attractive in some sporting contexts; and we have emphasized a fundamental constraint on any of the 'new ways of presenting research' that they too must allow the possibility of knowledge-generation. Like their scientistic opponents, postmodernist theorists of sport share a misguided view of what *truth* would be like, of the kind put aside by Ramsey's Maxim in chapters 5 and 6.

Part IV
Ethics for research

8   Voluntary informed
consent – not as good as gold

Introduction

In social-scientific research into sport, our concern with human subjects treated as people can be problematic: for instance, how can data that is sound be generated when one aspect of our interchange with our research subjects is inevitably *talk* in all its varieties? We might seem, though, to be on stronger ground when turning to the ethical treatment of research subjects. For here our problems might seem to more closely resemble those for natural scientific research into sport. This has been a widely debated topic, such that: "[s]tandards . . . for basic science research regarding the ethical design and conduct of research on human subjects are set out in several international codes . . ." (Stern and Lomax, 1997: 288). Moreover, the upshot is often stated bluntly: "[f]or all research involving human experimentation, informed consent *must* be obtained from subjects" (Stern and Lomax, 1997: 291; emphasis mine). And this can appear unproblematic to sports scientists. So that "[i]nformed consent *simply* means that the participant has given consent to take part in an investigation about which they have been fully informed" (Williams and James, 2001: 9; emphasis mine). However, much of the debate is misdirected since it too fails to grasp the full range of the possibilities provided through the recognition that our subjects are persons. And that in turn reflects the claims here to be "*fully* informed" (emphasis mine).

Still, it helps to look at what might be thought the simplest case: where the research design does not exploit this fact about one's subjects – indeed, the research might focus on the hand or the musculature; or the design might not consider the subjects directly as persons. And hence it limits the inputs it demands of them.

The basis for ethical considerations in research

But why do ethical questions arise in research with human subjects? Ethical issues arise, in general, when we confront (roughly) what we, or other persons, did or ought to do: that is, primarily in our interactions with one another. So, at the centre of such ethical problems for research is a tension, or possible conflict, between (on the one hand) the rights of subjects and (on the other) *inter alia*, the (public) right to know, as well as considerations of academic freedom. If there is a legitimate reason for thinking a topic worthy of research – a legitimate public right to know, as it were – then (to that degree) there may be ethical justification for infringing, or setting aside, the liberties or rights of those (humans) who will be subjects of the research. For ethical conduct can result from a kind of balancing of ethical forces: for example, when we speak of a line of conduct as "the lesser of two evils".

Of course, there are other ethical issues here. For instance, that researchers should behave with integrity, publishing only what they discovered, rather than fabricating results; or that researchers should not steal the research of others (either through plagiarism or misrepresenting authorship). But the central questions here will be those concerning the most potentially vulnerable participants in the research process: the research subjects. So we can return to our contrast between the rights of subjects and the public right to know.

Where the public right to know seems overwhelming – say, in respect of a cure for cancer – there might be correspondingly more reason to infringe the rights of subjects; or more infringement could be justified. But this will rarely be true of research into sport or leisure. At best, we should hope for research sufficiently well-justified as to warrant, say, giving up some of one's time to further it; or standing around in the cold – a mild discomfort, at worst. Further, the issue here concerns the moral rights of subjects, not the legal ones – better, the legal ones are taken care of in another way.

Insofar as a major concern here is with respecting the rights of subjects, and insofar as each of us is taken as able to look after his or her own rights (and even to permit the infringement of those rights if we choose), *informed consent* suggests itself as a safeguard precisely because it respects the autonomy of those subjects: each gets to determine what will happen to him or her; and can decide whether to stop or go ahead. In this sense, informed consent seems just ". . . a formulation of the widely recognized moral obligation to respect others and take into account their interests" (Homan, 2002: 25).

Discussions to motivate this place for informed consent often begin from research designs that are questionable, or defective, from an ethical point of view. These seem to show what can go wrong if informed consent is not sought: my personal favourite example is the research design (from 1971) whereby women were given a placebo at a family planning clinic, rather than birth-control pills . . . with an unforeseen (although extremely obvious!) side-effect – a number of the subjects ". . . became pregnant" (Bok, 1978: 71: quoted Homan, 1991: 97)! Mention of such cases is often used to insist that research subjects should not be abused, where the abuse consists (as here) partly in the subjects not knowing what was going on. Then this seems to suggest that if the subjects had known what was going on, and (especially) if they were prepared to go along with it, their rights would not have been traduced. As we will see, this is not so much mistaken as much harder to deliver than is sometimes supposed.

Two key contrasts

In arriving at this conclusion, our discussion of research design turns on two key contrasts. The first is between covert and overt research designs, where what is not *fully* overt research is thereby covert to some degree, giving a spectrum of cases of covertness. In this light, then, blanket condemnations of covert research will be unhelpful, especially once our high standard for full overtness is granted. Moreover, the character of fully overt research should be explained by reference to the informed consent of its subjects – this seems right since lacking such consent would imply concealment or deception.

The second contrast formalizes some earlier remarks (from chapter 3), contrasting 'real world' research (naturalism) with controlled research (experiment, and such like). Again, there is a spectrum here, especially for real world or naturalistic research: interviewing runners after a race (for instance) considers them, to that degree, outside of the world of their event. After all, they are running no longer. Research into sport must always have a real world dimension – the sport itself does not (typically) take place in laboratories. But then its real world status ensures that its exact situations are not repeatable; further, a role must be recognized for persons (as agents). Moreover, our perspective is reinforced by recognizing how the idealizations inherent in controlled research mean that the claims of other methodologies are regularly over-rated.[1]

Elsewhere, in considering the *Bitter Cold* television documentary (McFee and McNaught-Davis, 1997), a colleague and I discussed (primarily) the issues for the kinds of overt research design facilitated by its being a laboratory-based study. My concern in this work will be primarily with research covert to some degree (and its ethical demands) explored in chapter 9. But we begin from the overt case, since the other is covert (to whatever degree) primarily by contrast with that case. But I do not concede that "[i]n an experimental research report there is usually no need to describe how the investigator complied with ethical requirements. Typically, this is straightforward ..." (Smyth, 2004: 222–23). For here too ethical considerations are crucial. Further, such a discussion allows us to rehearse, in this context, some familiar considerations.

I will urge that voluntary informed consent (VIC) cannot function as its advocates imagine. If we read it so that (were it achieved) it would be a gold standard, we render its achievement conceptually impossible – nothing meeting those conditions could possibly be actualized, even in theory. For it then requires that a finite totality of conditions be met, when there is no such finite totality. Hence its constraints can never be satisfied, even in principle. So, on this reading of the requirements for VIC, it is impossible.

On the other hand, to interpret VIC so that its constraints could be met – if only in theory – removes the basis of its claim to function as a gold standard for the ethical treatment of research subjects. For one may have secured VIC (on *this* weaker understanding) and yet be behaving unethically towards one's research subjects. This follows from granting that something less than the *full* conditions for voluntary informed consent were met: that is, from recognizing that, say, one's subjects may still not know enough to have genuinely consented.

The practical strategy here, of course, treats what is required as what a reasonable person (say) would agree to: treatment (as a research subject) that would strike such a person as not infringing his/her rights. Of course, in some sense, this draws on ". . . a hypothetical reasonable person" (McNamee *et al.*, 2007: 86). That is, someone with suitable desires, with no defects in his/her capacity to reason (so he/she will not make logical errors), and no relevant defects in his/her understanding or knowledge of the relevant context (Harris, 1985: 196–200). In fact, this is less a positive standard than, first, an acknowledgement that matters can go badly when assumptions of this kind are not satisfied; and, second, a concession that my conclusions depend on those assumptions. This is plausible just as long as we idealize this reasonable person – basically, as me! Yet, without a guarantee of reasonableness on this occasion, it is difficult to move forward.

Recognizing, in these ways, that voluntary informed consent – our criterion for overtness – is not a gold standard for the ethical treatment of research subjects may open the door for some ethically-constrained covert research methods, my topic in chapter 9.

It is worth recording a large proviso, with two aspects: first, that the research topic itself must be worth pursuing – since there is, after all, to be some (albeit temporary and non-harmful) infringing of the rights of subjects, the potential outcome here must be worth the risk.[2] That condition may not always be met in covert enquiries concerning sport and/or leisure. For the tradition in the USA, which calls such research "deceptive", has this much correct: there is some traducing of the rights of subjects. Second, the effects on the subjects must themselves not be large: we must not be subjecting them to, say, life-threatening procedures. This second aspect of the constraint is – for the social sciences of sport and leisure – relatively easy to meet.

But these two aspects of the proviso put in opposite directions. Thus, suppose that there were good probabilities of finding a cure for a regularly fatal condition such as, say, breast cancer if a certain risky treatment could be tried on a small number of subjects (for instance, six): indeed, let this treatment be such that it guaranteed that half the subjects would die. And let it be granted that this research could not proceed in any other way. [Further, there is nothing covert here.] Now, here we have a case clearly permitted under the first aspect: this is clearly important work. But it would equally be very problematic under the second, since to kill people is certainly to traduce their rights. Moreover, this does not seem a case where one could plausibly consent – to do so knowing these possible consequences would be to cast doubt on one's sanity; and hence on one's ability to consent!

In such a case, the right line of conduct is unclear. Thankfully, research into sport and exercise can never face this kind of problem. Since its cause can never be this good, nor the potential benefits so large, it can never consider permitting this range of harm. That fact is useful when considering the question of covert research in chapter 9: if a good justification for doing the research can be found, and if its risks are within limits, why should we not proceed?

Informed consent in overt research?

(a) The place of (voluntary) informed consent (VIC)

The requirement for informed consent in research with human subjects is widely presented, through codes of practice, as fundamental: for instance, in the British Sociological Association (BSA) *Statement of Ethical Practice*:

> As far as possible sociological research should be based on the freely given informed consent of those studied. This implies a responsibility on the sociologist to explain as fully as possible, and in terms meaningful to the participants, what the research is about, who is undertaking and financing it, why it is being undertaken, and how it is to be promoted.

Or, again, in the Social Research Association (SRA) *Ethical Guidelines*:

> Inquiries involving human subjects should be based on the freely given informed consent of subjects. . . . [Subjects] should be aware of their entitlement to refuse at any stage for whatever reason and to withdraw data just supplied. Information that would be likely to affect the subject's willingness to participate should not be deliberately withheld, since this would remove from subjects an important means of protecting their own interests.

We should conclude that there is a consensus as to its importance. Indeed, Gratton and Jones (2004: 111), for instance, urge that "[t]he best approach to take is that of informed consent".

(b) What is 'informed consent'?

Explanations of both the nature and importance of informed consent regularly (and rightly) begin from the Nuremberg Code of 1947:

> The voluntary consent of the human subject is absolutely essential. This means that the person involved should have the legal capacity to give consent, should be so situated as to be able to exercise free power of choice, without the intervention of any element of force, fraud, deceit, duress, over-reaching or any other ulterior form of constraint or coercion: and should have sufficient knowledge and comprehension of the elements of the subject matter involved as to enable him to make an understanding and enlightened decision.
>
> (quoted in Homan, 1991: 69)

While we should recognize that there have been many later interventions, most notably the Helsinki Declaration (WMA, 2000), the basic principles are relatively unchanged. I offer the following summary, setting down some minimal conditions for counting as "informed" and for "consenting" (although, clearly, there are connections here – that one cannot be consenting if one is not informed as to the topic on which one's consent is asked; and that one will not count as informed if one is not in a position to consent, as [say] a child might not be):

Informed:

The subjects should be aware:

- that you are the researcher;
- as to the research topic/protocol;
- as to dangers, and such like – the risks, the potentials for harm, and so on;
- as to use of data: its publication, and so on, including their identification.

Consent (and voluntary):

- The consent given must be based on information or understanding (of topics on which subjects were informed); and
- the subject must not be coerced (or any such) into giving it; and
- the subject must be in a position to give it; and (therefore) can take it back 'at any time'.

Then the term "voluntary" (in VIC) is not irrelevant. For voluntariness implies both that one was not coerced or constrained – part of one's genuinely consenting – and that one's consent may be withdrawn at any time during the research process.

Useful parallels for the points about *consent* might be with a legal contract: the defeating conditions for contracts, helpfully stated as a positive-sounding condition that the contract must be "true, full and free", highlight ways in which a contract would be set aside if it was coerced (say, with bribery or threats), or if the signatory were a minor. Hence ways in which genuine consent is necessarily voluntary.

Any of these conditions might – if breached – lead to abuses in research; in particular, to abuses of the kind from which the discussion began. But these are not easy conditions to satisfy. As we shall see, what appears to be genuine voluntary informed consent (say, through the signed informed consent form) may fall far short of what is required. Yet only if *all* these conditions are genuinely met – and not merely when they appear to be – will we have voluntary informed consent.

(c) The seeming virtues of voluntary informed consent

It should be clear exactly what might be hoped for from voluntary informed consent; and why it might be thought a Good Thing. Thus, for instance, "[i]t is rooted in the high value we attach to freedom and to self determination .... When individuals involved in research risk limitation of their freedom, they must be asked to agree to this limitation" (Frankfort-Nachmias and Nachmias, 1996: 82).

In a similar vein, Penslar (1995: 125) rightly stresses the connection to: ". . . the principle of respect for persons. Respect for persons involves a recognition of the personal dignity and autonomy of individuals, as well as special protection for persons with diminished autonomy". Then the features of voluntary informed consent, as presented or developed here, justify that title: *consent* means that the subject is recognizing his/her own rights, and so on, and is safeguarding them; *informed* means that he/she is in a position to do so; *voluntary* reinforces the previous point.

It is widely agreed that ". . . informed consent should be much more than just signing a form" (Shamoo and Resnik, 2009: 259). But what more? Certainly, we cannot have VIC if the researchers are only paying lipservice to it. But the claim here is yet stronger. Perhaps, as Freedman (1979: 266a) urges, ". . . informed consent is seen as not merely a legal requirement, and not merely a formality: it is a substantial requirement of morality". But what exactly is its position? How might that be understood?

One thought, then, is that VIC achieves *all* that could be desired as to the ethical treatment of research subjects: thus, to ask about the ethical credentials of some particular research design is implicitly to contrast it with VIC. In this sense (the thought runs) VIC is a gold standard.

It is important to be clear just what is meant by a gold standard for the ethical conduct of research. This takes us back to the rights of subjects: for the thought, as Freedman (1979: 266b) puts it, is that: "[a] person who has the capacity to give valid consent, and who has in fact consented to the procedure in question, has a right to have that fact recognized by us". So this is not just the best we can get in respect of respecting our ethical obligations (as researchers) to our human subjects: rather, it idealizes the best there could be. So the gold standard metaphor takes VIC to give what could, in that sense, be cashed-out in terms of the gold of meeting our obligations to others, or of respecting them as persons. Thus ". . . *the process of informed consent must ensure comprehension, voluntariness, and disclosure in order to maximize protection from harm*" (Shamoo and Khin-Maung-Gyi, 2002: 39; emphasis original). Hence VIC sets the target for the ethical treatment of human subjects.

Some pitfalls of using VIC as an ethical safeguard

One set of difficulties concerns the degree to which the conditions imposed by such informed consent are genuinely (as opposed to apparently) met. For if they are not met, but researchers take the procedure to be informed consent, we have merely fools' gold. And if, as I shall urge, the problems are conceptual, rather than merely concerned with the practical performances of particular researchers, the danger for ethical conduct of research may be greater still. I will raise four such difficulties:

(i) Do subjects really understand the research protocol?

It is easy for researchers to have explained, say, only some of the experimental protocol (the rest being, say, a taken for granted in the research community), or offered explanations in a language unfamiliar to the subjects, or failed to mention an aspect to which the subjects would have objected, had they known. And this is as likely to be true for social scientific research as for the natural scientific, although perhaps the point is more readily seen in the latter case. The upshot is that the subject might not be properly informed: say, well enough informed to draw a conclusion (of his/her own) concerning the nature of this research. But this subject has nonetheless signed the form and, if asked, would agree that there was informed consent. The suggestion earlier that "[i]nformation that would be likely to affect the subject's willingness to participate should not be deliberately withheld" is all well and good: but the *researchers* decide what to tell the subjects – and, *a fortiori*, the subjects do not know what information they lack; do not know what questions to ask. Moreover, there may be issues which, although they end up not arising in practice, would have a bearing on subjects' willingness to participate: again, they remain uninformed! Thus, on the aforementioned model of VIC, any relevant 'informing' that is not done or that does not 'take' (whether or not it impacts on *this* trial or experiment) means that one does not, after all, have (full) informed consent. So this remains a very stringent requirement, almost never met in practice.[3]

(ii) Who decides what issues/dangers subjects need to be informed about?

In practice, the researchers decide which of the possible risks, dangers and the like subjects will be informed about: that is clearly not in the spirit of the informed consent programme outlined earlier, where the thought was that subjects must understand those issues which (if they knew them) would lead them to withdraw. But this is clearly problematic, at least in practice. At its most extreme are examples such as that from the *Bitter Cold* television documentary where a researcher urged:

> People [he meant "research subjects"] can get themselves into great states of apprehension about their fears, real or imagined. Fears do not kill you. The dangerous things in experimentation, objective ones like excessive rises or falls in body temperature, excessive rises or falls in blood pressure, ... are the things which ethical investigators have to make it their business to monitor extremely carefully.
>
> (BBC, 1986)

Unsurprisingly, the experiment this person was conducting caused some concern: I (for one) would not trust his account of the issues or dangers – and that is precisely what his colleagues (who were also his research subjects) felt. So I do not see informed consent in this case. This highlights, too, the place of trust in the practicalities of informed consent. But the moral is more general: only the researcher has any sense of what may occur, and hence any sense of how unpleasant it will be for subjects. Some subjects may be willing to tolerate some degree of unpleasantness – if it is in a good cause – but this requires trust that the discomfort is necessary and that all efforts have been made to prevent its being genuinely dangerous. Full VIC at the least requires explicitness here.

(iii) Can subjects really pull-out at any time?

Of course, one thinks first of cases of blackmail, or bribery, or threats of harm to oneself or one's loved ones: clearly these will (typically) be taken care of by informed consent. But coercion can take many forms, some mild: that does not excuse them, at least from the perspective of the model of (full) informed consent developed here. One's subjects may *be* (or at least *feel*) pressured into continuing in a number of subtle ways: for example, the thought of letting down others, the researchers, and so on. And even the good cause that grounds the research. Equally, when we encourage a subject who is, say, riding an exercise-bike to continue, our thought may be only that he should try as hard as he can – but he may feel he should continue beyond that. Again, there is a fine line here: we do not want subjects who bail as soon as the questionnaire (or the interview) gets too long – on the subjects' account of *too long* – but we must recognize how close we are to the point at which (justified) encouragement ("Why don't we have another drink and just finish this off") turns into something more. And, again, recognizing how that "something more" is a transgression against voluntary informed consent.[4]

(iv) Do subjects really know the fate of the data?

The issue of data-dissemination has at least two primary dimensions. The first concerns the prospects for publication (or other kinds of public dissemination) of the data. Very often, subjects do not know exactly what such-and-such a means of publication entails – of course, if they did, they might be perfectly happy to agree, but the requirements of informed consent are not met if they (in fact) remain ignorant.

This might be of special importance if the subjects themselves have a special role in respect of these data: if it comes from their oral history, or from participant-observation of a context in which they were active. Although I would insist on the researcher's ultimate responsibility for even these data (see chapter 10), these 'participants' may have a key role to play in accepting that does capture the relevant aspects of their lives (viewed through the researcher's lens to whatever degree). So these subjects may feel a particular attachment to these data; and hence particular concern as to where the data will appear; and perhaps how. Of course, sensitive researchers can both explain the research 'outlet' (for instance, that discipline's house journal), giving some of the reasons it was selected, and offer a kind of translation of any aspects of the data-presentation that were not clear. Here, I am simply stressing that this may prove difficult, but without it, one does not have full informed consent.

The second, and related, aspect turns on the questions of privacy and, especially, anonymity. Again, it is easy to think that the anonymity of one's research subjects can be guaranteed. But maintaining confidentiality here can be difficult in practice. Thus, imagine a sports psychologist who advertises his consultancy base, mentioning some particular team: say, the national cricket team. Now, imagine that one of his articles, suitably anonymized, discusses the relation between a sports psychologist and a major team from a team-sport, and includes information that a player on the team might wish to keep confidential. To repeat, the player is treated anonymously in the article. But clearly the members of the national cricket team would come under immediate scrutiny. In such a case, ethical behaviour requires more than just, say, anonymizing the research subject.[5] In another case, a researcher into physical education anonymized the area in which his study – which depended on collaboration with teachers in local schools – was conducted. Some of the data concerning socio-economic features of the education provision were deemed sensitive, hence the anonymity. But, since the geographical relations among the schools in this local town were important here, as reflecting economic divisions among the catchment areas of the schools, a first draft included a map of the area! When this was pointed out, the map was removed. Yet the author was identified as a lecturer at a particular Midlands university with a very developed interest in sport. If one looked at the environs of that university, it was not difficult for any fairly determined investigator (such as a journalist) to identify the schools from the study.

So there is no foolproof guarantee here if the data and the subject can possibly be connected – one cannot, say, preclude a determined journalist from finding out; although the best guarantee here may lie in a topic which gives the journalist no incentive! But, with no guarantees here, can I really inform the subject of what will happen to the data? To the degree that I cannot, the conditions (articulated earlier) for informed consent are not met. This problem does not disappear if the subject is told that the anonymity is only *conditional*, given that we cannot specify the conditions!

Outcomes for (genuine) voluntary informed consent

The four considerations just outlined highlight practical difficulties in meeting the conditions for VIC, as we have set them out (drawing on codes of ethical research practice, and the like). That suggests that one cannot be cavalier here. Each of the conditions for VIC summarized earlier can appear to be met, but without the subjects being genuinely informed or genuinely consenting to the treatment they received. In this sense, as Ingelfinger (1979: 264a) put it, "... it is not educated consent", despite appearances to the contrary (say, the signed form). Similarly, Onora O'Neill (2002: 43) urges that "... there are systematic limitations to the degree of justification that informed consent procedures can offer". For she points out that one consents to be a research subject under one description of the research protocol. Perhaps one would not have consented if offered some other description of that protocol.[6] But one can only ever be offered *this* description or *that* one: there is no complete or perfect description. So one cannot know if there is a true description of the research to which one would *not* have consented.

The research described in the *Bitter Cold* television programme seemed to offer ideal conditions for the success of informed consent: there was no question as to the research context; subjects had access to the protocols of experiments and sufficient scientific knowledge either to understand them or to find a man who does; any dangers could be discussed with the researchers (who were colleagues) in a shared language; the dissemination routes were clear – and would be foreseen when the subjects for one experiment became the researchers in the next. That is, the case seems explicitly to meet the conditions laid out earlier. Yet, even in what look like ideal conditions, ethical concerns were produced – I mentioned one earlier [(ii) in the previous section]. In fact, the concerns raised in that case were precisely the ones just outlined.

The upshot, then, is that (full) VIC does not seem a practical possibility: it is unlikely that *all* the subject's questions have been answered (including the ones he/she did not know enough to ask); and so the subject *could not* know what he/she was being asked to consent to. Hence there could be no informed consent. Moreover, if there is not full VIC then (by our initial contrast) the research design is not fully overt!

Actually, each of the aforementioned four points urges two parallel objections: first, the practical objection already raised – that one cannot guarantee that one's subject was either fully informed or fully consented (or both). Second, that there is no finite totality of conditions, such that being fully informed is knowing them *all* or fully consenting is consenting in respect of *all* of them – there is no *all* here. Hence, there is no fully informed or fully consenting. But without these, the requirements of voluntary informed consent as we have articulated them cannot possibly be met. And only under these constraints of full or genuine VIC was the 'gold standard' idea justified.

We could conclude that meeting the constraints on procedures for informed consent might still leave one short of genuine informed consent. In doing so, we object to the practicability of achieving informed consent. And only genuine informed consent would (might?) count as a gold standard – a model for the best there could be. But it is difficult to see how more could have been done than was done in the case of the research (from *Bitter Cold*) mentioned. The difficulty does not seem simply to concern how diligently we act. This moves us from a practical objection to a conceptual one; it highlights the danger in treating an abstract conception of informed consent as an ideal, forever inaccessible to humans. For, were that its status, it would have moved from (putative) gold standard to the philosophers' stone pursued by alchemists, to transmute base metal into gold.

If, instead, this case is regarded as doing the best that can (humanly) be done, we are then recognizing, first, a kind of (full) informed consent weaker than what, earlier, I called "genuine or full informed consent"; and, second, that such informed consent does not after all guarantee the rights of subjects, even in those cases most closely approximating fully overt research, such as that with elaborated 'informed consent' forms, conducted by obvious 'white coats' in the laboratories of sport and exercise science.

The earlier discussion in (c) above highlights the right rationale for the ethical treatment of research subjects, namely, as rooted in ". . . the principle of respect for persons" (Penslar, 1995: 125). But, since the rationale was there couched in terms of VIC, its real force was obscured. So a key question must be: *how do you respect persons in a world where you can neither (in principle) fully inform research subjects, nor get their full consent?*

Certainly, if the only (or best) way to respect persons were through VIC (as has been suggested), it might be impossible to conduct ethical research in sport (or more generally) – since one can never meet the constraints of (full) VIC, as developed here, where this difficulty would be conceptual, not practical. Our alternative must be to think again about what constraints these ethical ideas impose.

An impractical restriction?

Before doing so (in chapter 9), it is worthwhile putting aside explicitly the suggestion that my constraints on VIC are too severe or too extreme. As it was put to me, one theorist claimed never to have met an experimenter who, noticing the impossibility of full VIC, was 'significantly thrown by this realization'. That matches my own experience exactly. But then such experimenters have not been reading, or thinking about, their own claims to VIC as a gold standard. Indeed, this would be part of my evidence that there are researchers who do not sufficiently grasp their own research tradition, in which it can be claimed that "[i]nformed consent by participants is a necessary condition for ethically acceptable research" (Polgar and Thomas, 2008: 25) or that informed consent is ". . . one of the fundamental prerequisites for conducting research involving humans" (Penslar, 1995: 125). For example, in the UK the Code of Conduct of the British Association of Sport and Exercise Sciences (BASES) stated:

> No member may undertake any work without first having the informed consent of all participating clients. Informed consent is the knowing consent of a client . . . who is in a position to exercise free power of choice without inducement or element of force, fraud, deceit or coercion.
>
> (2000: 20)

This conscious echo of the Nuremberg Code seems to leave no 'wiggle room': the consent must be "knowing", which surely means both that one must know *that* one is consenting, and must know *to what* one is consenting; and, as the parenthetical remark about children makes plain, the ideal involves an agent competent to give the consent. The result is that "[a] central feature of modern biomedical research ethics is the notion of obtaining . . . voluntary informed consent from research participants" (Olivier, 2007: 31). Further:

> [c]onsent is deemed ethically acceptable if the participant receives full disclosure of relevant information, if the implications are fully understood, if the participant voluntarily agrees to participate, if opportunities to freely ask relevant questions are present throughout the duration of the project and if the participant feels able to withdraw from the procedures at any time.
>
> (2007: 31)

By implication, research is not ethically acceptable with one or more of these conditions absent.[7] Notice in particular the "full" and "fully" here; and the implication that the participant will know the "relevant questions". For these totalities ("full"), and this sense of abstract "relevance", are both what a gold standard requires and what I have shown cannot, in principle, possibly be met. Similarly, one specimen consent form published for the benefit of students asks subjects to agree that: "I have had full details of the test I am about to complete explained to me. I understand the risks and benefits involved, and that I am free to withdraw from the tests at any point" (Williams and James, 2001: 164). So "full" details are assumed. In another (Williams and James, 2001: 165), the subject is asked to concede that ". . . the research staff will have *fully* explained the procedures being used" (emphasis mine).

My critics might be excused for having failed to notice some of these commitments. Even when informed consent is the foundation of ethical research with human subjects, the power (and even the nature) of the commitments here are only directly apparent in small asides, or something similar. Thus, Thomas *et al.* (2005: 349) write that, in a certain circumstance, "the *whole* concept of informed consent must be observed . . ." (emphasis mine) – as though sometimes there might be a justification for 'making do' with second-best; yet thereby conceding that such practice is understood by contrast with "the *whole* concept". Accepting that "[t]he participants have the right to be informed of the purpose of the study" (Gratton and Jones, 2004: 112) implicitly contrasts cases where that right is respected with those where it is not. Or, again, Bryman (2001: 477) sometimes writes as though the sole source of an ethical imperative here resided with VIC: that is, as though it was the "[l]ack of informed consent" (Bryman, 2001: 481) that explained the "ethics (or lack of them)" of Laud Humphreys' covert research, to anticipate a case considered in the next chapter.

Moreover, those who criticize the ethical failures of others are, of course, implicitly appealing to standards of appropriate ethical conduct of research. Thus, the use of some physiological testing ". . . solely for selection purposes" (Doust, 1997: 100) is not ethical when the athlete is unaware of its purpose (or takes it to have another purpose). Nor will it be ethical to coerce the athlete to take such a test. Here again an implicit contrast to VIC, where the purpose was known, will be inflected by the conception of VIC assumed. This is another place where adherence to VIC as a gold standard may be visible, even in those who do not practice what they thereby preach.

Thus, researchers operating with these conceptions of ethical research are committed to the importance of VIC as a gold standard. Another group here certainly regard VIC simply as a tool for avoiding litigation: so I would need to argue that the obligation to conduct research ethically is itself an ethical obligation on researchers, not simply a legal one.

In the USA, the legal obligations here are typically the province of an Institutional Review Board (IRB: see, for example, Barnbaum and Byron, 2001: 166); but the IRB embraces the moral concerns too. A classic statement of the position is found in the papers of the University of Dayton IRB, which specifically mention sport (the IRB having a representative from the Department of Health and Sports Sciences). First, the centrality of VIC is urged:

> Participation of a human subject in research must be voluntary and the right to withdraw at any time must be provided. Information given to gain subject consent must be adequate, appropriate and presented in lay language appropriate to the subject population.
>
> (University of Dayton IRB)

Then some of the details of what information should be given to subjects is provided. Then we come to a revealing waiver:

> The IRB may waive some or all of the requirements of informed consent if the research could not practicably be carried out without the waiver, provided that (1) the research is designed to evaluate public benefit or service programs . . .; or (2) the research involves minimal risk, the waiver will not adversely affect the rights of subjects, and the subjects will be provided with additional pertinent information after participation, as appropriate.

Although "some or all of the requirements of informed consent" may be waived under certain circumstances, this is clearly the exception, where the desirable situation cannot be reached. Hence this IRB does regard VIC as offering the ideal of protection for the rights of research subjects here.

Many researchers in the USA seem inclined to regard VIC simply pragmatically, as that ensured through formal procedures as represented by IRBs, although it is often granted that ". . . informed consent issues are discussed with reference to 'principles', which are then translated in an applied manner by IRBs" (Shamoo and Khin-Maung-Gyi, 2002: 39). And such 'principles' would be our concern here. The legal framework in the USA thus allows part of the responsibility to be passed from researchers back to the institution. Still, to the degree that the approach is pragmatic, it implicitly concedes that informed consent as sought (or as achieved) is not, after all, a gold standard of ethical research with human subjects in general. And hence for the corresponding sport-related cases.

Whose interests are being safeguarded: researcher or subject?

That thought allows us to identify another way in which the ideal of voluntary informed consent is traduced in practice, focusing on one outcome of the giving of informed consent – namely, that:

> . . . informed consent shifts part of the responsibility to the participants for any negative effects that might occur in the course of the study. It also reduces the legal liability of the researcher because participants will have voluntarily agreed to take part in the research project.
>
> (Frankfort-Nachmias and Nachmias, 1996: 82)

Indeed, at a BASES-organized Sports Science forum under this topic, this last point is all that was discussed; as though all that mattered was avoiding litigation! But then the ethical imperative would no longer be driven by the need to protect the rights of subjects. So that concern would have been lost, submerged by an ethics-free prudential concern on the part of the researcher.

Now, universities (and funding bodies, both public and private) will want some safeguard against litigation from research subjects. And both covert and overt researchers will need to strive in that direction. Perhaps (indeed, undoubtedly) the provision of a document signed by the subject, voluntarily taking the rap for any consequences, will gladden the hearts of the funders' lawyers.

Of course, were I right, that paper is legally worthless: to bring this out, the signatory need simply assert that there was some aspect of which, after all, he/she was not fully or properly informed. Since there is no finite totality of such aspects, he/she has logic on his/her side. At best, the lawyers will urge the missing information was not in respect of *relevant* aspects – and then there will be numerous lawsuits disputing what is or is not relevant! But this has nothing to do with the ethics of informed consent, or of research more generally. (In fact, we rightly set aside such legal questions early on.)

A role for codes?

It might seem that the position advocated here gives the researcher insufficient guidance as to how one should behave in one's research, in order to behave ethically. In fact, that is not so, for three reasons. First, and in line with the aforementioned ideas, we must reiterate our concern with the ethical treatment of research subjects, contrasting that with the meeting both of legal obligations (although they need not conflict, the demands of law and of morality do not always coincide, as a matter of fact) and of requirements from one's ethics committee – that is all too often a matter of ticking some boxes, rather than safeguarding the rights of subjects.

Second, we should not assume that too much guidance is ever forthcoming: in particular, we should be aware that any set of (putative) rules will either remain silent or offer counter-intuitive 'guidance' in some cases – that rules cannot deal with all cases, since *all* rules admit of exceptions (McFee, 2004a: 46–49). And codes here operate as a kind of rule.

Third, and paradoxically, this recognition of the limitations of codes has a consequence running in practice in the opposite direction to the previous point: once the codes are recognized to never be exceptionless, they can be deployed as offering 'helpful hints and reminders' as to what one should do; or as considerations one might look to first. In this sense, we are in the same position – facing the same ethical imperative – whether or not we have been able to inform our research subjects. For (as we have seen) informing can never be a guarantee that the rights of subjects are respected, and not informing does not guarantee that their rights are not respected.

Conclusion

The major conclusions for this chapter are the ones touted throughout: that VIC cannot be the species of gold standard for ethical research sometimes hoped (or claimed), and that covert methods can have moral strictures.[8] My arguments and exemplifications for these conclusions should have suggested some guidelines for the ethical conduct of covert researchers, and for the modification of those guidelines (to be discussed in chapter 9). Central here was the recognition that ethical conduct may require a balancing of the rights of subjects and the 'obligations' of researchers. In addition, I have raised a number of specific questions which, if answered for a particular case (or in a specific context), will aid the researcher in maintaining the ethical standards of his/her research. Finally, I have suggested why VIC, earlier called "genuine informed consent", cannot (as theorized) be a gold standard (despite its claims): it is just an idealization – hence it is not as 'good as gold'.

9 Covert research into sport can be ethical

The connection of the covert to the naturalistic

For many of us, including some of those researching it, sport is crucially a human activity, taking place in diverse contexts. That fact is central to any investigation of sport, bearing on the methods appropriately used (and hence on the ethical issues confronted). For the slogan, deployed repeatedly, that for research purposes human beings be treated as though they were persons (Harré, 1983) acknowledges that we can interact with human subjects in ways impossible for one's interaction with the subjects of biology. One can ask one's subjects, and take note of their replies or other responses. That leads us back to naturalistic or real world research designs, by suggesting (correctly) that naturalism is usually a virtue here.

Further, we know that awareness of being observed can alter our behaviour. Someone observing one's teaching typically impacts on that teaching, at least for some time. Similarly, being closely observed as to one's table manners too is likely to alter one's behaviour – say, by making one nervous and hence clumsy. (Here too I speak from personal experience.) It is commonsense that, in a similar way, being researched will typically impact the behaviour of research subjects: at the least, it would be unsafe (in the legal sense) to assume it did not. Since, as we saw, the exact situation is not itself repeatable, the change (if any) is typically not checkable. We cannot run the experiment again since the subjects' knowledge of having been researched will not disappear. And using different people introduces an additional dimension of change.

In any case where knowing that one was being researched (knowledge of the topic, say) might be expected to alter the behaviour being researched, and hence bear on the findings, a degree of covertness is justified if that research is to go ahead. For instance, a researcher investigating subjects' mental training for sport used a design which had different interventions – but it was the impact on the subjects of these interventions that was really being studied. Had the subjects been told this, their knowledge would inevitably cloud the results of the research: were they responding to the interventions or to their own (supposed) place in the research process? One could never know. So, given this research is warranted, voluntary informed consent of subjects cannot be required, since it would preclude undertaking the research. Similarly, research involving attitudes will be compromised if the subjects, knowing they are being researched, do not respond (or behave) as they would have, had there been no research. Again, it would be unsafe (in the legal sense) to assume there was no such change of behaviour.

Moreover, the fact of being researched might intervene in many ways, to some degree or other. At one extreme, so-and-so does not regularly run his marathons wearing a portable heart monitor – can we really guarantee it will not alter his behaviour? Or, as one of my research students found out, in getting the thoughts of a runner while running, the tape-recorder may not prove problematic, but the need to speak while running (and to articulate clearly) makes the situation atypical. At the other extreme, the mere fact of opening a sports club for young people in a certain area is an intervention into the lives of those who attend – perhaps they really wished for such a facility, but perhaps they had no wishes either way, until the club 'appeared'. So here too there is a compromise with (full) naturalism. Thus researching people in naturalistic settings almost always alters that situation to *some* degree. Then the researcher aiming at as little disruption as possible often needs methods that are covert at least to some degree. Thinking that the very same thing could be researched in some other way (hence, regarding the covert research as second-best) is failing to notice this fundamental point.

Thus, (some) covert research designs are essential if we are to investigate 'real world' (or naturalistic) settings, such as sporting situations – granting that the research itself is desirable. And, since that covertness is unavoidable, we cannot regard it as somehow second-best, at least if we are to continue with such research.

Having shown that covert research is essential, I could stop. But it helps to say something about how ethical strictures might apply to some forms of such covert research.

Privacy in public spaces?

Let us begin with examples where ethical considerations are uppermost, asking which of the rights of subjects might be infringed (especially as we will not explore the foundation of rights as such). *Privacy* offers a useful example, since it is often invoked when raising the (supposedly) unethical behaviour of the covert researcher.

Private spaces (such as one's home) offer a fairly clear-cut line for the requirement to privacy: this is precisely what is appalling about (say) agents from some government department bugging one's home – indeed, it is what supports the term "bugging" here. But in public spaces the issues are much less clear.

One guideline for ethical research, applicable in other areas, is also germane here: that subjects do only what they would have done anyway – thus, in experiments, it is taken as read that if the subject normally lifts such-and-such weights, he can do so in the experiment. The demands of naturalism give this a new gloss: the subject is just doing whatever it is. So, if he is a marathon runner, and was planning to run this marathon any way, then the behaviour itself is partly detached from the ethical protocol: the researcher is not persuading, or coercing, or any such. Since the subject regularly does this behaviour – here, running his marathon

– in a public space, where overt observation might reasonably be expected, covert observation, say, cannot be especially morally reprehensible.

For example, Laud Humphreys (see Homan, 1991: 45; 101–2; Bryman, 2001: 477) did not need permission of those he observed in his role of lookout voyeur, or "watchqueen", in research into behaviours of gay men. Although "the men for whom he acted as a watchqueen were not given the opportunity to refuse participation in his investigation" (Bryman, 2001: 481), they were only engaging in activities in which they would have engaged in any case – so the research (in this aspect)[1] is not compromising the behaviour of these people, except in regards to their expectation of privacy.[2] But this was a public place of a kind.

However, the boundary between the public and the private is not as clear as has often been supposed. After all, one's so-called private space might also be private space for one or more others. (The moral there: do not live with social researchers.) Even given such points, the private/public barrier has been eroded – there are webcams in what might (otherwise) have been thought private spaces. And people shout their business into mobile phones on crowded trains. The idea of eavesdropping as faintly morally repugnant cannot long survive such practices. But that just says that the realm of the 'rights of subjects' (in virtue of their being human beings) is open to change.

A further complication seems to arise with using images (photographs, videos): there may be people in them who have not consented. At present, this often provides a difficulty for ethics committees (for instance, those at universities). But it should not. As long as we are discussing adults in public places, and methods of dissemination appropriate to academic research (rather than tabloid journalism), no (putative) right is being infringed. For we can have only a limited expectation of privacy in public places. At worst, this is only an infringement of one's sense of the extent of one's private space in that public place: as when someone sits next to you on a bus or train – conventionally, it is preferable not to do so, but one cannot command the use of the adjacent seat. (There is no equivalent to the towel or newspaper used to safeguard one's own seat: see Homan, 1991: 45.) This possibility should extend not just to observing but to recording, so long as anonymity is preserved. One's (unattributed) image should not be regarded as one's own property (unless perhaps one is a celebrity: say, an actor or a rock-star – but these are different cases).[3] Of course, such a photograph (say) may lead to one's being 'found out' in a place one had denied being: but an adult cannot feel (morally) aggrieved that it becomes known that he/she was in a public place, when it is clearly true. Moreover, we are specifying that the activities are not contrary to the law; and that the dissemination is of a respectful kind – for instance, in an academic journal or monograph (not the usual stalking ground of, say, jealous lovers). So, to repeat, there seems no ethical imperative requiring the permission of (say) those casually photographed in this way.[4]

Andy Sparkes (in conversation) provided an interesting case: some bodybuilders who, although they had no problems with being looked at or photographed, resented being asked – that was an intrusion too far! In this case, then, one's 'subjects' (in the photograph at least) felt more offended by the intrusion involved in seeking their consent. They might even have expressed their point as one concerning their privacy – the privacy implicit in completing one's workout untroubled by clip-board wielders, given that one has chosen it. Therefore, the search for voluntary informed consent (in practice) may conflict with our desire to safeguard the rights of subjects. And, however atypical such a case, it does conflict with the demand that informed consent is taken as a gold standard for the ethical treatment of subjects.

Clearly, there are ways of behaving ethically here without looking to informed consent: they basically amount to an injunction to *think about others* in ways one might if one were friendly with those people – recognizing, as Nagel (2002: 26) notes, the danger in an ". . . insistence on securing more agreement in attitudes than we need".

Ethically sound covert research: the basic idea

The basic idea is to limit the degree of infringement of rights of subjects, in cases where the research would be impossible if it were (fully) overt. For, clearly, covert designs can only be ethically justified where overt designs are impossible. In illustration, it is useful to return to the case where a researcher studied the impact of some interventions on subjects' mental training for sport. As we saw, this research could only have been carried out with a degree of covertness for, had the subjects been told the research design (and topic), their knowing would inevitably cloud the results of that research. One could never know whether the subjects' responses were to the interventions or to their own (supposed) place in the research process: in that sense, any conclusion would not have been (in the legal terminology) *safe*. The point is well-put in the British Sociological Association (BSA) *Statement of Ethical Practice*: ". . . covert methods may avoid certain problems. For instance, difficulties arise when research participants change their behaviour because they know they are being studied". In this way, employing such methods may be the only way to conduct research: if the research is warranted (given its infringement of the subjects' rights), it must be conducted covertly.

Of course, the qualification here – that the research itself be warranted (or, to put that another way, that the research question be worth asking) – implies another constraint, here working on the subjects' side of the contrast drawn initially. For there is no reason to even consider infringing the rights of subjects unless that constraint is met.

One argument in favour of the research in the aforementioned case is that it did not harm the subjects: that, indeed, the only infringement related to their being misled about the research topic. (And this case suggests some canons to deal with covert research: discussed later).

Homan (1991: 105–8) rightly distinguishes four 'principles' of covertness: *concealment* (not letting subjects know that they are being researched); *misrepresentation* (not letting subjects know the topic or protocol); *camouflage* (the aim to be invisible in the field one is researching); and the acquisition of confidential documents. Although these will all preclude *full* overtness, our argument must be that research deploying them can still be performed ethically.

Crucially, research such as this should not be regarded as 'second-best' because covert . . . as we recognized in granting the connection of the covert to naturalism in research. First, both the overt research designs and their covert counter-parts can leave subjects in the dark: for ethically-conducted covert designs, this should be regarded as a kind of white lie (in ways we will come to shortly), which does mislead the subject. The parallel for overt designs is a 'sin of omission' – there are topics on which the subject should be informed, or should have consented, for genuine voluntary informed consent, but where this has not occurred. (So the design is not fully overt.) As we know from chapter 8, there will *always* be such topics, since there is no finite totality of relevant matters for either informing or consenting. By its own lights, overt research should not have such omissions. Hence, by those lights, it too is necessarily flawed. Second, we recognized initially a conception of ethical judgement where the right thing to do in a certain situation might be just the best on balance: the 'lesser of two evils' (or the better of two goods!). As a result, the deception implicit in the white lie might, in some circumstances, constitute the (morally) right course of action. That is, it would be the right thing to do, despite involving (mild) deception. Clearly such a case would require some counter-balancing good. But the ethically-inclined covert researcher will explain his actions in precisely this way: there is sufficient reason (say, from the public right to know) to justify this level of deception.

Some practical options for ethically conducted covert research

As we have seen, there will never be easy answers as to how one should behave, given only some general injunction, such as *behave ethically*. But the rule of thumb suggested earlier – to treat the 'others' in one's research design as though they were ones' friends – does point towards some useful direction-markers, especially given those (also?) suggested by the aforementioned case of covert research (concerning mental training). So that ethically-conducted covert research should at least accept the following constraints: ensure no physical damage; debriefing; no exposé; give to subjects the other rights of persons. Each of these slogans will benefit from some elaboration

- *Ensure no physical damage* – minimally, to avoid obvious physical harms and minimize the risk of harms, both physical and psychological.

  Implementing this constraint is complicated because, of course, this is another place where there is no finite totality of conditions (here, of harms) to consider in avoiding damage or harm to subjects. So one cannot guarantee to avoid *all* harm to subjects. But the commitment here is just to do one's best: in alerting oneself to this requirement explicitly, one is bringing it to the forefront of one's attention. Clearly, covert research into sport would be unethical if it failed to safeguard the health and well-being of the subjects. Thus, a design which covertly gave its subjects what the researcher knew to be unsuitable coaching advice, or inappropriate training regimes, as part of the research process would be unethical; as would one which failed to safeguard the group of canoeists with whom the researcher had been playing the role of an established coach. Indeed, it would be inappropriate to undertake such a risky role unless one were in fact an experienced and knowledgeable canoeist (compare Donne, 2006).[5]

This is the single most important aspect here, as is shown by the case mentioned initially to introduce the supposed errors of covert research, in which researchers facilitated the unchosen pregnancies of their unwitting subjects. For this is something to which one would not consent if asked; and therefore one where the subject must rely on the researcher.

Again, a researcher investigating the 'black economy of football' (Sugden, 2002) might himself be at considerable risk, if many of the activities he witnesses are of doubtful legality, such as the sale of fake team shirts or forged tickets. But it will be important, too, that his subjects are not harmed as a result of the research process. Important here, as for all the cases discussed, will be minimizing the effects of being misled, among others.

- *Debriefing* – as much as is possible, to inform subjects 'after the fact'; this can be of the research topic, or indeed of any of the other aspects about which 'informed consent' would inform (as noted earlier). This is the best we can do: to tell the research equivalent of white lies and to banish the deception as soon, and as fully, as possible. The aim would be for the subject to leave the research site as fully informed as is consistent with the research protocol. So a covert researcher who feigned injury to study the interaction with the team's physiotherapist should not sustain that fiction beyond the point where the 'data-collection' was completed. Similarly for the researcher whose covert activities take place in some privileged position, especially if one's participant-observation (say) was conducted in some location in which the subject had a reason to expect was an 'insiders only' environment – for instance, where new training schedules were being implemented.

- *No exposé* – to present data fairly, and not sensationalize. We should see the detachment typical of academic disciplines as offering a useful constraint here: the manner of presentation characteristic of the discipline is unlikely to be unjust, and its locations typically scrupulous in reproducing work as written, and so on.

This is the most straightforward, contrasting academic research with, say, investigative journalism (Sugden, 2004). Even if the covert researcher presents herself as a journalist in order to gain access to information within, for example, the Olympic movement, her concerns will be to understand what is going on, rather than to uncover scandals. So the covert researcher will aim to present the results from the research dispassionately: the covertness involved has no implications for its presentation. And, to repeat, this will reflect the procedures usual within academic disciplines.

- *Give to subjects the other rights of persons* – to respect, for instance, the privacy of one's subjects in any case or respect in which one would grant privacy to other persons, unconnected with any study. This is perhaps, first, taking us beyond what we might do with friends and, second, recognizing that sometimes (as in this context) respecting the rights of others may not amount to granting those rights in *all* circumstances. In effect, this is not so much a specific requirement on the covert researcher who, as part of the covert activity, is deceiving the subject. But, as we have stressed, these are white lies, justified as the only way to research this worthwhile topic successfully. So it is a recognition that being a research subject in a piece of covert research means only that *those* infringements of one's rights are justified, to the degree that they are.

At least the first three of these proposed constraints correspond directly to some way that, if we did not follow it, we would be mistreating our friend (to some degree). In this sense, they both offer some practical help to the fledgling covert researcher and (more important) clarify the sorts of grounds from which – in his new situation – he should either apply and/or augment these suggested constraints.

It is interesting that Homan (2004: 219), who has practised it, regards covert research as "unethical" while granting that the covert researcher may ". . . honour the higher moral principles which . . . [ethical codes] are designed to safeguard". For Homan accepts that there can be ethical (he prefers "moral") constraints here. So that the researcher is paying due attention to the rights of his/her research subjects: the intention is to respect those rights. And the constraints suggested would not differ hugely from those endorsed in this text.

A useful guideline here, as for the ethical character of research behaviours, lies in the idea of its being excusable: yes, I have behaved badly (to some degree) but I explain – to my friend – and he excuses me. This is the ethical stance to which covert research designs must aspire: that the deception is excusable, once the value of the research is taken into account. And sensitively conducted research, treating one's subjects as one's friends, should meet this standard.

In practice, then, covert research might proceed ethically. Some 'principles' for such research have been suggested (without believing in moral principles).[6] I have also explained how my list might be modified in new or unfamiliar situations. In doing so, I have shown how ethical conduct here is not second-best to a gold standard of informed consent. I turn now to two further issues where the claims of VIC do not tally with aspects of its practice.

Covert or deceptive?

When research ethics are discussed in the USA, what this text has called "covert research designs" are more commonly referred to as "deceptive designs". The use of the pejorative term, "deceptive", seems to imply that such research designs are intrinsically unethical. This does not seem a good starting-place. As we have seen, such designs are inevitable in practice because the radical alternative – fully overt research designs – is both practically and conceptually impossible. But even if one sets a lower standard of overtness, attempting to align it more exactly with the practical possibilities, there will still be research topics within sport which (a) we regard as worthy of being pursued (they satisfy some appropriate curiosity) and (b) cannot be pursued without a higher degree of covertness than that permitted by (say) our modified version of VIC. One such – concerning the impact of some interventions on subjects' mental training for sport – was sketched earlier. The argument there was that this research could only have been carried out with a degree of covertness. Had the subjects been told the research design (and topic), their knowing would inevitably have, at the least, undermined one's confidence in the results of the research. For instance, were those the true results, or an artifact of the subject's view of what was wanted?

Further, my arguments justify my taking the much stronger view of the nature of overt research – as fully overt – than is common, by showing that what is not fully overt is thereby covert to some degree. Then a great deal of worthwhile research will fall under the general heading "not (fully) overt". Hence a blanket dismissal (as "deceptive") of covert research designs would be disastrous – and especially for those with a low degree of covertness (as in that sketched earlier).

Now, the concept of deceptive research (or deception research) is standardly introduced by citing horror-stories from covert research, cases which, in other places too, would be granted to be unethical – such as that of Laud Humphreys (used by Barnbaum and Bryon, 2001: 2) or Milgram[7] (used by Shamoo and Khin-Maung-Gyi, 2002: 18). Thus, to align covert research with the unethical. But this simply begs the question against covert research, at least *prima facie*.

Others, like Pattern (1994), also seek to rebut standard arguments in favour of covert (he would say "deceptive") research practices. Chiefly,[8] he concentrates on the suggestion, mentioned earlier, that such research "preserves greater experimental realism than alternatives" (1994: 113–14) – I would urge that it even permits the research to be undertaken! (That too would follow from our erotetic conception of research: what proceeded in a radically different way, or with a radically different epistemology, would be a different investigation.)

In spite of this tradition, room for debate on this topic has long been conceded. Thus, having recognized that "[d]eception is a word used to end arguments, not to begin them", Elms (1994: 121; emphasis original) states conditions (like those sketched here for covert research) for ethically justifiable research of this kind:

> *Deception is justifiable in social scientific research when (1) there is no other feasible way to obtain the desired information, (2) the likely benefits substantially outweigh the likely harms, (3) subjects are given the option to withdraw from participation at any time without penalty, (4) any physical or psychological harm to subjects is temporary, and (5) subjects are debriefed as to all substantial deceptions and the research procedures are made available for public review.*
>
> (Elms, 1994: 124; emphasis original)[9]

He then defends each of these conditions, to sketch a picture of an ethically defensible covert (he would say "deceptive") research design, recognizing that researchers differ from professional con artists not least in their ". . . principle motivations" and the commitment by researchers to ". . . seek publicity, in the form of presentations" (Elms, 1994: 137; 138).

One key feature here, perhaps explanatory of the US preference for the term "deceptive" or "deception", comes out when Schrader-Frechette (1994: 7), in talking about various stances on ". . . the defensibility of deception", urges that ". . . deception for the purposes of avoiding refusals to participate is never justified" (Schrader-Frechette, 1994: 8). But that was never one of the justifications that might be offered for covert research designs. Thus a major line of objection to deceptive research designs could have no purchase on the arguments for ethically-sound covert designs.

So here we see one virtue of the term "covert" (apart from its being less pejorative); namely, that one would not invoke it for some researcher who, in this way, was seeking to ensure he/she was not turned down by candidate subjects. Since that would be unjustified in terms of the research design itself, it would be closer to the kinds of unjustified misleading of subjects for which the term "deception" is well-suited. By contrast with such cases, Schrader-Frechette (1994: 8) grants that ". . . deception for the purposes of ensuring spontaneous reactions [roughly the cases envisaged here] may be justified".

Conducting research ethically

Finally, it is worth commenting briefly, in an explicit way, on how the conduct of research might not meet the standards implicit in the arguments for voluntary informed consent. The cases here could all be taken for examples of manipulating subjects. In fact, we have already commented on two such cases (in chapter 8): (a) where the practice of 'encouraging' subjects (for instance, to continue cycling on a bicycle ergometer) and (b) rehearsing, as a species of 'emotional blackmail', those who will be 'let down' if the subject does not continue. Both might conflict with the principle that the consent of subjects can be withdrawn at any time. Certainly, in both cases, pressure is applied in the direction of subjects' continued participation. Hence, at the least, subjects are manipulated. But strategies of manipulation are often used in, say, questionnaire design: questions the researcher regards as sensitive will be put at the end of the questionnaire, on the grounds that subjects who have already invested a deal of time in completing the questionnaire will not baulk at answering questions which, early on, might have made them refuse to start, or to continue. Here too the researcher is attempting to elicit from the subject information which, in the ordinary run of things, the subject would refuse to provide: it is akin to the 'emotional blackmail' mentioned earlier, and certainly amounts to persuasion, if not exactly to coercion. So these are ways in which overt research designs either fail, or come perilously close to failing, to meet their own standards.

It is regularly urged, though, that there is one case at least where the covert researcher (often) behaves badly, but which the overt researcher avoids: it concerns the invasion of privacy. And the complaint will be well-supported with examples of covert designs where privacy *is* invaded, from researchers hiding under dormitory beds (Homan, 1991: 96), through hiding in wardrobes dressed as

'aliens', in a study of cognitive dissonance (Homan, 1991: 102–3), to genuine telephone tapping and the like.

Now, the notion of privacy is a vexed one (discussed earlier: also Homan, 1991:
41–44; Nagel, 2002: 3–6). Yet can one sustain the charge that it is especially
abused by the covert researcher? I suggest not. Of course, I put aside cases where
there is genuine hiding in private or semi-private spaces of others (as exemplified
before). For not all covert research must be like this: some might (for instance)
only be covert in concealing the precise research topic, with no other deception.
And this last case is clearly not invading my privacy.

Moreover, parallel yet overt cases suggest that nothing here is distinctive. For I
am regularly assailed (as I suppose we all are) by phone calls offering me double-
glazing and, in shopping malls, by 'researchers' with a few questions, but often a
product in the background (to say nothing of the offers to modify my body-parts
with which the Internet seems to teem). These are an intrusion into my privacy –
merely that they bother me is enough. Here I resemble the body-builders in
Sparkes's anecdote discussed earlier (the only way I resemble them!): I do not want
to be bothered by these people. That these are not cases of research does not matter: I would be as bothered by telephone calls concerning some research project.
My point is simply that these perfectly overt practices have already annoyed me –
of course, I have not yet been asked to give my consent. But it never need get that
far: I am annoyed already!

Have these petitioners invaded my privacy? It is hard to say. At the least, I can
with some justice claim that they have importuned me in ways that are far from
respectful – that, roughly, they have not kept their distance; and that they should
have done so.

But need our covert researchers really do anything more than this? There is
deception involved in (some) covert research: that, say, you treat me in the workplace, or invite me into your home, under false pretenses. For this deception is of
the essence of (some) covert research. Still, is it really more than the deception
when the double-glazing salesman on the phone begins by telling me about the
promotion his firm is running in my area . . . that my whole house can be double-
glazed for free . . . if only . . .? Of course, he is fairly soon unmasked (if I listen long
enough) – some money is always to be paid: my successful covert researcher will
need to unmask himself. But the debriefing can include both the important issue
to which the research was directed (whatever the subject thought) and the sense
in which these were merely white lies – that one deceived no more than was
absolutely necessary, and only in the direction of the research protocol. Then the
parallel with the importuning seems strong enough to suggest that nothing here is
especially immoral.

Much of our interchange will be as honest as the research protocol permits: if I
conceal that I am a researcher, I may have to conceal, say, that I am engaged in a
PhD. But, for instance, I need not deny that I am a student – I can imply that I am
not presently studying. Whatever is undermined by such deception, it does not yet
amount to an infringement of privacy: I have merely lied to you a couple of times.
In this respect, I should conduct myself as truthfully as I can (because that will be

to behave as ethically as I can). And we have already discussed (in chapter 3) the obligation to mean what we say. Nor do we *never* lie at all to our friends, at least if this were taken to preclude exaggeration and such like. Thus, to repeat, I have lied to you, but only on the scale of perhaps concealing from you the details of your surprise party. Moreover, kinds of concealment which facilitate social interaction must be carefully distinguished from lying (see Nagel, 2002: 9–15), recognizing that neither concerns what is or is not private.

As mentioned earlier, this topic is usually introduced into discussions of the ethical weakness of covert research under the heading of the invasion of privacy. Yet covert methods, in involving deception, need not be infringing privacy at all (as we have suggested, mere deception need not). Even when privacy is at issue, we need not think in terms of its invasion – although the cases from which we began fit that bill, concern for one's subjects will require a sensitivity the term "invasion" belies. Still, if you invite me somewhere (say, your home) or treat me confidentially in, for instance, a workplace, my deception might indeed be an infringement of (or, worse, an intrusion into) your privacy. And that is ethically reprehensible. But only an exaggerated regard for the scope of privacy leaves this behaviour as inexcusable, given both the minor character of the infringement and the value of the research knowledge. At worst, my behaviour parallels the annoying opportuning – except that it has a justification, through the value of the research. So when what is excusable is actually excused (say, after the debriefing), no residual ethical difficulty remains.

There are two points here: the first is that, at least under one description, overt research: designs are not immune to some 'invasion of privacy'; the second is that covert designs, ethically conducted, neither require invasion of another's privacy (even when there is some deception involved) nor – if there is some infringement of privacy – need it be seen appropriately as an invasion. So this topic provides no special reason to criticize the conduct of covert research.

Some practical thoughts on research governance

As we have seen, research with human subjects is primarily social scientific research: that is, research into the actions of persons in social settings. In that sense, for sport, it will typically be naturalistic research where the setting are usually those of sports events or training, or leisure practices (especially physical leisure). Methods routinely used for generating qualitative data include overt observation; participant observation; interviews of various kinds, including focus groups; and questionnaires. Methods routinely used for generating quantitative data include questionnaires and structured interviews. And more might be said of all these. The key factor here is that none of these techniques is physically intrusive, none poses any direct threat to the health or well-being of the subject. So ethical considerations relate primarily to information and its uses, and to a more generalized respect for persons. The following might suggest the sorts of governance needed for a typical research group in a university (or similar institutional setting).

Disciplinary research in the social sciences operates under the ethical guidelines of the relevant academic disciplinary bodies; in particular:

- British Sociological Association (BSA) *Statement of Ethical Practice* – http://www.britsoc.org.uk/about/ethic.htm
- British Psychological Society (BPS) *Code of Conduct, Ethical Principles and Guidelines* – http://www.bps.org.uk/about/rules5.cfm
- Social Research Association (SRA) *Ethical Guidelines* – http://www.the-sra.org.uk/ethics.htm
- American Sociological Association (ASA) *Code of Ethics* – http://www.asanet.org/ethics.htm
- American Psychological Association (APA) *Ethical Principles of Psychologists and Code of Conduct* (2003) – http://www.apa.org/ethics/code2002.html

Such codes make clear that academic researchers recognize the primacy of the rights of research subjects. These subjects will be as fully informed as the situations permit, and their consent will be sought, where possible (or, to the degree possible).

But, as we have recognized, many of the research designs deployed in researching sport are covert or have covert aspects. So *fully* informing subjects, or obtaining their *full* consent, is not possible without compromising the research.[10] Here, researchers must be bound not merely by the codes of the relevant bodies (as earlier), but also by practical guidelines (or 'rules of thumb'), which emphasize constraints on ethically-conducted covert research (of the kind suggested earlier). As we have seen, the central thought here is to accord to one's research subjects any regard one would accord to one's friends, which may be more than we give to other people. Further, such research should not typically require of subjects that they perform actions they would not otherwise perform (excluding, say, the completion of questionnaires or of interviews).

Not withstanding the need to treat each case individually, researchers should recognize the obligation to ensure that any research project in which they are involved has been subjected to appropriate scrutiny in respect of its ethical design and conduct. For routine research designs – that is, research:

- not involving human subjects, or
- conducted overtly or mainly overtly, in line with the sets of guidelines listed earlier, or
- conducted covertly using only actions the subjects would normally perform (plus such overt techniques as questionnaires), and investigated in line with our conception of ethical covert research; *and*
- where the investigative techniques are clearly identified (roughly, by the aforementioned list) as either non-intrusive or only intrusive in an obvious way (as with an interview question on a sensitive topic), such that the subject can decline to answer.

Researchers should determine for themselves appropriate ways of conducting the research ethically, bearing in mind that (for these purposes) they are themselves experienced researchers.

In addition, some committee external to the research group in having members from other research groups (where appropriate), but including some of its members, might be set up, in order to consider any proposals; and such a committee would normally be asked to consider those involving external funding.

For research conducted involving some of the 'typical' purposes, settings, and participants described earlier, ethical approval would normally be given on the assurance of the researcher (although the practice of informal peer-consideration should mean that typical proposals have been seen by a number of such experienced researchers).

In any cases where subjects were asked to go beyond their normal range (except in the ways already noted), or where techniques other than those from the routine catalogue are to be deployed, the research protocol would be forwarded for consideration to the research group's 'external' committee, or some sub-group appointed by it. With research students, and perhaps some others, the permission may be delegated via the supervisory team.

If the difference of this protocol from that considered routine is deemed to be slight, ethical approval can be granted at this stage. If there is some remaining question, or if the protocol clearly goes far beyond the routine, the proposal should be referred to some external body: say, to the University or Faculty Research Ethics and Governance Committee.

Conclusion

The aim here has been to demonstrate that covert research can be ethically constrained, and to suggest both some of the principles which might guide that constraint as well as the governance procedures that might be employed. One theme has been that, for much research, there is little significant difference between the principles of ethical overt research and those of ethical covert research.

10 The researcher is not the research subject

Introduction

How ought a responsible researcher to behave, where doing otherwise means failing, for that reason, to research responsibly? This chapter explores one issue germane for many investigations into sport and leisure; indeed, one arguably central to research into social science. As we shall see, the researcher's commitments extend both to data-collection and to analysis, two contrasting phases of the research process. Further, the need for rigour in analysis of the data combines with that for the dissemination of research conclusions. Moreover, these are moral obligations, in ways the chapter may clarify.

In clarifying the researcher's role, I take for granted that some topics are, perhaps, bound to be the preserve of certain categories of researchers rather than others:[1] for example, that certain topics may require researchers of a certain gender or ethnicity. Much of this idea is familiar: for instance, as an insight (broadly) from feminism. But why exactly is it correct? Much research which is the implicit target of this chapter lacks any such good reasons for this restriction. Or, at the least, does not offer such reasons: instead, researchers simply derive this pattern from a commitment to, say, political correctness, or something similar. So it will be important to understand just why this restriction might arise, since any methodology which deploys or assumes it must do so for a good reason. But a more important part relates to the topic of this discussion: however daft one's reasons are for insisting on, say, the gender or ethnicity of the researcher, they will be compounded if one does not separate the data-collection role (or phase) from the analysis role (or phase).

My strategy in discussing this topic partly involves offering an account of this kind of restriction on researchers, and partly considering its rationale as it is worked-through in an abstractly-characterized case. Here, I focus on one species of explanation of this position, such that its basis resides in the need for an empathetic understanding of the situation of the researched – or, as I shall express it, the need to understand the *stories* of the researched. Of course, there are many kinds of research, even in the social sciences (broadly conceived), to which the considerations raised here will not apply: for example, historical research based exclusively on written sources. But it is important to re-iterate that the feature seized on here is characteristic of much research into sport and leisure: we need to look to cases where it is at least plausible that this person is the appropriate researcher because of such-and-such – where the lacuna represented by that "such-and-such" is filled-in by reference to gender, or ethnicity, or sexuality, or some such. That is, where we circumscribe facts about our researcher. Then we must ask why such a restriction could make sense (in cases where it does, and to the degree that it does). For the rationale for any constraint must, in some way, reflect the research-protocol: that the topic to be researched would be unclear, or less clear, to a person from another category within whatever general heading: ethnicity, sexuality, gender, and so on.

One way this restriction is made out aligns the topic for research with the perspective of one's subject or subjects: the *story* of those participants is the issue. Then one constraint on the research process is that it should begin from an account of the story which reflects the perspective on the relevant events offered by the subjects – that it should be *their* story! But we also grant that, often, that story must be recast for research purposes. Then the researcher's role involves the ability to do just that re-casting. So the researcher must be someone plausibly situated to understand that perspective, so as to re-cast it if that were needed, and (perhaps) to have access to 'collect' those data.

Roles for researcher and researched

What does this account of the relation of researcher to researched imply for the nature of their roles? Clearly, it presupposes (and rightly) a strong contrast between the roles of researcher and of researched, although this is not always understood. That fact is further obscured when the researcher is his own subject: say, in auto-ethnography (compare Collinson and Hockey, 2004), although not only there. For whenever the roles of researcher and of researched – or the different 'hats' for one person – must be sharply distinguished (as urged here), some claims that confuse the two must be rejected, if high quality research is to be conducted. (This is, in effect, a plea to retain the concept 'research subject', in the face of entreaties to turn all such people – for the social sciences – into, say, collaborators or contributors.)

The centre of my thought, then, is that this emphasis on difference of role follows from the proper understanding of the insight from which this discussion began: namely, that one may need a particular situation to make sense of the stories of one's research subjects. For it gives a particular account of one role of the researcher and (therefore) implies another. These would be research designs which involve giving credence – as 'informants' – to the participants in the research: many qualitative research designs do this to some degree, insofar as they recognize those participants as persons who can be asked questions and to whose responses one might profitably listen. Such a case presupposes that one's subjects have relevant knowledge and a certain grasp of the topic or situation: for instance, that they were themselves participants in such-and-such activity which is one's topic (say, the golf-like game *knur and spel*).

So, why does one need to make sense of those stories from the researched, even when one is broadly empathetic towards the researched? Why are these stories not transparent? We begin from the subjects having understanding. But they do not have a complete understanding. Here my point is not the conceptually fundamental one that they cannot know *all* about the topic, since there is no *all*; no finite totality of things to know or understand – although, of course, this is also true (see McFee, 2006b). Rather, if they have a complete understanding, what do you (as researcher) contribute in respect of their 'stories'? Here, although these stories pick-out the subject's version of his/her experience, they may well be presented in a manner the researcher understands as partial: for example, that the research subjects do not fully understand the mechanism of, say, their oppression, even when they recognize themselves as oppressed. Of course, this must be true if theoretical accounts of those (researched) subjects environments are ever revealing: for (*a fortiori*) the subjects do not know those theoretical accounts. Thus the researcher's obligation here is precisely to contribute the analysis – that is what it means to wear the researcher's hat.

Three moments of 'data collection' in oral history

We need a clear picture of such an investigation in a social scientific area. But using actual examples, at least of the mistakes here, will always be contentious: the dispute easily focuses on the example, rather than the point. So the presentation will remain abstract. In practice, then, the model must work something like this – taking, say, oral history as an example. The 'data-collection' aspect of this research can be conceptualized in three moments. First, the researched subject offers his/her story: even here, some sympathy with the subject is fundamental – without it, the researcher is less likely to recognize lies or evasions in the subject's telling; here too familiarity with one's subjects is likely to be advantageous. Once this phase is complete, the researcher then takes the subject's story away and, as a second moment, 'reformulates' it to bring out (say) its underlying causality – to turn its broad view of, for instance, oppression into (say) a more articulated account of the oppression inherent in patriarchy.[2] Now, at this stage, the researcher is, in effect, drawing together and re-drafting the subject's story. It is here that the need for the researcher's empathetic understanding is most obvious: without such understanding (or, at least, sympathy for the situation of the subject) the researcher will fail to capture the subject's story in constructing this revised form.

The third moment of this aspect of the research process must involve taking the revised story back to the subject: can he/she see his/her life in this story, at least once some of it is explained? If not, of course, we simply have an iteration of the process of re-drafting the story to bring out its theoretical underpinnings. Then the newly re-drafted version would be offered to the subject again. So let us assume that, after some explanation, the subject can see his/her life in the re-drafted version of the story: moreover, that he/she now sees this version as a more insightful account of what is happening than the first version. And, as mentioned earlier, the empathy with one's research subjects plays a crucial role here: in understanding the subject's story well enough to be able to re-draft it.

At this point, the subject's story is in an articulated form: and the subject is content that this is indeed his/her story despite some unfamiliar forms of expression. But this will still be expressed largely in the subject's terms. So it will certainly be possible that the manner of this account is still quite a long way from the austere language of the academic article. For example, it may be impossible to capture the subject's story without reference to his/her *patois* – and even to certain misconceptions about the world that the subject entertains (for instance, if the subject were committed to the falsity of the theory of evolution, this might come to be reflected in his/her story). So the condition here is that the story truly reflect the subject's view of the relevant events.

A lot more could be said in exposition of the features of such a story, but readers are asked to draw on examples with which they may be familiar to simply underline that, here, a complex and concrete 'product' is being described in a simplified and abstracted form. So that this is highly specific, particular to this occasion perhaps, and understood in a very sophisticated and theoretically-inclined fashion. In all of this, the subject has had a clear *hand*. Further, this situation would be expanded if the research subject were also the researcher: so that there is only one 'voice' here, as there is in, say, auto-ethnography. Hence this aspect of the research design (in social research) draws extensively on – and reflects – the subject's position.

This phase of the research amounts to getting *clear* the subject's story: and, in such cases, it makes good sense to go back to the subject (where one can) – at least in those cases where, as typically, writing-up the subject's story has involved going beyond the words the subject used. For if the subject can see his/her life in the researcher's re-drafting of it, that should give the researcher confidence that he/she has captured the subject's perspective (to the degree one can). Of course, this is not (yet) the moment of *research*: rather, the end (roughly) of a data-collection phase is reached.

The moment of research

We are now entering the other aspect of the research process, in which the researcher attempts to make sense of the data thereby acquired. This will involve the researcher in having the final decision-making. Indeed, it is this that justifies the researcher in claiming the research (and especially the findings) as his/hers. For this is how he/she is *responsible* for that research – otherwise, putting one's name to such research would simply be theft. It is also this feature that can, in some circumstances, justify the terms "flattery" and "betrayal" – which, recall, Alan Tomlinson (1997) uses in describing some of his own research situations. Of course, there is nothing inherently a betrayal in this process. But it is easy to see how this might come about: hence easy to see why the description is apposite – that the decision as to how the research is treated is (rightly) the researcher's decision, and not the subject's. Thus one can sympathize with those of Alan's subjects in his research into *knur and spel* in the Colne Valley who said, optimistically, "yer different t'others" (Tomlinson, 1997: 261; see also Tomlinson, 1992). But, as he ruefully records, "I wasn't so different: I knew I would evaluate and selectively edit the accounts" (Tomlinson, 1997: 261). Because, of course, that is the researcher's obligation. And this is true even when, as with auto-ethnography, there is only one person here, for there is more than one role. For the essence of the researcher's role is precisely in making these decisions. (On a parallel with the standard experimental design in natural science, we can separate, for analytical purposes, the 'generation of results' phase – in which the subject participates – from the 'discussion of results' phase, the province of the researcher.)

The presentation of conclusions

This responsibility for the researcher has a corollary: that the research conclusions should be presented, as far as is possible, in a manner accessible to other researchers. Of course, there may be a need, in a particular case, to include the researched's own story: and, as we have seen, this should be presented in a way that is both most transparent and most authentic to the subject's experience – consonant with the researcher's need to be as explanatory as possible. And this is underwritten by the empathetic understanding of the subject that is demanded by the possibility of being a researcher into at least *some* areas of social science. For that is the force of the insight from which this chapter began. But, now, when we turn to presenting the conclusions or implications, the primary consideration will be the accessibility of the structure to other researchers. Thus, for instance, if our subject does in fact reject evolution, that rejection should not be given credence: similarly, if he/she takes current misfortunes to be the result of a malign influence from a body with *no* influence here (as theory shows us), or if he/she draws comparisons which have neither clear substance nor explanatory appropriateness, such elements – present in the story, no doubt – must disappear from the analysis. This is the researcher's obligation: if you like, it is the content of the researcher's 'hat'. For the obligation here is no longer to the researched (the subject) but to the research community – to make sense of the material as best as one can, and to present that in as clear and structured a fashion as possible. For, to repeat, that is just a way to distinguish the roles of researched (or data-subject) and researcher or analyst.

Now this distinction is often not one readily employed (or even drawn) within the *text* of, say, a research paper. For, there, the data and its analysis will often be mingled – within what is sometimes called *rich* or *thick* description: which, in context, means *theoretically-informed* description. Here, the impact of the researcher's contribution may be less obvious, but not less important.

A qualification and another obligation

The concession from which we began – that some research, of its nature, can only be performed by researchers deemed appropriate in some way (for instance in terms of their gender or ethnicity) – might seem more powerful than it is. Thus, if it were necessary to be, say, a Victorian woman to do certain research, and also to understand the outcomes or results of that research, the world of Victorian women would be forever unavailable to the rest of us. Since this seems improbable, some other account must be sought. My thought, urged here, is that one may need certain sympathies to research Victorian women successfully. For only then would one be in a position to make sense of the data; say, the diary-writings of some Victorian women. This may well restrict who could conduct such research successfully. So we have here a clear justification for the insight from which the chapter began: in order to write coherently the *story* of such-and-such Victorian women, the researcher must empathize with the key concepts of such a person. But how would one be in a position which was as strong as possible for such empathy? Since one cannot be a Victorian woman, we make do with a position as close to that as practicable. For that is the best chance to locate the truth of her 'story' from her exposition of it.

Recognizing that such sympathy may often be sufficient is clarifying here. Not least, it identifies that one obligation of the researcher is *dissemination*. For, as described, the researcher is in a privileged position with respect to the research topic; and hence especially well-suited to elucidate that matter for the rest of us. So that the very restriction, in turn, obliges the researcher to present the outcomes of that research in a manner as widely available as possible, since this is not research those others could do for themselves. Then, although the audience for this work might turn still out to be small, it should be recognized as an obligation (by the researcher) to make the audience as large as possible: or, if this is different, not to artificially restrict it.

Further, seeing this as an obligation (or set of them) owed to the research community brings out that this obligation is ethical – it concerns what one *ought* to do. Indeed, those who do not acknowledge it thereby fail in their moral duty as researchers, which is an obligation to follow where the research leads (of course, to the best of their abilities) rather than being misled by extra-research commitments – as we would with justice, say, criticize a researcher who shaped his/her data in line with the dictates of the funding body.[3]

Again, the extreme case (and the one where back-sliding is easy) might arise when the researcher *is* the subject. These cases are often difficult to unpick in practice. But, for those of us who grant the possibility of such auto-ethnography, the worry is precisely that one might fail to keep the researcher's role detached from the subject's: for, if this goes wrong, the accusation of self-indulgence will be well-justified – (roughly) the subject's story (and, often, the subject's passions) will be unconstrained by the researcher's intelligence (compare Collinson and Hockey, 2004: 194–95). In the most extreme version of this case, there will be no usual research findings at all: at best, the subject's story – which dominates the work as I have been imagining it – will be used as data for a detached treatment by some other researcher.[4]

Issues of soundness and dissemination: the researcher's role

This point, too, highlights two further features of the researcher's 'hat'; or, better, two features of the final research output for which the researcher must take responsibility. For what goes for auto-ethnography holds more generally. First, the subject's 'flights of fancy' (in explanation) must be controlled in the final discussion.

Of course, it may be revealing that the subject sees his/her situation in terms of that from, for instance, the history of the field (say, sees herself as in the position of some specific figure, such as Sir Thomas More[5] or Martin Luther King, or a figure in some specific position – say, as like the aforementioned Victorian woman): that is, this can be a revealing aspect of the subject's story. But the researcher must decide the degree of credence to give to such claims, before including them in any analysis. And that will mean treating judiciously the subject's claims – or, more bluntly, rejecting some of them. Second, the subject's mode of expression must be written-through to present it to the research community. Again, this will always be done to the degree and in the ways that this is possible. But a consequence of the restricted scope of researchers from which we began – that, typically, only certain researchers could consider certain topics – is that the presentation of research is designed to make that set of research findings open to as wide a range of the 'research interested' as possible; not least because, on this conception, there will be those who – despite their other gifts – could not have done this research themselves.

Here, too, one might think of the virtues of research teams: roughly, you (as my research partner) keep me on the 'straight-and-narrow' of the subject's story. But the very constraints that make you the right person for that role need no longer apply to me – at least, if we are confident of our capacity to work together.

As noted initially, there are many kinds of research – even in the social sciences (broadly conceived) – to which the considerations raised here will not apply: the example offered there was of historical research based exclusively on written sources. We are now able to explain one difference. For such a case lacks *two* features of the case from which I began: first, it does not seem plausible that any particular group of persons, understood in terms of broadly unchangeable features, is better (or worse) placed to make sense of those written sources – only the knowledge of, say, Latin of the requisite period is required; and, second, there is no sense in which the topic is so-and-so's perspective on events, where this is contrasted with what he/she (but typically *he*) would say. For here we have his/her words to go on; and little else.[6] So there can be no question of trying to check that he/she would go along with our developed account of his/her 'story'. And this, in turn, suggests the connection, already mooted, between the need for particular categories of researcher and the requirement for empathy with research subjects. For where the *requirement* for empathy with subjects becomes attenuated, there seems no basis to insist on a researcher from a certain (unchangeable?) category.

Thus the selection of oral history as my example was no idle choice: the requirement that one re-draft the subject's history (or 'story') while retaining its authentic flavour requires of the researcher just the kinds of understanding of the subject's situation from which we began. This suggests that this is indeed a plausible rationale for that restriction on the scope of the researcher's interests (as suggested earlier). Further, it suggests that where no such rationale can be constructed – as it could not be for the historical investigation as I imagined it above – there will be no legitimate theoretical basis for restricting who is suitable as a researcher, but only the practical obligations noted initially. So, although the *arguments* developed here for the obligations on researchers will not always apply, first, when they do, they clarify the role of the researcher; and, second, when the arguments do not apply, we could – on another occasion – look for arguments to similar conclusions in those cases also.

My claim, throughout, is that this is how a responsible researcher *ought* to behave: that to do otherwise is to fail to be a responsible researcher – and to fail for that reason. And we have seen that the researcher's commitments extend (at least arguably) to the dissemination of research conclusions, as well as to rigour in analysis. In recognizing these as moral obligations – or obligations to the research community – we elaborate what is involved in being a (genuine) researcher.

Part V

Conclusion

11 In summary

This work has offered a radical re-thinking of the ethics of research for social scientific research into sport, as part of an equally radical re-thinking of the epistemological stance of such research. Although its thesis is the necessary integration of these issues, for analytical purposes the presentation has abstracted one issue from the other, attempting to divide the topics in ways revealing for (would-be) researchers.

This text urges the distinctive epistemological assumptions of researches into the social scientific aspects of sport, ignored at researchers' peril. Given the 'question-and-answer' (that is, *erotetic*) relation between research questions and research methods in sport, 'qualitative research' into sport is best recognized as research dealing with persons *viewed as persons*. But such interpersonal conceptions automatically import an ethical dimension; and much of this research must involve a degree of covertness. How can such research designs be accommodated, given the scientism prevalent in sports studies?

As an epistemological argument, the presentation is largely given abstractly. One part of that argument lies in recognizing just how pervasive such scientism is: even an explicit rejection of scientism (fuelled by postmodernism, perhaps) can still take its bearings from a scientistic account of *truth* – that is what is being denied! Further, such denial can seem to be a rejection of the concept of truth. But the search for truth is fundamental to any research worth the name. So a second element of the argument articulates a conception of *human truth*. Such a conception can be given a philosophical underpinning by a particularist contextualism, merely sketched in the text.

A third consideration lays out the distinctiveness of this account of truth, highlighting its appropriateness to social research, given its congruence with the picture of research into persons from which the book began. In doing so, it lays the groundwork for a defence of an ethically-constrained covert research; and sketches some guidelines for the ethics of covert research.

More specifically, this book argues for a number of specific theses. These include:

- its defence of a conception of truth (and knowledge) in social research, against both its postmodernist detractors and the advocates of a scientistic conception of truth and knowledge.

- its demonstration that social research into sport (and into sporting topics) must recognize its erotetic character – that its methods are inflected by the questions they are suitable to address: that is, they originate as answers to these questions.
- that, as a result, combination of methods is only possible when the methods are clearly answers to the same question; or address the same issue. And this will rarely be so.
- its principled rejection of the taking of voluntary informed consent (VIC) as a 'gold standard' for ethical research with human subjects; that view of informed consent assumes (falsely) that there is a finite totality of considerations to address, so that (in principle if not in practice) one could address them *all*. Removing this assumption undermines the claims of VIC to be a gold standard here.
- its defence of the potential for ethically-conducted covert research designs, a prerequisite for genuinely naturalistic research into sport.
- its consideration of the researcher's obligations to the research community of which he/she is a part; thereby distinguishing the researcher's role as analyst from his/her role as data-collector.

This text is silent on many key topics: in particular, it does not say how to investigate in line with its principles. But it has offered (and defended) rules of thumb here, for use in evaluating such methods: that one's subjects be treated as persons; that their answers (their *talk*) be treated as the *talk* of such persons; and seen in relation both to the erotetic structure of the research question and the context within which that question arises.

Appendix

Considerations of exceptionlessness in philosophy: or, everything goes with beer

Preamble

On one conception, philosophy is concerned with conceptual connections (all right so far!) which are *exceptionless*, so that:

- one can refute supposed or claimed conceptual connections by noting counter-examples (and hence raising exceptions);
- the preferred conceptual connection is entailment – which is exceptionless;
- we can recognize definitions as logical equivalences; as concise yet comprehensive accounts of such-and-such (having an 'exact fit': McFee, 1992a: 16–17; McFee, 2003). And this is another way to identify them as exceptionless.

This view of definitions explains why a (supposed) definition should be rejected if it *allowed in* cases that were not of the idea defined or if it *excluded* cases that were.

But some *conceptual connections* in philosophy, although real enough, are not exceptionless. Thus Austin (1962: 144) asks us: ". . . whether it is true that all snow geese migrate to Labrador, given that perhaps one maimed one sometimes fails when migrating to get quite the whole way ". For it seems true both that snow geese migrate to Labrador and that this claim is not exceptionless. If conceptual connections of the kind explored by philosophy are not always exceptionless, then the model of definition just noted cannot be the dominant force in philosophy it sometimes seems. Similarly, since less weight can then be given to counter-examples, less weight also accrues to those thought-experiments refuted by the finding of an exception. Such considerations problematize the place of exceptionlessness in philosophy.

Part One: Introduction

On some occasions, "all" and "every", and similar terms, are not used exceptionlessly: hence analyzing their use as (always) exceptionless may mislead. In my non-professional moments, I am happy to assert:

a   Everyone likes Chinese food;
b   Everything goes with beer.

I have had occasion to assert each of these, in contexts where, if pressed, I would claim the *truth* of what I said. (With regard to the second, I especially recommend chocolate with beer.) Later in this discussion, I will return to contexts for using these claims. In those contexts, saying that these claims were *true* amounts to recognizing that anyone wanting to dispute them – probably just a friend who studied philosophy – should (rightly) be dismissed as a pedant, with no place at our celebration.

But whenever I feel privately happy with such claims, the demon of philosophy appears on my shoulder, asking me (first) whether it is really true that every single person likes Chinese food. Surely someone, somewhere, does not. And, even were this is not currently true in practice, surely it must be true *in principle*: even were my claim *presently* true of the world's population, it seems logically possible that someone *not* liking Chinese food might be born tomorrow. So the demon's thought is that this claim about the pervasive attraction of Chinese food cannot be true because it admits of counter-examples. Hence, it is either false as it stands or (since it might be or become false) not the sort of claim one should accept without qualification.

Equally, for my second case, the scope of the *everything* must be restricted: roughly, to foods and drinks.[1] Then what does and does not count as *beer* for these purposes must be determined (factoring in, for example, the claim by Canadian friends that American beer is the result of filtering Canadian beer . . . through a horse). Even with such points accommodated, there are foodstuffs which – at least in the minds, or on the palates, of some judges – do not go with beer. Our concern here, in either case, is not with these as matters of taste, or discernment, or discrimination. Putting such considerations aside again leaves potential counter-examples: hence, the thought that my claim is not exceptionless. Again, this is urged in principle, if not in practice.

All this concerns the demon, of course, just because (from his perspective) philosophy does – or anyway should – concern itself with the *exceptionless*, since exceptionlessness is one mark of (conceptual) necessities.

At this point, the demon reminds me that students in my predicate-logic class treat a statement such as "Everyone likes Chinese food" as urging that all persons like Chinese food (since this is one way to produce a categorical version).[2] And would in turn treat *that* claim using the universal quantifier: "For *all* X . . .".[3] So their account of the claim would cast doubt on its truth – at least in principle – since that account takes (or stresses) *exceptionlessness* as a feature. Moreover, such students (it might seem) typify one powerful inclination within the project of philosophy.

My debate with the demon comes to this: in making my claims, did I *really* say or assert what he is keen to deny? Or, even if I did not, *should* I have done so, if I were only more thoughtful, more consistent, and so on. In part, this debate concerns how to translate English into quantifier-speak, but I shall not pursue that point. Yet it also concerns when to raise objections, and what sort of objections, to general claims: ultimately, a debate about the scope or purpose of claims made in philosophy.

Part Two: Ziff's cheetahs

It has long seemed to me that the answer to the demon's queries is that I did not claim, say, or assert what he is denying, where the reasons for this might be philosophically revealing, in addressing the place of exceptionlessness in the project of philosophy. Philosophy has for some time recognized questions here concerning the exceptionlessness of claims beginning "all" or "every". As Austin (1962: 143) reminded us, first, faced with the claim that "all snow geese migrate to Labrador", we remain unfazed ". . . that perhaps one maimed one fails when migrating to get quite the whole way". Equally, we understand the person who – defending the claim that all swans are white – asserts that he was not talking about swans in Australia. For clearly there was no intention to discuss swans *everywhere*: he would, with justice, respond that his claim was not "about possible swans on Mars" (see Austin, 1962: 143). But comments such as Austin's have not been widely explored. First, the primary feature of statements (of which the claims just mentioned are clear examples) is still the capacity to be either true or false. Second, much philosophy continues as though the units of truth and falsity here, the statements, were really just sentences; that is, just linguistic units. Disputing the first of these (at least conceived detached from contextual standards of truth and falsity) will do something to unsettle the second.

So, first, I rehearse some of the discussion, from Paul Ziff (1972),[4] of the assertion that *a cheetah can outrun a man*. This, I take it, is something we would all be prepared to assert, at least in our pre-reflective moments. Of course, in not using the words "all", "every", and so on, this claim does not obviously intersect with issues of exceptionlessness. But it has a kind of generality – for instance, it is not just about Herbert, our pet cheetah. Ziff's point is that this claim is not equivalent to "any cheetah (or every single cheetah) can outrun any man", even though it is sometimes treated that way. So it has generality without universality, a thought to elaborate.

In discussing his claim, Ziff makes six crucial points, here merely stated (since later discussion both elucidates and justifies them):

- the claim itself is ". . . as standard as can be" (1972: 128);
- we grant that the claim can be used to say something true;[5]
- we are not *excluding* very fast human runners (Olympic champions, say), cheetahs with broken legs, cheetahs wearing leg-weights (what Ziff [1972: 128] calls "an encumbered cheetah"), or even the slow horned cheetah (1972: 139);
- we are also not *failing to consider* such cases, as though they might have slipped our mind;
- our remarks are not equivalent to asserting that, if we put a man and a cheetah on a racetrack, the cheetah *will* outrun the man – for a cheetah turned loose might just sit "lazily in the sun" (1972: 128). As Ziff (1972: 128) puts it, ". . . 'can' is not 'will'";
- what we *said* cannot be translated (without change) into some other form of words: especially not in terms of merely "some", and so on. My point here

(with Ziff) is partly that we need a way to say what we *did in fact* say, in saying that. Of course, this discussion is not about words as such, but about the contrasts those words are (sometimes) used to draw. So this point amounts to claiming that something importantly distinctive is being said. Then, looking for an analysis, or some such, means finding something equivalent.

This last insight, fundamental here, really needs careful consideration. But a few (haphazard) examples make the point. Thus, the claim was not that *some* cheetahs can outrun men – then we could ask *which*; and we have no more specified *that* (nor intended to, nor needed to) than we have filled-out to which cheetahs (or men) our original claim referred. So anything in that direction makes what was said *specific* in ways it presently was not. Thus it cannot be equivalent to what was said initially; and, for that reason, must be rejected

Our original claim did not imply some exceptionless connection or relation. That point is quite general. For instance, Ziff (1972: 132) considers the claim: "A tiger is a large carnivore". This too is a standard sort of claim taken as true. But Ziff correctly urges that it is not *exceptionless* – especially given the powers appropriated to itself by philosophy. First, a newborn tiger is a tiger all right, though not a large carnivore (1972: 129). Granting that case gives 'open season' for thought-experiments: we can consider (say) "an adult tiger . . . shrunk to the size of a newborn tiger" (1972: 132), and so on. Faced with such a case, one might – in the spirit of disambiguation (see later: Part Three) – assert, "A normal unshrunken adult tiger is a large carnivore". But did we really mean that initially? Clearly not, for thoughts of, for instance, *shrinking* (or *not* shrinking) had not crossed my mind.

What goes for tigers as large carnivores goes for cheetahs outrunning men: we must rule out not only encumbered cheetahs but (Ziff's list): ". . . foot-bound [since birth] unencumbered cheetahs . . . three-legged cheetahs, cheetahs being forced to run after being force fed and so on and on" (Ziff, 1972: 129). The "so on and on" is revealing in two ways. First, it highlights, quite correctly, that there is no finite totality of such (imaginable?) cases to consider: that "so on and on" could never be turned into a complete list of them. Any list drawn up will (in principle) admit of yet more cases. Second, it recognizes that there is no single *principle* for generating such cases. So all (apparent) counter-examples cannot be dealt with in a uniform way: for instance, by specifying that our cheetah is not encumbered. For that still admits of plenty of ways of identifying a particular cheetah not fitting our (general) bill – say, the three-legged cheetah, still (after all) a cheetah!

Suppose we arrive at some cheetah-ly equivalent of the general formula, "a tiger is a large carnivore", true in the ways that this assertion is true. (Here our best example to date was a highly qualified claim about unshrunken adult tigers.) Then, in this new claim (whatever it was), we have said of cheetahs what we *originally* claimed, in saying they could outrun men. Anyone happy with *this* transformation accepts that this new version was what was *really* meant all along.

That seems at least one bridge too far. For, typically, some highly qualified version (say, speaking of "some cheetahs", for instance) does *not* bring out what was meant all along. To elaborate this idea, Ziff (1972: 129) comments:

It is true that some – never mind which – cheetahs can outrun a man. But it is also true that some – never mind which – men can outrun a cheetah (namely those able ones racing against disabled cheetahs). And it is also true that some – never mind which – cheetahs cannot outrun a man and some – never mind which – men cannot outrun a cheetah. So[,] so far[,] men and cheetahs would seem to be on a par with respect to running. But they are not: a cheetah can outrun a man. [my commas]

This last assertion is what we wanted to say all along. Since it does not amount to either or both of the others, we have not yet arrived at what we do want to say. Yet both claims rightly put aside by Ziff in that passage aim at exceptionlessness. And our 'summary' here more or less reiterates our original assertion. But what did that assertion amount to? How does it relate to the powers and capacities of extant cheetahs?

Suppose that, as a result of disease, only a few weak cheetahs were left in the world. All (or anyway most) men could outrun these poor specimens. Does that necessarily mean that, now, cheetahs *cannot* outrun men? No, it does not. To clarify that point, Ziff (1972: 129) considers the assertion: "Cheetahs don't have horns". Again, we would be willing to assert this; and doing so seems right. But what should then be made of a cheetah with grafted horns, say (Ziff, 1972: 128)? Or even a result of genetic engineering? Certainly, these are not typical cheetahs. Perhaps that thought can move us forward.

In this context, I am reminded of a kind of joke: asked, on average, how many arms a human being has, you might be inclined to answer, "two". And certainly Jo and Jane Normal, average human beings, have two each. But perhaps you are wrong (ha! ha!). For if we look, instead, to the *average* in the sense of the statistical mean ... well, I imagine that few (perhaps no) human beings have three arms, but there are definitely a large number with fewer than two arms – as a result of injury and such like. So, for humans, the *statistical mean* for arms will certainly be less than two.

This, of course, highlights something about our target in claiming that a cheetah can outrun a man: we were looking for a kind of *average* man and a kind of *average* cheetah – but not in the statistical sense of the term "average". (This might even be, on a parallel with dog shows, the 'breed standard' for cheetahs, or whatever.)

For it is typical cheetahs in typical conditions – don't want anything too hilly, perhaps – that can outrun typical men. In addition to its *not* being what was said initially, such a claim seems rendered true *by definition*: that all these *typicallys* guarantee it. My original claim might have been false: at the least, it seems contingent. (After all, that I commented on Chinese food and not, say, on Indian food was supposed to reflect differentially 'how the world is'.)

Explaining that thought a bit may help. For our concerns here might vary. In teaching a biology class, and wanting to show our students a cheetah, which of the powers, capacities, features, properties, and so on, of *cheetahs* – instantiated in some cheetah or other, including the drugged and encumbered ones – will we select? Our purposes certainly do not require *all* of the properties of extant cheetahs, both because, for many of these properties, lacking them would not mean that the animal was *not really* a cheetah and because some will conflict with others (say, height or age) without this being problematic – our chosen cheetah will not exemplify these features to our class. To answer this concern, some but not all of the characteristics of extant cheetahs are required. But the cheetah chosen will, of course, instantiate some characteristics not, in this way, required of it as a sample. It will, for instance, be of a certain age. (We only rule out very young and very old – for a cheetah!) And the context creates the requirements. Thus, for these classes, an unencumbered, four-legged, two-eyed, unhorned cheetah is certainly required – that one will (if it wants to) outrun the kind of man needed when exemplifying *homo sapiens* to these same students.

Complications arise, though, when something *other* is wanted of our cheetah: for instance, a guard-cheetah to keep our property safe. Now fierceness, or perhaps the appearance of it, might be prized over some of the aforementioned features. Our cheetah isn't required to run-down any burglars, just to scare them away. We might, therefore, not care if this cheetah could outrun the man mentioned previously. Indeed, we might be happy to find it staying put, guarding us. Again, a fierce but one-eyed cheetah, although pretty useless in our biology class, would be perfectly 'adapted' to the tasks now set for it (see McFee, 1992a: 108–9). Is it a cheetah? Certainly! But does it have all the properties of the abstraction from cheetah-hood, the 'breed standard' for cheetahs? No – in particular, this cheetah would not, and could not, outrun the 'breed standard' for *homo sapiens*. But who ever said it would or should? I certainly did not, although – as mentioned earlier – I agree that a cheetah can outrun a man.

First, this conception of a *breed standard* is therefore a normative one, highlighting some features *good* of cheetahs (or whatever) in some contexts. Second, we cannot give it genuine descriptive substance while insisting on exceptionlessness. Third, our picture of generality here cannot be expanded by expanding the *breed standard* either in length or into a disjunctive form (say) – there is no finite totality of such properties, such that noting them would say *all* we could say about (in this example) cheetahs: there is no *all* here.

I draw four morals from this consideration of ideas developed from Ziff's chapter:[6]

1   The claim made (about the cheetah) is not equivalent to the disambiguated versions, those using "some", and so on – to say more about that, I turn (in the next section: Part Three) to more general comments on disambiguation strategies.

2   It is revealing here that no finite totality of properties circumscribes either the exceptions to our original general claims (that everyone likes Chinese food; that everything goes with beer) or the 'class' of cheetahs.

3   Something revealing in this case applies to many occasions either when the terms "all" or "every" are used or when the use of such terms might be thought (say, by die-hard logicians) to be implied. And, again, I will comment on this later (Part Four).

4   Our conclusions here extend beyond these few cases: as Ziff (1972: 129) puts it, "[t]hese cheetah cases are not curious[,] special or rare".

Part Three: Defeating disambiguation – some morals from Travis

One response here might *seem* (it seemed to Ziff, 1972: 131) the route of disambiguation: making explicit further specifications which – it might be claimed – were implicit in what was said. In some cases, this is just what is required: say, a question about the temperature of your Indian food becomes confused with a similar-sounding (because orthographically indistinguishable) comment about its degree of spiciness – "Is that vindaloo hot?" Moreover, this kind of implicit disambiguation seems to apply to, say, the assertion "I want to buy some alligator shoes" (see Ziff, 1972: 63).

For only occasionally do we need to add, "Yes, *of course* for my alligator". But these are cases of a clear and recognizable *ambiguity* (at least once it is pointed out). Disambiguation in such cases may do all that is required, giving the illusion that such a disambiguation strategy *always* works: that is, in every case, that disambiguation clarifies what was *really* said or meant.

This strategy might *seem* suitable to deal with our cases concerning the general attractiveness of Chinese food or the compatibility of beer. It might seem that – once exceptions are recognized – *disambiguation* makes these claims exceptionless, on this new understanding. This strategy works in cases where, say, "all" or "every" can be replaced with "some". Not *all* swans are white, but *some* (and perhaps *most*) are.

To give us cause for suspicion of the general force of such disambiguation strategies, Ziff showed that, faced with (apparent) exceptions to the claim about a cheetah outrunning a man, disambiguating the original assertion did not readily preserve our sense of it as *true* or appropriate. But our response to the thesis about disambiguation should be careful. If the issue is whether, *in a particular case*, generating a particular puzzlement, we can always (or, at least, generally) resolve the perplexity through disambiguation, I would agree – that is much of the usefulness within philosophy of the drawing of distinctions.

But often more is required: a disambiguation such that no perplexity whatever can remain. Can we deal with *all* perplexity in this way, globally rather than case-by-case? This I deny, with my reasoning reflecting, in two different (though related) ways, the fact that no finite totality of candidate counter-cases exists here. The more direct response points out that disambiguations between notions or 'senses' deal only with *this* case (the case before us), since the manner of drawing the distinctions *here* is set by this context: that is, by this puzzlement or perplexity. There can be no guarantee that it could (or would) deal with other cases. And new cases, unconsidered cases, can always arise. So, as Travis (1997: 119) notes, this "... is a dead end", because our newly-drawn contrast must now be confronted with "... novel cases, which it may count as describing correctly or not" (1997: 119).[7]

This introduces Travis's view of the occasion-sensitivity of what is said: that the same string of words might, on a different occasion, amount to something different

– indeed, might even have a different truth value. Thus, consider the contribution of colour-shades, stains, holes, fading and such like that would permit correctly asserting, on one occasion, that a particular curtain was red, but where, on another occasion, that same combination would make it *false* that the curtain was red, given who now was asking, or the interest in redness on that occasion. So these different occasions set different constraints on the redness of the curtains. As Austin (1970: 130) noted:

> The statements fit the facts always more or less loosely, in different ways on different occasions for different intents and purposes. What may score full marks in a general knowledge test may in other circumstances get a gamma. And even the most adroit of languages may fail to 'work' in an abnormal situation.

The thought of some exceptionless account of the relation of statements to facts here seems unsustainable.

The other response (taken more directly from Travis) focuses closely on how the disambiguation strategy seems to exploit a natural or obvious way to distinguish cases. But is this really always so? Recognizing that what was previously called "gold" (and taken for one substance) was actually two substances – with different chemical composition, atomic number, and so on – what should be done? Which of them should continue to be called "gold", which should be called something else; for instance, "fools' gold"? As Dummett (1978: 428–29) noted: "What is clear, at any rate, is that the word 'gold' did not, in advance of the introduction of a theory and technique of chemical analysis, have a meaning which determined the course to be followed". For that decision suggests that the term "gold" always *really* meant the element with such-and-such atomic number, rather than the compound. Indeed, we might continue calling them both "gold" (as though it were some larger covering concept), and then distinguish *within* that category: say, between assay gold and fools' gold. But *must* one of these be what was meant all along? The disambiguation strategy assumes that there were two different ideas, each clear, distinct and non-occasion-sensitive, which need to be distinguished from each other. That is not our view.

Moreover, it seems implausible that semantics alone will distinguish, for all cases, one option (and not the other) as *true*. Consider a different example (Travis, 2008: 112): "the leaves are green", said of painted leaves – now, is this just plain true or plain false? Part of the difficulty is that we cannot decide *which*, since it seems natural to say one on a particular occasion and the other on another occasion. But if we cannot decide which is (obviously) right, then neither can be *obviously* right.[8]

At first blush, disambiguation seems to offer a promising way forward: we could talk of, say, "painted-green leaves" – although this too might not be unproblematic; for instance, some (otherwise) green leaves might be painted green (which would then be, as it were, double-green).

To consider the adequacy of the disambiguation option, consider one of the (apparently) disambiguated pair: if we can generate occasion-sensitivity in respect of it, then the disambiguation strategy looks unhelpful. So our argumentative tactic is, for each of the different so-called *senses* of "green", to find it still amenable to occasion sensitivity. Of course, one cannot *prove* that such still-contentious cases can always be found; but it looks promising. As Travis (1985: 200)[9] urges, "[d]istinctions in the same and other veins can be proliferated indefinitely … as ambiguities in expressions of a language cannot". Hence occasion-sensitivity should be distinguished from (mere) ambiguity.

First, even if disambiguation sorts out this case, one cannot be sure that it sorts out *all* such cases. For any level of 'grid', a yet finer mesh might be needed to avoid, once and for all, unclarity or ambiguity. And, if this is so, the idea of an ultimately fine mesh is needed – but we have no basis for such a conception.

Second, if disambiguation works for *these* purposes or in *this* context, it deals (completely) with the issue in *this* context, for our puzzle is the one *now*, the one in this context. As a result, the puzzle depends on the context. Then both the puzzle and the relevant disambiguation are occasion-sensitive: "If you call a leaf green, the leaf must count as green for what you said to be true. But *when* must it so count? There is more than one thing to be said in calling a leaf green" (Travis, 2008: 278; emphasis original). As Travis notes, there are a wide variety of cases here, including the term "green" used to mean inexperienced ("But that is a different kind of green!"). Still, even sticking to some version of (roughly – but much turns on how rough) green-coloured and leaves, there are green leaves painted green as well as brown leaves painted green; also leaves dyed; and naturally occurring green leaves. In this last camp, there are those uncontentiously green, and those contentiously green ("Isn't this one a little yellow?"; "Hasn't that one started to turn red?"). And many more. For some purposes, what I happily (and rightly) call "a green leaf" will not count for you – neither my painted leaf nor my yellowing (but still green) leaf works as an example for your biology class. And you have no truck at all with my jade leaves!

A case both simpler and nearer to that desired by the advocates of the disambiguation strategy helps consolidate our response. In some cases, a hearer may not know how to take an utterance which is in fact clear once the context is taken into account – it might have misled *me*, but it is not *misleading*. Suppose I am assistant to both a marine biologist and a cook (McFee, 1992a: 121; Travis, 2008: 189–90; Austin, 1962: 65–66); both are interested in red fish – the cook in a surface swimming red fish, the biologist in a deep swimming one. Now the instruction, "Bring me a red fish", is clear once I know which of my masters uttered it. Although I might end up confused (I don't know who said it), it is not *confusing*: I might be unable to fulfill the task but – in this case – what I am being asked is perfectly clear, in the sense of prescribing one behaviour as a satisfactory response. The differential interests of biologist and cook yield different interests (or different questions, or different issues) even though both result, for me, in the request, "Bring me a red fish". But particularizing the matter offers this clarity: once I know who said it, then whatever follows will follow. So, in each 'world', there is really no ambiguity. There is, in general, no prior way of guaranteeing in which of these worlds we find ourselves; still (in practice), participants in that world need not be perplexed.

One cannot simply dismiss the issues raised as merely pragmatic (rather than semantic)[10] nor treat them as amenable to solution through disambiguation – which may have been a first thought faced with the red fish case: that just referring to "surface-swimming red fish" would make the occasion-sensitivity disappear. So that what I hear would determine which fish to bring without needing to explore the occasion or the speaking. As we have seen, this answer is inadequate for a number of reasons:

a   What is said was *always* clear in these cases; once we know what occasion this is, or what 'world' we are in, the order or claim becomes clear (and clearly either satisfied in such-and-such way or truth/false [respectively]). So there is really no *ambiguity* to be remedied.

b   There is no natural or obvious way to distinguish cases. In my red fish story, in trying to simplify, I indicated how the expressions might be taken. But, in general, we lack a sense of the precise number of possibilities here – for this reason, my artificial cases (with, seemingly, only two outcomes possible) aids recognition of occasion-sensitivity while clouding our understanding of it.

c   Were there really just two options here, we should be able to say which is the correct one on a particular occasion, which is wrong. As Travis (2008: 112) notes, ". . . one must choose in a principled way. What the words mean must make one or other disjunct plainly, or at least demonstrably, true". And there seems little hope of this.

d   If we take some term in English to be *ambiguous* (and therefore amenable to disambiguation), ". . . there must be a way of saying just what these ambiguities are: so a fact as to how many ways ambiguous they are" (Travis, 2008: 112). And, again, there seems no hope of finding some fixed number here.

e   Further, the new terms, now suitably disambiguated, are still amenable to occasion-sensitivity – as when the cook would ask for a surface-swimming, red-skinned fish if he were making fish tacos and a surface swimming, red-fleshed fish if he were making fish stew. Having disambiguated the expression "red fish" once still leaves two occasions, with different satisfaction-conditions, where I bring *red fish*; and on which the word "red" means *red*, "fish" means *fish*, and so on. The artificiality of the case should not disguise its power. For we cannot in general predict how certain expressions might be used (that is what Chomsky calls "creativity" [Lyons, 1970: 86]: that particular terms can be understood in indefinitely many sentences, most of which we have not previously encountered). Moreover, we cannot predict which of the many understandings of a particular situation is the appropriate one for a particular occasion – although (consonant with earlier points) that we would typically understand it when we encountered it!

As this line of reply emphasizes, the notion of an 'ideal language' that could deal with all cases (including the new ones) is a fiction, because there is no finite totality of conditions to be met in describing a particular scene; and, relatedly, that even if a particular issue could be accommodated by, say, modifying what was urged (so that it covered exclusively *some* of the cases originally envisaged: for instance, by specifying which kind of red fish), the problem simply recurs – the point is that there is no basic level of description or explanation here (see McFee, 2000: 130–31). We cannot simply disambiguate [see (c) earlier] down – or up – to that level: there will always be a sense of, say, the term "green" which escapes such disambiguation:

> To grasp a thought is to grasp what it would be for things to be in a certain way – that way things are according to it. To grasp that by grasping what being green is, one must grasp the appropriate way of counting as green or not; a particular way in which facts about [say] the leaf may count for or against its being as it is according to that thought.
>
> (Travis, 2008: 284)

This conception of meaning and understanding would be radically revisionary of many of the questions or issues or assumptions of much philosophy of language (at least, in the Anglo-American analytic tradition).

Part Four: "All", "every", and contexts

The argument of the previous part extends the considerations from Ziff (Part Two), by showing us flaws in the general disambiguation strategy as clarifying what was said: say, in claiming that a cheetah can outrun a man.

What has all this discussion demonstrated in respect of the implication of *all* or *every* shown to be misplaced by the cheetah example? In particular, what, on that basis, can be said about apparent counter-cases to the claim that everyone likes Chinese food or that everything goes with beer? Ziff (1972: 136) notes: "Speaking of a cheetah, as one does when one says 'A cheetah can outrun a man', is like modelling a cheetah in clay or like doing a pictorial representation of a cheetah". Certain things which must be true of any particular cheetah (either it is or is not one metre high at the shoulder, say) need not be determinate for the cheetah in "A cheetah can outrun a man" – they amount (in terminology from Ziff [1972: 136]) to *conceptions* of a cheetah. Our counter-cases make determinate some or other feature of this conception, a feature that *will* be determinate for any extant cheetah. This allows us to recognize that claims about such conceptions are not exceptionless, where "exceptionless" means that there can be no counter-cases to them. But such claims should be read differently. For (recall) there is no finite totality of properties here, either as part of this conception or applicable to extant cheetahs. Hence the conception cannot cover *all* cases. As Ziff (1972: 139) notes: "No picture captures everything: even the best picture of a cat won't purr". Also, there is no *all* or *every* here: there are features which, given the interest taken or the question asked (or answered), are important or central – and other features are important or central on other occasions, in respect of the raising of other issues. (This is just occasion-sensitivity: see Part Three.)

The scope of the "all" or "every" is then understood via a consideration of the context in which the assertion, or question, is raised. On some occasions "Everyone does such-and-such" will mean "Every single person, without exception, does such-and-such",[11] but there will be other contexts too.

In what contexts of their utterance might my candidate claims about Chinese food or about beer be appropriately thought *true*? How exceptionless do these contexts require them to be? It might have seemed – since this idea was introduced (from Ziff) in Part Two – that some sleight-of-hand was implicit in my repeated assertion that, properly understood, these claims of mine were *true*.[12] I will discharge that obligation here by offering a brief sketch of at least one context for each of them, presented through dialogue, while granting that a large number might be constructed, in all directions.

a   "Let us buy Chinese food for this motley crew of visitors – we do not know much about their specific requirements or tastes; but everyone likes Chinese food."

b   "No, it is not essential to open a bottle of (expensive) wine to go with this food, especially as – if you do so – you will need a bottle of a different wine with the next course (if you are consistent). Beer is OK, honestly – everything goes with beer." [And, in imagining the beer in front of us, this is a context where the content of the term "beer" is clear!]

As my earlier characterization recognized, the claim that a cheetah can outrun a man has *generality* without universality. This also fits exactly what to say, in the contexts in which they are plausible (better *true*) of my two claims:

a   Everyone likes Chinese food.
b   Everything goes with beer.

It would be misplaced to offer, in criticism of me, the claim that *everyone* just means "every single person", that *everything* just means "every single foodstuff", suggesting that I revise my comments accordingly (or read them that way). For what I meant is certainly not equivalent to these revised claims – as the possibility of counter-cases to these claims (but not to mine) illustrates. If it is urged, instead, that my claim too is susceptible of counter-cases, that amounts to revising the terms of our example. For commonsense took my original claims to be *true*.

In justification of such 'commonsense' (were justification thought necessary), we might even *explain* why these are just the things to say in this context. For instance, I want to be as inclusive as possible for those to whom I am giving this food: they are not just my Friday philosophy class, nor my friends from next door, but a wider (and unspecified) group. And yet others may arrive. Moreover, if they do, my claim is that they will be happy with my selection. The practice of ordering Chinese food in such contexts is, I am asserting, a sound one – for everyone likes Chinese food. So there will be no dissenters;[13] there will be some food for the vegetarians, and so on. Since no particular group is identified (such that I could say,

"All my Friday philosophy class like Chinese food"), my *thought* here must be something general and expansive. The issue of its exceptionlessness does not arise in this context. (Who would raise it but a philosopher-manqué – and my people know better than literalism!) Were the issue of exceptionlessness to arise, I could console myself by pointing out that my expansive, general *everyone* does not, after all, invoke a finite totality. So it is not as though – had I wished to ascertain the truth of my claim about Chinese food – I should (or could) explore *all* the people who could (in principle) show up for dinner, to see where they stand *vis-à-vis* Chinese food: for their likes or dislikes are beside the point – I need only consider those who might plausibly show up. (To put it formally, a *principle of total evidence* is at work here.)[14] So I cannot be criticized for, as it were, *failing* to consider some group of only *logically possible* dinner guests.

Second, our comments here had a point: we were not merely 'flapping our gums'. Hence we need some way to assert what I said, in claiming:

a Everyone likes Chinese food.
b Everything goes with beer.

And many candidate assertions – including one with the term "some", or one that *is* shown false by counter-cases (as mine is not) – are not equivalent to that from which I began. So one cannot simply reject (as somehow ill-formed) my original assertions. That is one aspect of Ziff's recognition that such claims are ". . . as standard as can be" (Ziff, 1972: 128): they do not turn on complexities of grammar or syntax, for example.

Moreover, we do have a reason to say what was said. And can imagine it being challenged: "Well, in this vegetarian enclave, that is not true – since all the Chinese food you can buy near here contains meat".[15] In context, this challenge would make me withdraw my claim *here*. Yet it would not preclude my making a claim in the same words on another occasion (as long as I was in a different place!). Nor would it incline me to add, as a parenthetical remark, "Except for such-and-such". For that gives my assertion false specificity: there are, no doubt, other such enclaves of which I am unaware (so the specification to just *this one* is misplaced). Again, my claim in the new place does not bear on the old enclave, one way or another – its members are too far away to get here for dinner. So I am neither *including* the case of that enclave nor *failing to mention* it: it is not relevant to the generality towards whom my new assertion is directed. Thus I am justified in sticking to my assertion (on the new occasion) even when I have encountered what *others* might take as a counter-case.

In this way, the force of my claim about Chinese food is clear: it is general but not universal or exceptionless. And, in context, it is true. Or, at least, that would be the best way to characterize it, if pressed.

Then, even if the expression is used (slightly aggressively?) to suggest that a dissenter is, somehow, weird – because everyone likes Chinese food – the thought still preserves a kind of generality: it does not deny the existence of the dissenter, who is (after all) right there in front of the person making the assertion. So one way not to be 'weird' would involve accordance with the 'breed standard' in liking Chinese food.

At this point, we can return to the thought of my claims as *contingent* (see Part Two). For what is really happening? In Ziff's case, some features are extracted from extant cheetahs in claiming that a cheetah can outrun a man. Since we begin from the extant cheetahs, we will not (say) include the possession of horns – although, of course, cheetahs might have been different. In that context, this matter is empirical: this process is a kind of generalization across cheetahs. Then, we are in the hands of the changes in our world – as it changes, we revise what to say about it. As Austin (1962: 76–77) remarked about talking cats:

> Suppose that one day a creature of the kind we now call a cat takes to talking. Well, we say to begin with, I suppose, 'This cat can talk.' But then other cats, not all, take to talking as well; we now have to say that some cats talk, we distinguish between talking and non-talking cats.

Our comments assume (or build in) a certain stability to the powers and capacities of the cheetah population, real or imagined (or future). In this sense, my claim (like Ziff's) must be revised were these generalizations no longer broadly true: that is, if cheetahs could not, in general, outrun men or if people did not show a marked preference for Chinese food.

However, the assertion itself (in either case) is not such a generalization: as I put it earlier (Part Two), Ziff's remark pertains to 'breed standard' cheetahs and 'breed standard' men. That is a way of saying that the claim is not, after all, straightforwardly empirical, if that means that it must be susceptible to counter-cases (or, better, it is a reason to reject that conception of the *empirical*: compare Travis, 2004).

Further, as Austin goes on to illustrate, the contours of concepts here too can be responsive to the values or priorities of people:

> . . . we may, if talking becomes prevalent [among cats] and the distinction between talking and not talking seems to us to be really important, come to insist that a *real* cat be a creature that can talk. And this will give us a new case of being 'not a real cat', i.e. being a creature that is just like a cat except for not talking.
>
> (1962: 77; emphasis original)

The scope of what is said cannot be completely detached from the interests and concerns of those saying it: this goes for our claims about *all* or *every* as much as for the remarks about cheetahs (or cats).

Am I saying, using Ziff's terminology, that a *conception* of *all* or of *every* is at work here? I prefer to put the point another way, since the terminology does not quite fit. At the least, we have identified both the generality of my claims and the fake universality in some of the exclusions noted earlier. For it seemed I was not entitled to claim *everyone* or *everything* unless I had checked – and put aside – all the potential counter-cases. That is mistaken. With no finite totality of such cases (no *all* here), that requirement is spurious. We can never consider *all* cases (or *every* case) because there is no *all* (nor *every*): unconsidered cases could always arise, as we saw earlier. Thus we cannot legitimately be criticized for failing to consider them *all*. (Indeed, a more sophisticated account of the philosophy of logic here might suggest our view – that these claims here are not exceptionless – as the only defensible one.) Thus, if we took *all* and *every* always to be necessarily exceptionless (as earlier), there would always be exceptions, in some contexts, to claims deploying them. Hence, in those contexts, the terms would be useless. Yet they are useful in my contexts: they say (in these contexts) just what I need said.

Of course, I am not asserting that in no contexts should terms such as "all" or "every" be taken exceptionlessly. Instead, my position involves waiting to see. Of course, in certain contexts – say, those of natural science (see McFee, 2000: 126–31) – exceptionlessness is secured by fiat. But we cannot always argue seamlessly from the presence of the terms "all" or "every" (and so on) to a conclusion about exceptionlessness.

Thus far, my claims about (say) *everyone* were, in context, not to be read exceptionlessly; this reflected a wider issue concerning the scope of general claims. At root, both points are explained by *occasion sensitivity*. We have seen, though, a kind of constraint on such occasions: that we read them charitably. Hence, if it makes no sense to talk (exceptionlessly) of *all people* in this context (as liking Chinese food) – because there is no finite totality – then that cannot be a way to understand what was said in using those words on that occasion.

Part Five: Conclusion

Ziff (1972: 141) offers a useful slogan, summarizing my overall point here that "[o]ne speaks and hopes to be understood". At issue in considering (say) my major claims about the attractiveness of Chinese food and the general compatibility of beer with other foodstuffs is (first) what I said – in saying those words on that occasion – and (then) the truth of what I asserted. In line with Ziff's slogan, you must understand this in order to understand what I said. To understand what I said is, in part, to take from my saying those words, in that context, both what I meant and where I was right (when I was). Here, some pitfalls to this kind of understanding are discussed: in particular, those associated with assumptions of exceptionlessness, especially in making sense of the generality in claiming (in context) both that *everyone* does such-and-such – in my case, liking Chinese food – and that cheetahs have so-and-so properties (in this case, that they can outrun men). Insights from the second were deployed to help us with the first. In neither case is the claim as merely about *some*, or this or that specific group. In both cases, what was said was (in context) arguably *true*. Further, you will misunderstand if you take them differently: in particular, if you assume that such general claims were (or were supposed to be) exceptionless.

A thesis of this Appendix has been that terms such "all" and "every" do not necessarily indicate exceptionlessness, and that other locutions operate similarly.

Our example was: "A cheetah can outrun a man". Moreover, this is an unproblematic feature of our understanding – and hence of our language. That suggests a commitment here to occasion-sensitivity, at least as an agenda for research. But why should we care? Does this leave us anywhere useful? For philosophy is not, in general, much vexed by either the speed of cheetahs or the tastiness of Chinese food.

The short answer is that a tendency within (especially) philosophical readings of some claims treats *every* claim of this kind as exceptionless. A symptom here involves the search for counter-examples to these claims. Then claiming such exceptionlessness can seem a philosophical error. In saying that men did such-and-such, was I really ignorant of the two men who did not? How could I miss (or, worse, ignore) such an obvious counter-example? Well, the 'error' requires that, in saying "All men . . ." (for example, are selfish), I meant it *exceptionlessly*. In part, then, the concern is to capture what was said or meant in context, rather than to import from outside a reading of what was said. This is one place where the occasion-sensitivity of the remarks is crucial. Thus, as Travis recognizes:

> The point is: whether *that* is so depends not merely on the fact that it is *this* that is to be so or not, and on the way things are, but also on what one is to count as things being that way, where this last is a genuinely substantive question.
>
> (2008: 300–1; emphasis original)

So my asserting, "Men are selfish" is not equivalent to claiming that *all* men are selfish, where that "all" is read as exceptionless: this is the moral from Ziff's tales of cheetahs. Then, even had I said, "All men are selfish", that too should not (in all contexts) be taken as an exceptionless claim: that is the moral from my claims about beer, or about Chinese food – saying these things need not commit one to the exceptionless reading.

Coda: one example – Freud's claims

An exceptionless reading is sometimes imposed on an author's remarks even when there is (or seems) compelling evidence in the opposite direction. Thus, Freud's ideas are commonly presented as offering exceptionless generalizations, which are then assailed with counter-examples. The finding of such exceptions offers one way to read the Popper-inspired criticism that Freud's work is not *falsifiable* (compare Cioffi, 1970). But in general, and throughout much of his work, Freud fairly careful considered the scope of his claims: in particular, he was aware that those offering *summaries* of his chief ideas tended to muddy those ideas in the process. (And he understood why.) As he wrote:

> . . . qualifications and exact particularisation are of little use with the general public; there is very little room in the memory of the multitude; it retains only the bare gist of any thesis and fabricates an extreme version which is easy to remember.
>
> (Freud, [1905] 1953: 267)

So that what is taken from his theoretically-precise accounts becomes, instead, something inexact when presented to a general audience. Thus, for instance, Freud carefully denied the idea of a 'Freudian symbol' for dreams,[16] although that appears one 'legacy' of his work.

Much general, abstract criticism of Freud (as of psychoanalytically-inclined psychology) is precisely directed at its failures to *generalize* fully or at its (supposed) spurious exceptionlessness. In particular, it was claimed that Freud's work could never be scientific because, by its nature, science works with exceptionless generalizations ("laws"). Then Freud is criticized either for not dealing in such exceptionless generalizations or, in aiming to deal with them, for producing general claims that were *false* (because not exceptionless).[17] We now know enough about spurious exceptionlessness to require a fuller scholarly treatment of exactly what Freud was *really* asserting before, in these ways, convicting him of the sin of claiming exceptionlessness for some thesis that admits of exceptions (and especially obvious exceptions).

I hold no particular brief for Freud or for psychoanalytically-inclined psychology: that is just an example here. Certainly meeting the criticisms of Freud noted here would not be to meet all lines of criticism. But a judicious weighing of Freud's claims involves us reading him aright. That takes us back to Ziff's slogan, quoted at the beginning of this section. As noted in McFee (2004c), judicious attention requires the sort of close reading of Freud offered to other theorists, as a criterion of our taking them seriously. Then another constraint on understanding (with Freud as my example) lies in not mistaking an exceptionless claim for one that is not (and was not meant to be). In particular, those recognizing occasion-sensitivity should be more hesitant about raising accusations of failing to be exceptionless. These are points to convey to my philosophical demon.

Notes

1 A vision of the ethics and epistemology of qualitative research into sport

1 Indeed, many experienced researchers, having not addressed these issues in their training, could benefit from them.

2 The term "subject" is also preferred by others, even those thought respectable guides to the responsible conduct of research in the USA: thus, see Shamoo and Resnik (2009: 236ff.) – their chapter is called "The Protection of Human Subjects in Research".

3 I am describing Anglo-American traditions. The situation may be expressed differently in continental Europe, where the term "science" is viewed in a more encompassing fashion: for instance, as *Wissenschaft*. But the contrasts discussed here typically remain.

4 My primary concern here is with designs for empirical research into sport: social-scientific disciplines such as sports sociology or some varieties of sports psychology are typical. Since sports history and sport philosophy might engage in similar enquiries, they are not excluded.

5 For instance, Gratton and Jones (2004), often excellent, might be augmented in this respect.

6 In the 'pure' versions of key disciplines, such as sociology, my claims may appear less revolutionary than they do – if I am right – in sport-related fields; perhaps because, in the parent disciplines, such points are broadly familiar.

7 Non-numerical Unstructured Data Indexing, Searching and Theorising (NUD*IST) – for me, the name is somewhat confusing! See Gratton and Jones, 2004: 225–26.

8 As Kenny (1980: 29) notes, "[a] generation ago philosophers insisted on a sharp distinction between morality and ethics". The influence of Marxism and logical positivism, both major forces in philosophy in the late twentieth century, partly explained the prevalence of the contrast then, since "… both … in different ways were sceptical about the reality of moral questions" (Nagel, 2002: 77).

9 Two chief kinds: those relating assertion to truth-telling mean that we should mean what we say; and those relating to our treatment of others mean they should get a fair hearing.

10 O'Neill (2002: 35) raises the issue of priority among the principles here. Although research with human subjects has no specific connection to the moral context, it must aim at human good – as, say, exercise research with medical applications need not.

11 See especially the essays collected in Travis, 2008; also Travis, 2004.

12 The explanation of cinematic narration as a series of question-and-answer relations offers another simplified erotetic context (Carroll, 2008: 134–44).

13 I am only highlighting how someone might come to the solutions of this piece of research, not suggesting the actual research is flawed in these ways.

14 Example from Matt Davies, reported (and quoted) in Blackburn, 2001.

15 Contrast Dennett, 1991: 5 on "computational explosion": see McFee, 2000: 24; 116.

2 Research must answer its question

1 Is this a *different* question? Or does that same question, in that new context, mean something different? This distinction seems without difference – like asking whether the term "bank" has two meanings or whether there are two words, orthographically indistinguishable.

2 Descartes' writing offers this insight: when Descartes' critics claimed that, on his view, animals could not *think*, they wrote urging the credentials to thought of their various pets. But Descartes connected thinking in the relevant sense with being a moral agent. So, rather than simply deny what they asserted, he highlighted what (at the time) was an accepted consequence of being a moral agent – he suggested quickly baptizing these pets, or (as moral agents) they would go to Hell! A secular version of Descartes' point seems right.

3 The reciprocal relation here is important for, say, grounded-theory approaches: as one comes to the question, the appropriate methods too become clear.

4 Except that some early research in sports coaching used precisely this method! [Detail withheld to protect the guilty.]

5 As one of my research students did. Whatever one makes of this, it at least coheres with our emphasis on *talk*.

6 Strictly, the truth-bearer is the utterance, not the sentence.

7 The final nail in the coffin of *triangulation*, in this context, was meant to be a short piece (McFee, 1992b) explaining clearly, to those not seeing it for themselves, why its earlier advocates had dropped the notion. It remained un-nailed!

8 Although the point is good for *all* research, our concern here is with social research into sport. Since a slightly different form of argument is required for natural-scientific research into aspects of sport, the restriction to the social-scientific is retained.

9 Other cases work roughly similarly. For example, Lincoln and Guba (1985: 305) talk of ". . . determining the point of origin of a radio broadcast by using directional antennae set up at two ends of a known baseline". But my sketch is sufficient to introduce our points.

3 The issue of 'the qualitative' is not helpful

1 See here Morgan (2006: xiii) writing of students' ". . . unwillingness or incapacity to view sports from a moral vantage point".

2 The most general 'principles' may be exceptionless, but lack content. For example, "Be nice to others", gives no guide to conduct – almost certainly requiring different behaviours in different contexts. For more articulation of particularism, see Dancy, 2004.

3 An anecdote may clarify: when two Oxford philosophy professors were on the same exam board, the particularist J. L. Austin (in a lull in the proceedings) asked his colleague, Richard Hare, how he would respond if offered a bribe by one of the candidates. Hare, an advocate of *principles* in the sense denied here, replied that his answer would be: "I do not take bribes as a matter of principle". By contrast, Austin remarked that his own reply would be, "No thanks".

4 Given the content of, say, the photographs in the book, the ethological investigations of the 'Manwatcher' are better called "womanwatching": see Morris, 1977.

5 As published by Roethlisberger and Dickson (1939). Gillespie (1991: 182–89) offers detailed study of this case, ". . . still among the most frequently cited and most controversial experiments in the social sciences" (Gillespie, 1991: 1). See also Toulmin, 2001: 97–98 (despite my extensive use of Toulmin here, I found Gillespie's discussion independently).

6 Harré and Secord (1976) certainly resembles my position: (a) my account of treating research subjects as people comes from them; (b) an elaboration of my concept of persons could usefully begin from their "Summary of the Anthropomorphic Model of Man"

(1976: 86–87); (c) we agree that "[l]ay explanations of behaviour provide the best model for psychological theorizing" (1976: 29) – although I find more place for technical expressions from, say, psychoanalysis; and (d) ". . . a co-operative enterprise between psychologists, philosophers and sociologists" (1976: 2) is required for making sense of the social world.

7 The 'construction' metaphor is very misleading: compare Ward (1997: 774) for the extreme version (which he calls "standpoint epistemology") on which "all knowledge is localized perspective" and therefore can be dismissed. But agreeing on the importance of "localized perspective" does not mean that, once we are in that context, claims from that perspective cannot be true. Hence, Ward's second point does not follow from his first (see also chapter 6): the "therefore" is misplaced.

8 This journal, it must be admitted, was selected partly because of its conservative view of sound 'qualitative' research – this feeling (shared with others) partly motivates the publication in 2009 of a new journal, with (it is to be hoped) a less conservative line: *Qualitative Research in Sport and Exercise*.

9 For a brief description, see Fielding and Lee (1991: 197–98); Punch (1998: 290–91).

10 As Bryman (2001: 407a) noted, ". . . most of" the consideration of NVivo also bears on NUD*IST, with which it shares many features.

11 Although some moral status in respect of their welfare may be attributed, they are not agents here (any more than, say, natural phenomena, such as earthquakes).

12 I won't comment directly on this completely daft idea, which comes to a self-refuting relativism: see chapter 6.

4 Research must aim at truth

1 This is confusing by contrast with my real beliefs (if any) – say, in God. "Beliefs" in the philosophers' sense are just what one would assert, if asked, better viewed as *what I think* than what I believe.

2 Even if, say, Newton's astronomy had hopes of changing human practices for the better, on the basis of changed knowledge, that knowledge required application in some way – the transformation was not the knowledge *itself*.

3 For example (Toulmin, 1972: 124): "the theoretical concepts of Einstein's relativistic physics [say] may perhaps be incompatible with those of Newton's classical physics in the first sense [as theoretical principles]; yet supporters of the two positions shared enough disciplinary aims [the second kind of difference] for them to be able to discuss, in a vocabulary intelligible to both sides, which of the two theories 'did a better explanatory job' for theoretical physics".

4 In practice, testing of *reliability* (in this sense) is not always rigorous: sometimes "minimal steps may be taken to ensure that a measure is reliable . . ." (Bryman, 2001: 74). But this does not weaken our conceptual point.

5 A personal favourite: Sparkes (2002: 203) writes, without much explanation, of *voluptuous validity*.

6 See, for instance, the view of science from Williams and James, 2001: 4–5 (quoted chapter 5).

7 Einstein was famously dismissive about the results of experimentation; and Darwin ([1872] 1993: 620) confidently set aside apparent falsification:

> With respect to the lapse of time not having been sufficient . . . [for evolution to have taken place] . . . this objection, as urged by Sir William Thomson, is one of the gravest as yet advanced. I can only say, firstly, that we do not know at what rate species change as measured by years, and secondly, that philosophers [scientists] are not as yet willing to admit that we know enough of the constitution of the universe and of the interior of our globe to speculate with safety on its past duration.

And Darwin was proved right when the discovery of radioactivity provided more heat-sources than Thomson assumed.

8 As Wollheim (1993: 111) notes, the sceptical possibility of *suggestibility* can operate similarly for psychoanalysis. Following Fine and Forbes, he remarks how "suggestibility starts off . . . as a mere place-holder for sceptical doubt. But gradually it escalates. Its claims upon our credence grow: its content is inflated. Soon it appears as an alternative theory to psychoanalysis, replete with its own hypotheses".

9 For scholarly defence of Nietzsche's perspectivalism along similar lines (against that sometimes extracted from his "Truth and Lies in the Moral Sense"), see Clark 1990: 127–58.

10 The suggestion that differences here might reflect taste or 'styles of writing' (Richardson, 2001: 877; Sparkes, 2002: compare chapter 7) is even more puzzling.

5 Scientism is a bad model for truth (and natural science)

1 The term science here usually means natural science. Those presenting the positions under discussion usually have natural science as their concern, often rejecting the claims to *scientificity* of social science.

2 This text is often recommended to students of sports science, including sports psychology.

3 Thus I agree that "[m]ost scientists do not . . . realize how anti-scientific Popper's views actually are" (Searle, 2008: 23).

4 Lest it be claimed, against me, that Creation Science has not gone down this route, readers should look at the literature on (so-called) Intelligent Design: much of its rhetoric is precisely that it meets criteria for scientificity. For a robust rejection (in layman's terms), see the papers in Brockman, 2006.

5 Thus Popkewitz (1984: 32) writes of paradigms in "the social construction of rationality", commenting that "[t]he discourse of science contains different and sometimes conflicting assumptions about what constitute social facts *par excellence* . . ." (Popkewitz, 1984: 35).

6 My thanks to Mike McNamee for recognizing the value in stressing this point here, when these ideas appeared in *Sport, Ethics and Philosophy* (Mcfee, 2007).

7 A counter-theory, that sociology is still in a pre-science phase, is preposterous: at the least, no serious sociologist should be willing to adopt it.

8 McNamee *et al.* (2007: 199 note 4) write:

> The frequency with which authors either misconceive what Kuhn meant (and thereby manifest their failure to have read him . . .), or indeed fail to notice that his views were significantly altered in later texts . . . indicates a lack of first-hand knowledge of Kuhn's work.

I would like to think that my ideas about Kuhn may have contributed to the writing of this note.

9 Compare here Silk *et al.* (2005: 5):

> It was the work of Thomas Kuhn (1962) which brought the concept of a paradigm into the popular lexicon of research design.

10 Contrast McFee, 2000: 117–26 for a discussion of the inexhaustibility of description.

11 I ignore Popper's, since his 'misunderstanding' of Kuhn is so explicit it seems willful (see Popper, 1983: xxxi-xxxv). Indeed, Popper's scholarship is often highly insecure in his criticisms of others – to which at least some listened (and more will, should the policy of taking critique of inductivism as endorsing falsificationism discussed earlier in this chapter become widespread).

12 Hence his restriction to ". . . taxonomic or kind terms" (Kuhn, 2000: 92).
13 As Kuhn states them:

- A theory should be accurate.
- A theory should be consistent.
- It should have broad scope: in particular, a theory's consequences should extend far beyond the particular observations.
- It should be simple, bringing order to phenomena that in its absence would be individually isolated and, as a set, confused.
- A theory should be fruitful of new research findings.

He adds, first, that ". . . these facts of scientific life have philosophic import" (Kuhn, 1977: 325); second, that they do so by offering *values* to which scientists appeal to justify (or explain) their decisions in theory-choice. For these considerations must be made concrete in a particular case: then scientists might well dispute whether this theory is genuinely (say) *simpler* than that one, and so on.

14 As the previous note shows, Kuhn (1977: 322–25) writes clearly and sharply on any such regulation being a topic for discussion or debate – as to, say, whether this scientific theory or that one is the simpler on a particular topic, given that simplicity is a virtue of such theories.

15 For Kuhn, only some experiments count as 'crucial experiments'. As he explains, "crucial experiments – those able to discriminate particularly sharply between two paradigms – have been recognized and attested before the new paradigm was ever invented" (Kuhn, 1970: 153).

16 Sometimes Popper (1963/1999: 313; emphasis original) recognizes this limitation of his position:

> . . . many people have been moved to say that even though we do not know how near we are to or how far we are from the truth, we can . . . *approach more and more closely to the truth*. I myself have said such things in the past, but always with a twinge of bad conscience.

Again, "what can in principle be . . . overthrown and yet resists all our critical efforts to do so may quite possibly be false, but is at any rate not unworthy of being seriously considered and even perhaps believed" (Popper, 1963/1999: 309).
But sometimes Popper (1963/1999: 306) writes in a different vein:

> The status of truth in the objective sense . . . may be compared to that of a mountain peak which is permanently, or almost permanently, wrapped in clouds. The climber may not merely have difficulties getting there – he may not know when he gets there, because he may be unable to distinguish, in the clouds, between the main summit and some subsidiary peak. Yet this does not affect the objective existence of the summit . . .

For this analogy, whether or not "it may be impossible for the climber ever to make sure he has reached the summit" (Popper, 1963/1999: 307) makes a lot of difference: for this means that he can never be confident in the *truth* of any claim in science.

17 Of course, others (for instance, Imre Lakatos) who contributed to the philosophy of science could have been discussed here. The prominence of the term "paradigm", especially in social-scientific contexts, explains my choices here.

18 Another general example: Peter Medawar's paper "Is The Scientific Paper a Fraud?" from Medawar, 1990.

6 Postmodernism and truth-denial as a kind of scientism

1 Compare McFee, 2004a: 173–74.
2 Rorty acknowledges this conclusion by taking as his hero the ". . . 'strong poet'

rather than . . . the truth-seeking 'logical', 'objective' scientist" (Rorty, 1989: 53) – where the scare quotes indicate his hesitation about the possibilities of *objectivity*, and the like.

3   As we have made clear, that is not our position.

4   Kuhn (1970: viii) – quoted chapter 5: ". . . the practice of astronomy, physics, chemistry or biology normally fails to evoke the controversies over fundamentals that today often seem endemic among, say, psychologists or sociologists".

5   Indeed, Sparkes (1992: 11–12) offers some elaboration here, by discussing a number of other accounts, but without ever coming down on a clear defence of any.

6   For a recent case of treating the idea of a paradigm as (a) unproblematic in social science, and (b) as helpful, see Phillimore and Goodson, 2004.

7   Some (especially Sokal and Bricmont, 1998: 71–78; especially 75) claim that, for Kuhn, ". . . changes of paradigm are due principally to non-empirical factors" – I wonder what page-references support that "principally"! At the least, they also discern another trend ("moderate Kuhn") within the work.

8   At least defeasibly: see McFee, 1992a: 61–63; McFee, 2004a: 150.

9   Arguably the etymology of the term "etymology".

10   How Freudian do we want to be? Of course, forgetting can be revealing too: and that is one reason why one's narratives are often best reflected upon with others.

11   Thus Kuhn, 2000: 189: "In applying the term 'incommensurability' to theories, I'd intended only to insist that there was no common language within which both could be fully expressed and which could therefore be used in a point-by-point comparison between them". Also, with Feyerabend (1987: 272), I take incommensurability to be a rare occurrence . . . (see McFee, 1992a: 306).

12   This feature of understanding is very badly modelled as, say, translating from one language to another; and even worse as a set of symptomatic responses.

13   Here, I assume this: an elaboration would begin by highlighting characteristic flaws in the epistemology of quantitative social research.

14   As Bryman (2001: 470) notes, the term "reflexivity" has two related uses here: on this one, researchers are part of the social world they study; on the other, the *talk* they research is constitutive of that social world – introduced in chapter 3 in discussion of Declaration.

15   That is to say, the human behaviour here should be seen as *actions*, with the implied normativity (McFee, 2004a: 5–7).

7   Truth-denial is not just a style of writing

1   See Cavell, 1969: 32. This is true in two ways: in practical terms, our words are what we mean, other things being equal; and the alternatives are morally reprehensible outcomes such as lying, frivolousness or self-deception.

2   Gilbourne and Triggs, 2006 might provide a related example; some of the conceptual material is presented in Gilbourne, 2009.

3   Quoted Baxandall, 1985: 69. Compare also the account of Picasso's problems, and their solutions: Baxandall, 1985: 64–66.

4   The others are: "as . . . a source of factual information"; "as . . . a source of propositional understanding" (Davies, 2001: 270).
      [But neither of these are of any use to us!]

5   The insight which (no doubt) the writers of such dramas might come to, as a result of the writing and discussion, can also be set aside. These might be real gains, but there is no reason to suppose that *one* kind of writing, or even writing at all, *necessarily* connects with this increase in understanding.

6   Schön is writing quite generally about (at least) those professions that essentially involve action/practice; and describing *professions*, in the technical sense: on that

notion, see (for instance) Koehn, 1994 *passim*; especially, p. 59; pp. 174–81. But the sport-field contains a number of professions, or quasi-professions.

8 Voluntary informed consent – not as good as gold

1 Two such thoughts: (a) *control* in experimentation is achieved only through the use of *ceteris paribus* clauses (McFee, 2000: 117–23) – hence, it is an idealization; (b) all research deploys (if implicitly) a principle of total evidence (Carnap, 1950: 211).

2 This is sometimes expressed in terms of *beneficence* (see chapter 1; O'Neill, 2002: 35): but, for me, the benefit here need not be directly a moral benefit: that it was causally efficacious might well be enough, if that causality had a bearing on human welfare (say, through treating disease).

3 This reiterates the powerful philosophical point made elsewhere (see chapter 1; McFee, 2000: 117–23): that there is no finite totality of information which could (in principle) be provided – hence I can neither know (for sure) what *this* subject lacks nor provide him with *all* the information (since there is no *all*). Parallel difficulties beset (at least) *all* the considerations raised here against the achievability of this version of VIC.

4 I think *this* kind of transgression is in fact widespread – although my evidence is all anecdotal.

5 An interesting question: could one identify the sports psychologist from this (anonymous) description? If so, let me assure all readers that this person has not acted through his writing as I describe, and would not do so.

6 Hence O'Neill (2002: 157; italics original) concludes that "[g]enuine, ethically significant consent cannot . . . be achieved by aspiring to some formulistic . . . conception of *complete* or *exhaustive* description of the proposed research". But it can only be a 'gold standard' on precisely that assumption!

7 But Olivier (2007: 35) adds that "[i]f this is deemed inappropriate, you need to justify the exception".

8 Both points are crucial since, if VIC indeed functioned as a gold standard (once properly implemented), covert research should be regarded as ethically second-class (as Homan, 2004 seems to regard it).

9 Covert research into sport can be ethical

1 Humphreys also recorded number plates, etc. from cars – a very different case! See Homan, 1991: 102.

2 On this point, contrast Frankfort-Nachmias and Nachmias (1996: 87) – although they concentrate on just part of his design.

3 Not least because there might be some justified public 'right to know', and certainly some public interest, in aspects of this person's life: that is what makes him/her count as a celebrity.

4 In doing so, my position reflects the arguments in Nagel, 2002; especially 3–30; 41ff.

5 The similarity is that, in this case too the covert research design presented the researcher as less capable – and therefore less able to safeguard his fellows – than was the reality.

6 See the discussion of particularism in chapter 3; McFee, 2004a pp. 141–44.

7 Unlike many authors on this topic, I have not here used Milgram's experiments (clearly described by Homan, 1991: 161–65). Although these experiments have received 'bad press' for their failure of overtness, that largely misses the more positive history of the case: see McNamee (2002: 10).

8 Pattern also recognizes an appeal to the "logic of the experiment", such that knowing one was part of studies of trustworthiness or obedience would be introduce factors potentially contrary to that research design. He puts this aside both with the usual gesture to Milgram and with the (odd) suggestion that a dispute about the *logic* of

an argument should say more about ". . . entailment or conceptual connection" (1994: 112).

9 Since our research, into social-scientific aspects of sport, is less invasive than others that might be imagined, my treatment (while granting point [3]) does not stress it; and it treats [5] as "to the degree that this is possible".

10 It is actually conceptually impossible, since the requirement to inform *fully* imports the (false) assumption of a finite totality of options to consider (as earlier objections make plain).

10 The researcher is not the research subject

1 If your research requires talking to women in their changing room, it is an obvious practical advantage to be a woman. If your research design requires asking, say, certain group-members about their sexuality, it may be an advantage (even essential) for it to be clear that one is not being judgemental – and that may require sharing the group's sexual preferences! [And this is the sort of case being considered.]

2 Thus, a writer (say, Andrea Dworkin) who recognizes that there must be something amiss with the 'stories' of those women who have professed themselves happy with a life in pornography or prostitution will (rightly) set these 'stories' aside – they cannot provide genuine data.

3 It is a salutary reminder (for those of us who take this for granted) that, say, political correctness is a powerful force here – and not always one to the good.

4 Such cases always seem to begin by reminding us of the connection between the personal and the political!

5 The producer of the film *Chariots of Fire* (1981), David Putnam (quoted Tomlinson, 1999: 233), apparently thought of the protagonists of his film that way: as embodying ". . . instinctively honourable values" (Yule, 1988: 174) like those of Thomas More.

6 As Lindsey Davies wrote of her task in setting novels in Flavian Rome, it is difficult to reconstruct the spoken language: ". . . people spoke another language, one which has mainly survived either in a literary form or as tavern wall graffiti" (Davies, 2007: 322). Sophisticated written texts and graffiti provide at best an indication here.

Appendix

1 And I am not committing myself to the thesis from Sondheim's *Sweeney Todd: The Demon Barber of Fleet Street* (1979) that ". . . everybody goes down well with beer".

2 Compare Wisdom (1969: 42–43), discussing the Hilaire Belloc lines:

> The llama is a hairy sort of woolly fleecy goat
> With an indolent expression and an undulating throat
> Like an unsuccessful literary man.

Wisdom comments: "'The llama', used Belloc's way, means 'Llamas' or 'Every llama', just as the phrase 'The heart' used in medical textbooks means 'Every heart'".

3 For instance, characterizing *Principia Mathematica* (second edition), Ramsey (1931: 114) writes: ". . . Mr. Russell would say 'Unpunctuality is a fault' really means something like 'For all x, if X is unpunctual, x is reprehensible' . . .".

4 Sadly, few students of philosophy today read carefully that chapter of Ziff's work.

5 See also Austin, 1962: 143–45 on "France is hexagonal". We might agree that "Lord Raglan won the battle of Alma" (which means, "agree with the person who said it", or, "agree that it was true") while granting that "there would no question of giving Raglan a medal for it" (Austin, 1962: 144).

6 There is a great deal of other insight in Ziff's chapter, rewarding detailed attention.

7 As Travis (2008: 99 note) says, of another example: "I will not pause to argue against the heroic view that that just means that no one can ever speak truth in calling something round".

8 The remainder of this section reworks, with various expansion and contractions and other revisions, McFee, 2004a: 48–52.

9 This passage was excluded when the paper was 'reprinted'.

10 Another useless strategy: to deny that these are genuine *meaning*-connections, invoking "implicature" (Grice, 1989: 24–31): such ideas are annihilated by Travis 2008: 19–64; 65–93.

11 Amusingly, someone reading this claim over my shoulder asked, "What about the married ones?".

12 Recall that Austin (1970: 143) commented, of a similar case, "[i]t is a rough description; it is not a true or false one". Yet he goes on to grant that *true* should be thought of as standing for ". . . a general dimension of being the right or proper thing to say as opposed to the wrong thing, in these circumstances, to this audience, for these purposes and with these intentions" (Austin, 1962: 145). But this is just the kind of occasion-sensitive understanding which makes what I said, on that occasion, (plausibly) *true*.

13 For this reason, "Most people like Chinese food" would not do.

14 As Carnap (1950: 211) states it, "in the application of inductive logic to a given knowledge situation, the total evidence available must be taken as the basis for determining degrees of confirmation". So what we cannot presently know we must treat as irrelevant.

15 The example recalls the occasions when my friend Bob Goldman wanted to voice just such an objection.

16 Thus he did write "this symbolism is not peculiar to dreams" (Freud [1900] PFL Vol. 4, 1976: 467). For there is a fund of such symbols to be learned in myths, folklore, and so on – which partly explains their generality: 'we' read the same myths, etc. and myths draw on what is human (feelings, etc.). Further, "many of the symbols are habitually or almost habitually employed to express the same thing" (Freud [1900] PFL Vol. 4, 1976: 469). But asked whether we should interpret *all* dreams in this fashion, Freud replied: "No, not at all . . ." (Freud [1933] PFL Vol. 2, 1973: 4).

17 Both kinds of criticisms, and others, are re-cycled with animus in Gellner (1985: 150–203), although focused on the Freudian or psychoanalytic *movement*, rather than Freud specifically.

Bibliography

The publisher has no responsibility for the persistence or accuracy of URLs for external third-party internet websites referred to in this book, and does not guarantee that any content on such websites is, or will remain, accurate or appropriate.

Alderson, J. and Crutchley, D. (1990) "Physical Education and the National Curriculum" in N. Armstrong (ed.) *New Directions in Physical Education*, Vol 1. Rawdon: Human Kinetics, 37–62.

Anderson, A. G., Knowle, Z. and Gilbourne, D. (2004) "Reflective Practice for Sports Psychologists: Concepts, Models, Practical Implications, and Thoughts on Dissemination", *The Sports Psychologist*, Vol. 18, No. 2, June, 188–203.

Austin, J. L. (1962) *Sense and Sensibilia*. Oxford: Clarendon Press.

—— (1970) *Philosophical Papers* (Second Edition). Oxford: Clarendon Press.

BASES [British Association of Sport and Exercise Sciences] (2000) *Code of Conduct*. Leeds: BASES.

BBC [British Broadcasting Corporation] (1986) "Bitter Cold", *Horizon*, BBC2, Monday, 13th January; producer David Parer for the Australian Broadcasting Corporation [*Horizon* editor: Robin Brightwell].

Baker, G. and Hacker, P. (1984) *Language, Sense and Nonsense*. Oxford: Blackwell.

Bambrough, R. (1969) *Reason, Truth and God*. London: Methuen.

Barnbaum, D. R. and Byron, M. (2001) *Research Ethics: Texts and Readings*. Upper Saddle River, NJ: Prentice Hall.

Baxandall, M. (1985) *Patterns of Intention*. New Haven: Yale University Press.

Blackburn, S. (2001) *Being Good*. Oxford: Oxford University Press.

Bloor, M. (1997) "Techniques of Validation in Qualitative Research: A Critical Commentary" in G. Miller and R. Dingwall (eds) *Context and Method in Qualitative Research*. London: Sage, 37–50.

Breakwell, G. Hammond, S. and Wood, P. (eds) (1995) *Research Methods in Psychology*. London: Sage.

Brockman, J. (ed.) (2006) *Intelligent Thought: Science versus the Intelligent Design Movement*. New York: Vintage Books.

Bryman, A. (2001) *Social Research Methods*. Oxford: Oxford University Press.

British Sociological Association (BSA): Statement of Ethical Practice — [available at http://www.britsoc.org.uk/about/ethic.htm].

Burroughs-Lange, S. G. and Lange, J. (1993) "Denuded Data! Grounded Theory using the NUDIST Computer Analysis Program in Researching the Challenge to Teacher Self-Efficacy posed by Students with Learning Disabilities in Australian Education" [available at: http://eric.ed.gov/ERICWebPortal/contentdelivery/servlet/ERICServlet? accno=ED364193; accessed: 15 January 2009].

Carnap, R. (1950) *Logical Foundations of Probability*. London: Routledge & Kegan Paul.

Carroll, N. (2008) *The Philosophy of Motion Pictures*. Oxford: Blackwell.

Carter, T. F. (2008) *The Quality of Home Runs: The Passion, Politics, and Language of Cuban Baseball*. Durham: Duke University Press.

Cashdan, A. and Whitehead, J. (1972) *Personality Growth and Learning*. London: Longman.

Cavell, S. (1969) *Must We Mean What We Say?* New York: Scribners.

Chalmers, A. F. (1999) *What is This Thing Called Science?* (Third Edition). Milton Keynes: Open University Press.

Cioffi, F. (1970) "Freud and the Idea of a Pseudo-science" in R. Borger and F. Cioffi (eds) *Explanation in the Behavioural Sciences*. Cambridge: Cambridge University Press, 471–99.

Clark, M. (1990) *Nietzsche on Truth and Philosophy*. Cambridge: Cambridge University Press.

Cohen, L. and Manion, L. (1980) *Research Methods in Education* (Third Edition). London: Routledge.

Collingwood, R. G. (1938) *The Principles of Art*. Oxford: Clarendon Press.

Collinson, J. A. and Hockey, J. (2004) "Autoethnography: Self-indulgence or Rigorous Methodology?" in M. McNamee (ed.) *Philosophy and the Sciences of Exercise, Health and Sport*. London: Routledge, 187–202.

Cook, T. D. and Reichardt, C. S. (1979). *Qualitative and Quantitative Methods in Evaluative Research*. London: Sage.

Dancy, J. (2004) *Ethics Without Principles*. Oxford: Clarendon Press.

Darwin, C. [1872] (1993) *The Origin of Species*. [A reprint of the sixth edition]. New York: The Modern Library.

Davies, D. (2001) "Fiction" in B. Gaut and D. Lopes (eds) *The Routledge Companion to Aesthetics*. London: Routledge, 263–73.

Davies, L. (2007) *Saturnalia*. London: Century.

Dennett, D. (1991) *Consciousness Explained*. London: Allen Lane.

Denzin, N. K. (1997) *Interpretive Ethnography*. London: Sage.

Donne, K. (2006) "From Outside to Quasi-Insider at Wodin Watersports: A Reflexive Account of Participant Observation in a Leisure Context" in S. Fleming and F. Jordan (eds) *Ethical Issues in Leisure Research* (LSA Publication No. 90). Eastbourne: Leisure Studies Association, 63–81.

Draper, E. A., Fisher, L. A. and Wrisberg, C. A (2005) "Professional Women's Career Experiences in Sport Psychology: A Feminist Standpoint", *The Sports Psychologist*, Vol. 19, No. 1, March, 32–50.

Doust, J. (1997) "The Physiological Assessment of Athletes" in A. Tomlinson and S. Fleming (eds) *Ethics, Sport and Leisure: Crises and Critiques*. Aachen: Meyer & Meyer, 95–110.

Dummett, M. (1978) *Truth and Other Enigmas*. London: Duckworth.

—— (2004) *Truth and the Past*. New York: Columbia University Press.

Dunn, J. G. H. and Hart, N. L. (2004) "A Qualitative Investigation of Personal-Disclosure Mutual-Sharing Team Building Activity", *The Sports Psychologist*, Vol. 18, No. 4, December, 363–80.

Edwards, A. (1999) "Reflective Practice in Sport Management", *Sport Management Review*, Vol. 2, No. 1, 67–81.

Elliott, J. (1976). "Developing Hypotheses about Classrooms for Teachers' Practical Constructs: An Account of the Ford Teaching Project", *Interchange*, 7, 2; reprinted in

S. Kemmis *et al.* (eds) *The Action Research Reader*. Victoria, Australia: Deakin University Press, 1982: 293–311.

—— (1991) *Action Research for Educational Change*. Milton Keynes: Open University Press.

Elms, A. C. (1994) "Keeping Deception Honest: Justifying Conditions for Social Science Research Strategies" reprinted in E. Erwin, S. Gendin and L. Kleinman (eds) *Ethical Issues in Scientific Research: An Anthology*. New York: Garland, 121–40.

Engels, H-J, Wirth, J. C. and Haymes, E. M. (1996) "Metabolic and Ventilatory Effects of Caffeine During Light Intensity Exercise in Trained and Sedentary Low Habitual Caffeine Users" in R. Maughan and V. A. Rogozkin (eds) *Current Research in Sports Science*. New York: Plenum Press, 321–32.

Evans, L., Hardy, L. and Fleming, S. (2000a) "Intervention Strategies with Injured Athletes: An Action Research Study", *The Sports Psychologist*, Vol. 14, No. 2, 188–206.

Evans, L., Fleming, S. and Hardy, L. (2000b) "Situating Action Research: A Response to Gilbourne", *The Sports Psychologist*, Vol. 14, No. 33, 296–303.

Fasting, K. (2000) "Seeing and Being Seen: Body Fashion in Female Recreational Sport" in S. Scraton and B. Watson (eds) *Sport, Leisure Identities and Gendered Spaces*. Eastbourne: Leisure Studies Association, 151–61.

Feyerabend, P. K. (1987) *Farewell to Reason*. London: Verso.

Fielding, N. and Lee, R. (1991) (eds) *Using Computers in Qualitative Research*. London: Sage.

Fleming, S. (1995) *Home and Away: Sport and South Asian Male Youth*. Aldershott: Avebury.

Frankfort-Nachmias, C. and Nachmias, D. (1996) *Research Methods in the Social Sciences* (Fifth Edition). London: Arnold.

Freedman, B. (1979) "A Moral Theory of Consent" reprinted in R. Munson (ed.) *Intervention and Reflection: Basic Issues in Medical Ethics*. Belmont, CA: Wadsworth, 266–75.

Frege, G. (1984) "On Concept & Object" in his *Collected Papers on Mathematics, Logic and Philosophy*. Oxford: Blackwell, 183–94.

Freud, S. [1933] (1973) "New Lectures on Psychoanalysis", *The Penguin Freud Library*. Vol. 2. Harmondsworth: Penguin. – cited as PFL.

Freud, S. [1900] (1976) "The Interpretation of Dreams", *The Penguin Freud Library* Vol. 4. Harmondsworth: Penguin – cited as PFL.

Gamow, G. (1962) *Biography of Physics*. London: Hutchinson.

Gellner, E. (1985) *The Psychoanalytic Movement*. London: Paladin.

Gibbard, A. (2000) "The Reasons of a Living Being", *Proceedings and Addresses of the American Philosophical Association*, Vol. 76, No. 2, 49–60.

Giddens, A. (1989) *Sociology*. Oxford: Polity Press.

Gilbourne, D. (2000) "Searching for the Nature of Action Research: A Response to Evans, Hardy and Fleming", *The Sports Psychologist*, Vol. 14, No. 2, 207–14.

Gilbourne, D. (2009) "Embracing the Edge of Darkness: Representing Multilayered Context in Sport", Inaugural Lecture, Cardif School of Sport, UWIC [Wednesday, 13 May].

Gilbourne, D. and Triggs, C. (2006) "Your Breath in the Air", Autobiography, Auto-Ethnography and Verbatim Theatre combined with Fictional and Theatrical Techniques to form a full-scale ethno-drama production on the desperation and joy associated with soccer fandom. [Unity Theatre Liverpool, 16–19 May]

Gillespie, R. (1991) *Manufacturing Knowledge*. Cambridge: Cambridge University Press 1991.

Gratton, C. and Jones, I. (2004) *Research Methods of Sport Studies*. London: Routledge.

Grice, P. (1989) *Studies in the Ways of Words*. Cambridge, MA: Harvard University Press.

Hanson, N. R. (1958) *Patterns of Discovery*. Cambridge: Cambridge University Press.

Hardy, L., Jones, G. and Gould, D. (1996) *Understanding Psychological Preparation for Sport: Theory and Practice of Elite Performers*. Chicester: Wiley.

Harré, R. and Secord, P. (1976) *The Explanation of Social Behaviour*. Oxford: Blackwell.

Harré, R. (1983) "An Analysis of Social Activity" in J. Miller (ed.) *States of Mind: Conversations with Psychological Investigators*. London: BBC, 154–72.

Harris, J. (1985) *The Value of Life*. London: Routledge.

Homan, R. (1991) *The Ethics of Social Research*. London: Longman.

—— (2002) "The Principle of Assumed Consent: The Ethics of Gatekeeping" in M. McNamee and D. Bridges (eds) *The Ethics of Educational Research*. Oxford: Blackwell, 23–39.

—— (2004) "Is Research with and on Students Ethically Defensible?" in M. McNamee (ed.) *Philosophy and the Sciences of Exercise, Health and Sport*. London: Routledge, 219–33.

Howe, P. D. (2004) *Sport, Professionalism and Pain: Ethnographies of Injury and Risk*. London: Routledge.

Ingelfinger, F. J. (1979) "Informed (But Uneducated) Consent" reprinted in R. Munson (ed.) *Intervention and Reflection: Basic Issues in Medical Ethics*. Belmont, CA: Wadsworth, 264–65.

Ingham, R. (1990) "Leisure and Wellbeing: A Perspective from New Social Psychology" in J. Long (ed.) *Leisure, Health and Wellbeing*. Eastbourne: Leisure Studies Association, 233–51.

Johnson, J. J. M., Hrycaiko, D. W., Johnson, G. V. and Halas, J. M. (2004) "Self-Talk and Female Youth Soccer Performance", *The Sports Psychologist*, Vol. 18, No. 1, March, 44–59.

Kenny, A. (1980) *Aquinas*. Oxford: Oxford University Press.

Koehn, D. (1994) *The Ground of Professional Ethics*. London: Routledge.

Krüger, A. (2004) "What's The Difference Between Propaganda for Tourism or for a Political Regime? Was the 1936 Olympics thye First Postmodern Spectacle?" in J. Bale and H. K. Christensen (eds) *Post-Olympism? Questioning Sport in the Twenty-First Century*. Oxford: Berg, 33–49.

Kuhn, T. S. (1970) *The Structure of Scientific Revolutions* (Second Edition). Chicago: University of Chicago Press.

—— (1977) *The Essential Tension: Selected Studies in Scientific Tradition and Change*. Chicago: University of Chicago Press.

—— (1987) *Black-Body Theory and the Quantum Discontinuity, 1894–1912*. (Revised Edition) Chicago: University of Chicago Press.

—— (2000) *The Road Since Structure: Philosophical Essays 1970–1993*. Chicago: University of Chicago Press.

Laudan, L. (1982) "Science at the Bar – Causes for Concern", *Science, Technology and Human Values*, Vol. 7, No. 41, 16–19.

Lincoln, Y. and Guba, E. G. (1985). *Naturalistic Inquiry*. London: Sage.

Los Angeles Times (2005) "2 out of 3 Doctors Recommend Reading This", *Los Angeles Times*, 10 January, E14.

Luntley, M. (1995) *Reason, Truth and Self*. London: Routledge.

Lyas, C. (1999) *Peter Winch*. Teddington: Acumen.

Lyons, J. (1970) *Chomsky*. London: Fontana.

Lyotard, J-F. (1984) *The Postmodern Condition*. Manchester: Manchester University Press.

McFee, G. (1992a) *Understanding Dance*. London: Routledge.

—— (1992b) "Triangulation in Research: Two Confusions", *Educational Research*, Vol. 34, No. 3 (Winter), 215–19.

—— (1993) "Reflections on the Nature of Action-Research", *Cambridge Journal of Education*, Vol. 23, No. 2, 173–83.

—— (1994/2004) *The Concept of Dance Education*. London: Routledge [Expanded Edition: Pageantry Press (same pagination)]

—— (2000) *Free Will*. Teddington: Acumen.

—— (2002) "It's Not a Game: The Place of Philosophy in the Study of Sport" in J. Sugden and A. Tomlinson (eds) *Power Games: A Critical Sociology of Sport*. London: Routledge, 117–37.

—— (2003) "Art, Essence and Wittgenstein" in S. Davies (ed.) *Art and Essence*. Westport, CT: Praeger, 17–38.

—— (2004a) *Sport, Rules and Values*. London: Routledge.

—— (2004b) "Normativity, Justification and (MacIntyrean) Practices: Some Thoughts on Methodology for the Philosophy of Sport", *Journal of Philosophy of Sport*, Vol. XXXI, No. 1, 15–33.

—— (2004c) "Why Do Sports Psychologists Neglect Freud?" in M. McNamee (ed.) *Philosophy and the Sciences of Exercise, Health and Sport*. London: Routledge, 85–116.

—— (2006a) "Right Reason: Searching for Truth in the Sports and Exercise Science", *European Journal of Sport Science*, Vol. 6, No. 1, 65–70.

—— (2006b) "Ethical Considerations and Voluntary Informed Consent in Research in Sport" in S. Fleming and F. Jordan (eds) *Ethical Issues in Leisure Research* (LSA Publication No. 90). Eastbourne: Leisure Studies Association, 13–30.

—— (2007) "Paradigms and Possibilities: Or, Some Concerns for the Study of Sport from the Philosophy of Science", *Sport, Ethics and Philosophy*, Vol. 1, No. 1, April, 58–77.

—— (2008) "The Researcher's Hat: An Ethical Issue for Conducting and Reporting Research", *Leisure Studies Association Newsletter*, No. 79, March, 39–43.

—— (2009) "The Epistemology of Qualitative Research into Sport: Ethical and Erotetic?", *Qualitative Research in Sport and Exercise* Vol. 1, No. 3, November, 297–311.

McFee, G. and McNaught-Davis, J. P. (1997) "Informed Consent? A Case Study from Environmental Physiology" in A. Tomlinson and S. Fleming (eds) *Ethics, Sport and Leisure: Crises and Critiques*. Aachen: Meyer & Meyer, 111–25.

McGinn, C. (1992) *Moral Literacy; or, How to Do the Right Thing*. Indianapolis, IN: Hackett.

McNamee, M. (2002) "Introduction: Whose Ethics, Which Research?" in M. McNamee and D. Bridges (eds) *The Ethics of Educational Research*. Oxford: Blackwell, 1–21.

—— (2004) "Positivism, Popper and Paradigms" in M. McNamee (ed.) *Philosophy and the Sciences of Exercise, Health and Sport*. London: Routledge, 1–20.

McNamee, M., Olivier, S. and Wainwright, P. (2007) *Research Ethics in Exercise, Health and Sports Sciences*. London: Routledge.

Magee, B. (1973) *Popper*. London: Fontana.

Marsh, P., Rosser, E., and Harré, R. (1978) *The Rules of Disorder*. London: Routledge.

Masterman, M. (1972) "The Nature of a Paradigm" in I. Lakatos and A. Musgrave (eds) *Criticism and the Growth of Knowledge*. Cambridge: Cambridge University Press, 59–89.

Medawar, P. (1990) *The Threat and the Glory: Reflections on Science and Scientists*. London: Oxford University Press.

Morgan, W. J. (1994) *Leftist Theories of Sport: A Critique and Reconstruction*. Chicago: University of Illinois Press.

—— (2006) *Why Sports Morally Matter*. London: Routledge.

Morris, D. (1977) *Manwatching: A Field Guide to Human Behaviour*. London: Jonathan

Cape.

Moxon, D. (2000) *Memory*. London: Heinemann.

Nagel, T. (2002) *Concealment and Exposure, and Other Essays*. Oxford: Claredon Press.

Noakes, T. (2004) "Can We Trust Rehydration Research?" in M. McNamee (ed.) *Philosophy and the Sciences of Exercise, Health and Sport*. London: Routledge, 144–48.

Nussbaum, M. (1990) *Love's Knowledge: Essays on Philosophy and Literature*. Oxford: Oxford University Press.

Olafson, G. A. (1991). "Triangulation in Comparative Research: Mixing Qualitative and Quantitative Methods" in K. Hardman and J. Standeven (eds) *Sport for All. Into the 90s: Comparative Physical Education and Sport*, Vol 7. Aachen, Germany: Meyer and Meyer, 39–44.

Olivier, S. (2007) "Ethics and Physiological Testing" in E. M. Winters A. M. Jones, R. C. Richard Davison, P. D. Bromley, and T. H. Mercer (eds) *Sport and Exercise Physiology Guidelines*, Vol. 2. London: Routledge, 30–37.

O'Neill, O. (2002) *Autonomy and Trust in Bioethics*. Cambridge: Cambridge University Press.

Parry, J. (2004) "Must Scientists Think Philosophically about Science?" in M. McNamee (ed.) *Philosophy and the Sciences of Exercise, Health and Sport*. London: Routledge, 21–33.

Pattern, S. C. (1994) "On the Supposed Indispensibility of Deception in Social Psychology" reprinted in E. Erwin, S. Gendin and L. Kleinman (eds) *Ethical Issues in Scientific Research: An Anthology*. New York: Garland, 111–19.

Penslar, R. (1995) (ed.) *Research Ethics: Cases and Materials*. Bloomington: Indiana University Press.

Phillimore, J. and Goodson, L. (2004) "The Inquiry Paradigm in Qualitative Tourism Research", in J. Phillimore and L. Goodson (eds) *Qualitative Research in Tourism: Ontologies, Epistemologies, Methodologies*. London: Routledge, 30–45.

Polgar, S. and Thomas, S. A. (2008) *Introduction to Research in the Health Sciences*. Philadephia, PA: Elsevier.

Popkewitz, T. S. (1984) *Paradigm and Ideology in Educational Research*. London: Falmer Press.

Popper, K. (1963/1999) *Conjectures and Refutations*. London: Routledge.

——— (1968) *The Logic of Scientific Discovery*. London: Hutchinson

——— (1983) *Realism and the Aim of Science*. [Postscript to the Logic of Scientific Discovery, Vol. 1]. London: Routledge.

——— (1985) *Popper Selections*. David Miller (ed.). Princeton: Princeton University Press.

Punch, K. (1998) *Introduction to Social Research*. London: Sage.

Putnam, H. (1981) *Reason, Truth and History*. Cambridge: Cambridge University Press.

——— (1990) *Realism with a Human Face*. Cambridge, MA: Harvard University Press.

Putnam, R. (1996) "Creating Reflective Dialogue" in S. Toulmin and B. Gustavsen (eds) *Beyond Theory: Changing Organizations Through Participation*. Amsterdam: John Benjamins, 41–52.

Quine, W. V. (1986) *Philosophy of Logic* (Second Edition). Cambridge, MA: Harvard University Press.

Ramsey, F. P. (1931) *The Foundations of Mathematics*. London: Routledge & Kegan Paul.

Richards, L. and Richards, T. (1991) "The Transformation of Qualitative Method: Computational Paradigms and Research Processes" in N. Fielding and R. Lee (eds) *Using Computers in Qualitative Research*. London: Sage, 38–53.

Richardson, L. (1996) "Educational Birds", *Journal of Contemporary Ethnography*, Vol. 25, No. 1, 6–15.

——— (2000) "Writing: A Method of Enquiry" in N. Denzin and Y. Lincoln (eds) *Handbook of Qualitative Research* (Second Edition). London: Sage, 923–48.

—— (2001) "Poetic Representations of Interviews" in J. Gubrium and J. Holstein (eds) *Handbook of Interview Research*. London: Sage, 877–91.

Roberts, T. (1998) "Private Autonomy and Public Morality in Sporting Practices" in M. McNamee and S. J. Parry (eds) *Ethics and Sport*. London: Routledge, 240–55.

Roethlisberger, F. and Dickson, W. (1939) *Management and the Worker*, Cambridge, MA: Harvard University Press.

Rorty, R. (1989) *Contingency, Irony and Solidarity*. Cambridge: Cambridge University Press.

Rowntree, D. (1981) *Statistics without Tears: A Primer for Non-Mathematicians*. London: Penguin.

Ryle, G. (1990) "Jane Austen and the Moralists" in his *Collected Papers*, Vol. 1. Bristol: Thoemmes (reprint of Hutchinson edition), 276–91.

Schmidt, K. (2007) "Steroids: Take one for the team", *Los Angeles Times*, Sunday, 14 October, M9.

Schön, D. (1983) *The Reflective Practitioner*. New York: Basic Books.

—— (1987) *Educating the Reflective Practitioner*. San Francisco: Jossey-Bass Publishers.

Schrader-Frechette, K. (1994) *Ethics of Scientific Research*. Lanhan, MA: Rowman & Littlefield.

Searle, J. (2008) *Philosophy in a New Century*. Cambridge: Cambridge University Press.

Shamoo, A. E. and Resnik, D. B. (2009) *Responsible Conduct of Research* (Second Edition). Oxford: Oxford University Press.

Shamoo, A. E. and Khin-Maung-Gyi, F. A. (2002) *Ethics of the Use of Human Subjects in Research*. New York: Garland.

Sibley, F. (2001) *Approach to Aesthetics*. Oxford: Clarendon Press.

Silk, M. L., Andrews, D. L., and Mason, D. S. (2005) "Encountering the Field: Sports Studies and Qualitative Research" in D. L. Andrews D. S. Mason, and M. L. Silk (eds) *Qualitative Methods in Sports Studies*. Oxford: Berg, 1–20.

Smith, B. and Gilbourne, D. (2009) "Editorial", *Qualitative Research in Sport and Exercise*, Vol. 1, No. 1, March 2009, 1–2.

Smyth, T. R. (2004) *The Principles of Writing in Psychology*. Basingstoke: Palgrave.

Sokal, A. and Bricmont, J. (1998) *Intellectual Impostors: Postmodern Philosophers' Abuse of Science*. London: Picador.

Sparkes, A. C. (1989) "Paradigmatic Confusion and the Evasion of Critical Issues in Naturalistic Research", *Journal of Teaching in Physical Education*, Vol. 8, No. 2, 131–51.

—— (1992) "The Paradigm Debate: An Extended Review and a Celebration of Difference" in A. Sparkes (ed.) *Research in Physical Education and Sport: Exploring Alternative Visions*. London: Falmer Press, 9–60.

—— (1998) "Validity in Qualitative Inquiry and the Problem of Criteria", *The Sports Psychologist*, Vol. 12, No. 4, 363–85.

—— (2002) *Telling Tales in Sport and Physical Activity*. Champaign, IL: Human Kinetics.

Spracklen, K. (1995) "Playing the Ball, or the Uses of League: Class, Masculinity and Rugby – a Case Study of Scudthorpe" in G. McFee, W. Murphy and G. Whannel (eds) *Leisure Cultures: Values, Genders, Lifestyles (LSA Vol. 54)*. Eastbourne: Leisure Studies Association, 105–20.

Spurway, N. (2004) "Can Physiology be Both Popperian and Ethical?" in M. McNamee (ed.) *Philosophy and the Sciences of Exercise, Health and Sport*, London: Routledge, 34–55.

(SRA) Social Research Association: Ethical Guidelines [available on http://www.the-sra.org.uk/ethics.htm]

Stenhouse, L. (1978) "Case Study and Case Records: Towards a Contemporary History of

Education", *British Educational Research Journal*, Vol. 4, No. 1, 21–39.

—— (1980) "The Study of Samples and the Study of Cases", *British Educational Research Journal*, Vol. 6, No. 1, 1–6.

Stern, J. E. and Lomax, K. (1997) "Human Experimentation" in D. Elliott and J. E. Stern *Research Ethics: A Reader*. Hanover, NH: University Press of New England, 286–95.

Sugden, J. (2002) *Scum Airways: Inside Football's Underground Economy*. London: Mainstream.

—— ((2004) "Is Investigative Sociology Just Investigative Journalism?" in M. McNamee (ed.) *Philosophy and the Sciences of Exercise, Health and Sport*. London: Routledge, 203–18.

Sugden, J. and Tomlinson, A. (1998) *FIFA and the Contest for World Football: Who Rules the People's Game?* Cambridge: Polity.

—— (2002) "Theory and Method for a Critical Sociology of Sport" in J. Sugden and A. Tomlinson (eds) *Power Games: A Critical Sociology of Sport*. London: Routledge, 3–21.

Taylor, C., Appiah, K. A., Habermas, J., and Rockerfeller, S. C. (1994) *Multi-culturalism: Examining the Politics of Recognition*. Princeton, NJ: Princeton University Press.

Thelwell, R. C., Weston, N. J. V., Greenless, I. A., and Hutchings, N. V. (2008) "A Qualitative Exploration of Psychological-Skills Use in Coaches", *The Sports Psychologist*, Vol. 22, No. 1, March, 38–53.

Thomas, J. J., Nelson, J. K., and Silverman, S. J. (2005) *Research Methods in Physical Activity* (Fifth Edition). Champaign, IL: Human Kinetics.

Tomlinson, A. (1992) "Shifting Patterns of Working Class Leisure: The Case of *knur* and *spel*", *Sociology of Sport Journal*, Vol. 9, No. 2, 192–206.

—— (1997) "Flattery and Betrayal: Observations on Qualitative and Oral Sources" in A. Tomlinson and S. Fleming (eds) *Ethics, Sport and Leisure: Crises and Critiques*. Aachen: Meyer & Meyer, 245–64.

—— (1999) *The Game's Up: Essays in the Cultural Analysis of Sport, Leisure and Popular Culture*. Aldershot: Arena.

—— (2005) *Sport and Leisure Cultures*. Minneapolis: University of Minnesota Press.

Toulmin, S. (1972) *Human Understanding*. Oxford: Clarendon Press.

—— (1996) "Concluding Methodological Remarks" in S. Toulmin and B. Gustavsen (eds) *Beyond Theory: Changing Organizations Through Participation*. Amsterdam: John Benjamins, 203–25.

—— (2001) *Return to Reason*. Cambridge, MA: Harvard University Press.

Travis, C. (1985) "On What is Strictly Speaking True", *The Canadian Journal of Philosophy*, Vol. 15, No. 2, 187–229.

—— (1997) "Reply to Simmons" *Mind*, Vol. 106, No. 1, 119–20.

—— (2004) "The Twilight of Empiricism", *Proceedings of the Aristotelian Society*, Vol. CIV, 245–70.

—— (2008) *Occasion-Sensitivity: Selected Essays*. Oxford: Clarendon Press.

University of Dayton: IRB [available on http://campus.udayton.edu/~gradsch/research/instructions.html].

Ward, S. (1997) "Being Objective about Objectivity: The Ironies of Standpoint Epistemological Critiques of Science", *Sociology*, Vol. 31, No. 4, 773–91.

Wheaton, B. (2002) "Babes on the Beach: Women in the Surf: Researching Gender, Power and Difference in the Windsurfing Culture" in J. Sugden and A. Tomlinson (eds) *Power Games: A Critical Sociology of Sport*. London: Routledge, 240–66.

Williams, B. (2002) *Truth and Truthfulness: An Essay in Genealogy*. Princeton: Princeton University Press.

Williams, C. and James, D. (2001) *Science for Exercise and Sport*. London: Routledge.

Wisdom, J. (1969) *Logical Constructions*. New York: Random House.

Wittgenstein, L. (1969) *On Certainty*. Oxford: Blackwell.

Wittgenstein, L. (1993) *Philosophical Occasions 1912–1951*. J. Klagge and A. Nordmann (eds). Indianapolis: Hackett.

Wollheim, R. (1993) *The Mind and Its Depths*. Cambridge: Cambridge University Press.

WMA [World Medical Association] (2000) Declaration of Helsinki: Ethical Principles for Medical Research Involving Human Subjects.

Yule, A. (1988) *Enigma: David Putnam – The Story So Far*. London: Sphere Books.

Ziff, P. (1972) *Understanding Understanding*. Ithaca, NY: Cornell University Press.

Zukav, G. (1979) *The Dancing Wu Li Masters: An Overview of the New Physics*. London: Hutchinson.

Index

Printed in the USA/Agawam, MA
August 9, 2013

578744.155